AMERICAN POPULAR HISTORY AND CULTURE

edited by
JEROME NADELHAFT
UNIVERSITY OF MAINE

A ROUTLEDGE SERIES

Other Books in This Series:

Hollywood and the
Rise of Physical Culture

Heather Addison

ROUTLEDGE
NEW YORK & LONDON

Published in 2003 by
Routledge
29 West 35th Street
New York, NY 10001
www.routledge-ny.com

Published in Great Britain by
Routledge
11 New Fetter Lane
London EC4P 4EE
www.routledge.co.uk

Routledge is an imprint of the Taylor & Francis Group.
Printed in the United States of America on acid-free paper.

10 9 8 7 6 5 4 3 2

Library of Congress Cataloging-in-Publication Data

Addison, Heather.
  Hollywood and the rise of physical culture / Heather Addison.
     p.   cm.
  ISBN 0–415–94676-X (hardcover : alk. paper)
  1. Motion picture actors and actresses—United States—Health and hygiene. 2. Motion pic-
ture actors and actresses—United States—Recreation. 3. Physical education and training—
California—Los Angeles—History—20th century. I. Title.
  PNI998 . 2 . A26 2003
  791.43'028'092273—dc21

                                                                        2003007180

To my husband, Richard,
and my sons, Connor and Justin

Contents

List of Illustrations

Acknowledgments

The University of Kansas has been generous in its funding of this work. While I was a graduate student there, I received a dissertation fellowship that allowed me to do crucial archival research at the Margaret Herrick Library in Beverly Hills, California, and the Warner Brothers/First National Archive at the University of Southern California. I owe many thanks to my graduate advisors at Kansas: Dr. Charles Berg, Dr. William Tuttle, Dr. Catherine Preston, Dr. Edward Small, and Dr. John Tibbetts, all of whom read this manuscript in its developmental stages and offered constructive suggestions for its improvement.

I would like to thank Western Michigan University and the Department of Communication for a reduced first-year teaching load that has given me the time and opportunity to revise this study for publication.

My close friends and family, especially my husband, Richard, and my sons, Connor and Justin, have been understanding and supportive, and I would like to express my gratitude to them.

Portions of this book, in earlier versions, have appeared in the following sources: "Capitalizing Their Charms: Cinema Stars and Physical Culture in the 1920s," *Velvet Light Trap* 50 (Fall 2002): 15–35. Copyright 2002 by the University of Texas Press. All rights reserved. "The Rise of 'Reducing': Hollywood, the Body, and Early Consumer Culture," *Hollywood Goes Shopping: American Cinema and Consumer Culture* (Minneapolis: University of Minnesota Press, 2000): 3–33. Copyright 2000 by the University of Minnesota Press. All rights reserved. I am grateful for the permission to reprint this material.

CHAPTER 1

Cinema and Physical Culture

Eternal vigilance in the diet is the price of liberty from the ogre, obesity.... The saddest sight in the world is that of a pretty girl eating marshmallow sundaes.

— Corliss Palmer (screen actress), *Motion Picture Magazine*, 1921

I hope to bring a fresh perspective to a vexing theoretical question: What is the relationship between cinema and physical culture? (Here, "physical culture" is an umbrella term for those activities that attempt to modify the size or shape of the body to improve health or appearance. Typically such activities, which include dieting, muscle-building, and aerobic exercise, attempt to trim body fat and/or improve muscle tone, though they can also include attempts to gain weight.) Since early in the twentieth century, cultural commentators have speculated on the connections between film (as well as other mass visual media) and physical culture. Such speculation typically involves analysis of film content as well as broad assumptions regarding the ubiquitous nature of cinema and its ability to send messages about physical ideals to the public. The argument is as follows: Over the past century, movies (as well as television and popular magazines) have presented images of young, slim, well-toned male and female bodies. As movies and other mechanically or electronically reproduced visual media have proliferated, physical culture has become more common, making it seem likely that such media are at least partially to blame for our era's interest in weight control.[1] Film content—specifically, the tendency of commercial cinema to glamorize slender, muscular bodies and to marginalize heavier bodies—is presented as "proof" of this influence. Such an approach is evident as early as the 1920s and as recently as the end of the twentieth century. "The movies, which set standards of beauty for more people and to a far greater degree than the stage, have emphasized slightness, thinness, to such an extent that any other kind of figure looks strangely overnourished to American eyes," claims author Catherine Brody in a 1926 article in *Photoplay Magazine*.[2] Similarly, W. Charisse Goodman describes the research for her 1995 book *The Invisible Woman: Confronting Weight Prejudice in America* as follows:

1

I did my research. I watched the commercials. I studied the billboards, magazine articles and ads. I carefully noted the size of characters in dozens of movies and television shows. I cut out article after article until my apartment became a miniature paper warehouse.... Time after time I typed into my computer, 'Ad for Product Such-and-Such, featuring thin woman only,' 'movie featuring thin women only,' or 'movie featuring fat woman as minor character/stupid/loser/sexless sidekick'.... Message to all large women: You're not sexy. The only beautiful woman is a thin woman.[3]

Most work on film and physical culture has been done by scholars outside of the film studies discipline. Sociologists and social psychologists have used quantitative studies to assess the relationship between mass visual media and physical culture, although such studies tend to be correlational in nature.[4] While the last three decades have seen an explosion in work on the body, serious considerations of the relationship between film and physical culture are notably absent. Most film scholarship on the body is feminist in orientation and uses psychoanalytic theory to argue that the cinematic female body exists as the object of the male gaze.[5] This feminist work, which emerged in the mid-1970s and early 1980s, functions primarily to denaturalize sexist filmmaking practices, not to identify the impact of cinema on physical culture. In the 1990s, scholars began to focus on the male body and constructions of masculinity,[6] although recent film scholarship on the body is not limited to exclusively psychoanalytic approaches.[7] However, the focus is still on the body's symbolic manipulation in cinema, on how and why the body has meaning in film and the limits of that meaning.

In the 1970s and beyond, social historians and feminist scholars began to study the history and politics of physical culture as they attempted to account for the twentieth century's interest in weight loss. Hillel Schwartz, Roberta Pollack Seid, and Peter N. Stearns, who have produced excellent histories of twentieth century dieting, argue that consumer culture has been the driving force behind the modern aversion to fat.[8] Consumers spend money "improving" their bodies because they are urged to be continually dissatisfied with their appearance; they may also reduce their weight to compensate for consumerist excesses. Schwartz, Seid, and Stearns spend little time discussing film, perhaps because they consider its effects limited. Brief passages do imply that, like Brody and Goodman, they deem content analysis an appropriate method for understanding the relationship of film to physical culture. Seid explains, "In the popular media, the overweight are treated with ... contempt. Heroes and heroines are never fat. It would violate the very canons of the medium. On television or in the cinema, the fat are usually comic characters, buffoons or servants, and often their weight is one of the main comedic subjects."[9] Feminist scholars, who have produced dozens of books on the subjects of fat, dieting, and eating disorders, including Susie Orbach's *Fat Is a Feminist Issue*, Marcia Millman's *Such a Pretty Face: Being Fat in America*, Kim Chernin's *The Obsession*, Naomi Wolf's *The Beauty*

Myth, and Susan Bordo's *Unbearable Weight*, also marginalize film as they attempt to subvert prejudices about physical perfection.[10] The chief goal of these books is to emancipate women from unnecessary dieting. When causation is discussed, it is usually gender specific. For example, Susan Bordo argues that the female ideal of beauty becomes more slender and childlike during periods when women's social and political power increases.[11] Nevertheless, the brief discussions of film that do appear in these works of feminist advocacy are clearly content based.

What I wish to suggest is that a new approach is warranted, an approach that does not simply footnote the influence of film as self-evident based upon brief content analyses. Motion picture content, though it is an important influence on the public, cannot serve as evidence of its potential effects on human behavior. Furthermore, a focus on films precludes a consideration of the American motion picture industry as a complex institution. For instance, early fan magazine articles that detailed stars' diet plans may have exerted an equal or greater influence on fans' dieting decisions than film content. Lary May, Mike Featherstone, and René Girard have provided at least a partial model for looking beyond film content to examine the potential impact of cinema on physical culture. In *Screening Out the Past: The Birth of Mass Culture and the Motion Picture Industry*, May suggests that Hollywood, which became the de facto capital of the American film industry by 1920, created a "consumption allure" not only in films but also in the lifestyle it established. This consumption allure, claims May, included new desires for a "perfect" body.[12] Featherstone tries to situate the body in consumer culture, arguing that cinema as well as mass advertising urge a critical attitude toward the body and self to encourage consumption of "body improvement" products.[13] Finally, in an essay in the recently published book *The Body Aesthetic*, Girard claims that "mimetic rivalry" is responsible for the "epidemic" of competitive dieting in the twentieth century, a rivalry founded on a physical ideal established by Hollywood stars as well as an attitude of eternal dissatisfaction cultivated by consumer culture.[14] In this study, I elaborate on the suggestive methodology of these scholars by going beyond their insightful yet speculative considerations of Hollywood lifestyle, advertising, and stars' physical ideals. To do so, I have identified a historical period that lends itself to an analysis of the relationship between cinema and physical culture.

The post—World War I era is ideal for such an investigation. During this time, a "reducing" (dieting) craze emerged, primarily amongst white, urban, middle-class Americans, and became what is arguably the first major physical culture fad in the United States. Relatively brief yet intense, this craze developed in a time when the potential influence of Hollywood cinema was not complicated by the presence of other moving visual media such as television or the Internet. It began slowly in the mid-1910s, peaked in the mid- to late 1920s, and then waned in the early 1930s as the Great Depression stifled interest in weight loss. This was also the period when American commercial cinema established its position as *the* mass medium for visual entertainment. By the 1920s, the center of American film production had been established in southern California, where the studio system, with its vertically integrated spheres of production, distribution, and exhibition, held sway. (In this system, a few major companies owned studios, distribution networks, and theater chains, thus effectively controlling the film industry.) Known as "Hollywood," this southern Californian film colony churned out hundreds of films each year, and weekly audiences across the United States ranged in the tens of millions. Hollywood was also the site where the industry's huge profits were conspicuously consumed.

Those historians who mention cinema in their discussions of physical culture typically use such terms as "Hollywood," "Hollywood cinema," and "cinema" interchangeably, apparently under the assumptions that (1) film, if it exerts any effect upon physical culture, does so in a uniform manner, regardless of specific circumstances of production, distribution, and exhibition, and (2) what is true for Hollywood cinema is true for all cinema. Such assumptions discourage an examination of Hollywood as a unique, multilayered institution. In this study, the term "Hollywood" will include not only the films produced in southern California, but also the stars who appeared in such films; the media that existed to promote the film industry (for example, fan magazines); and the geographical area as well as the lifestyle in and around Hollywood, California. As Lary May notes:

> Other countries also centralized studios, but in America the production site was surrounded by a community where the stars really lived the happy endings, in full view of the nation. Here moviedom became much more than something seen on the screen, or touched in the theater. At a time when the birth of the modern family and consumption ideals might have remained just a cinematic fantasy [the 1910s and 1920s], Hollywood showed how it could be achieved in real life.[15]

In other words, Hollywood was more than a production site. It was also a place where stars consumed their wealth and displayed their bodies. It became both a symbol and an index of physical culture. Paradoxically, the clearest and most direct evidence of Hollywood's pronounced association with physical culture can be found *not* in the films it produced, but in materials traditionally considered secondary sources. Such evidence includes advertisements promoting physical culture (which appeared much more frequently in motion picture fan magazines than in other popular magazines); star publicity (which continually highlighted stars' struggles to maintain perfect forms); star contracts (which featured clauses that could be invoked if a performer gained weight); and the motion picture camera (which was and still is reputed to add weight to screen performers, requiring them to "reduce" to appear normal).

THE REDUCING CRAZE

Prior to the turn of the twentieth century, fat had largely positive associations in American culture. According to historian Hillel Schwartz, nineteenth-century Americans did not seek to be thin; rather, they sought to enjoy the sensation of lightness produced by properly digested food. (It was during the nineteenth century that Sylvester Graham, J. H. Salisbury, and W. K. Kellogg first produced their easily digested crackers, beef, and cereal.) Americans valued wholesome appetites and feared "dyspepsia," a disease marked by "chronic sensations of heaviness and sinking." Gluttony, not fat, was to be avoided. Indeed, notes Schwartz, gluttony was associated with thinness (undigested food).[16] Seid claims that there were "slenderness vogues" during the 1800s, but notes that they primarily aimed for an impression of lightness, since it was a feeling of heaviness—not fat—that was considered unhealthy. Women did want small waists, but mechanical means of achieving them were considered perfectly legitimate. At the close of the nineteenth century, there was an opulent bodily ideal; abundant flesh "symbolized all that was best in middle-class life, especially its comfortable prosperity."[17] Men were encouraged to develop a "dignified paunch"; for women, "the fashionable ideal was Junoesque: an amply bosomed, tall, statuesque figure."[18]

Around 1900, "a range of attacks on fat began to emerge ... not only in fashion or in specific slimming devices, but in diverse public comment as well."[19] The reason for this shift is a matter for some debate. Seid believes that industrialization, mechanization, and mass production between 1880 and 1920 brought new aesthetic standards and bodily ideals as people admired the efficiency of the machine age. "Artists became enchanted with speed, motion, and pure energy.... Concerns about the body reflected concerns about the country, which was seen as suffering from overproduction and inefficient consumption.... The ideal body became more slender."[20] Schwartz and Stearns both identify consumerism as the driving force behind the new aversion to fat, although it is Stearns who emphasizes the role of dieting as moral compensation for material excesses:

> What was happening was a major redefinition of modern consumerism from its more tentative origins in the late eighteenth to the early nineteenth centuries.... Consumerism began to take a new place in establishing personal meanings, as people window-shopped to create fantasies for themselves, urged consumer training on their children, began even to surround infants with store-bought items.... Dieting was ideally suited to an American need for an implicit but vigorous moral counterweight to growing consumer indulgence.[21]

Though this distaste for fat may have begun at the turn of the nineteenth century, Stearns, Schwartz, and Seid all agree that the 1920s was a crucial period of amplification. "The Roaring Twenties were also the calculating, calorie-controlled, ounce-conscious Grim Twenties," declares Schwartz.[22] Seid refers to the reducing craze of the 1920s as the "first powerful slenderness craze" and claims that it was "more widespread than any before it,"[23] while in *Fat History* Stearns notes that although diet campaigns initially developed in the period between 1890 and 1910, they "intensified in the 1920s and particularly after World War II."[24] During the 1920s, rounded slenderness became the new physical ideal for women, supplanting the voluptuous hourglass figure of the Victorian era; for men, a well-sculpted body with no superfluous fat became preferable to the jovial corpulence that had once been associated with prosperity. As an "ex-fat man" noted in *The Saturday Evening Post* in 1927:

> Back in the year 1912, or thereabouts, I noted the interesting fact that the world seemed to be populated mostly by persons belonging to one of two classes—fat persons who were trying to get thin and thin persons who were trying to get fat.... I discover, in my examination into this problem in 1927, that the basic situation has changed radically.... Now I find that the world is populated largely by fat people trying to get thin and by thin people trying to get thinner. Fat seems to have gone out of fashion all along the line.... Consequently, this is the period of reduction, especially the period of female reduction.... I know, as a layman who has made a study of the matter for years, what every dietitian, doctor, chemist and physical expert knows, if he knows anything—that fat is fatal, that it is dangerous, that it is a physical crime.[25]

If the number of articles in popular periodicals is any indication, Americans did become more aware of fat between 1900 and 1930. In the periodicals indexed by the *Reader's Guide to Periodical Literature*, only eleven articles under the heading of "Corpulence" were published in the years from 1900 to 1909; from 1910 to 1919, there were twenty-six such articles, and from 1920–1929, forty-five articles about corpulence appeared. Many of these articles were personal reducing stories accompanied by diet plans. All of them acknowledged a new standard of slenderness:

> The slim figure is in the ascendant.... Fat is now regarded as an indiscretion, and almost as a crime.... Yet within living memory it was no disgrace to depress the scales to the extent of twenty stone [280 pounds] or more.... Fat ... was indulgently tolerated, and even respected.[26]
>
> One of the greatest bugaboos in the world, so far as modern men and women are concerned, is *fat*. Probably half the people in this country are worrying about their weight.... A few of them want to add more pounds, but with most of them the pressing problem is one in subtraction.[27]
>
> Bulk for bulk's sake is a thing of a dead era. Reducing has become a national pastime. People now converse in pounds, ounces, and calories. The

most hated remark in the country today is, "You are a little fatter than when I last saw you."[28]

One author noted that even ex-President William Howard Taft, a man once respected for his imposing figure, had decided to reduce. "He has, by strict attention to business, lost six inches in girth.... Clearly the garments of the White House period are of little use in the emaciated condition of Mr. Taft, who is now a mere starveling of eighteen stone [252 pounds] or so."[29]

In 1926, *Photoplay Magazine* ran a series of extensive, sensational articles on the dangers of "reduceomania" and noted that the American Medical Association had called a special conference on weight reduction to address the dangerous health risks of quack reducing methods. The results of this conference were published in *Your Weight and How to Control It*, a volume edited by Dr. Morris Fishbein, who was also the editor of the *Journal of the American Medical Association*. This book denounces the "fad for slenderization":

> The Adult Weight Conference discussed many interesting and hitherto not fully understood facts. All the doctors agreed in condemning the craze for the boyish form and the barber-pole figure at any cost. Men and women, especially women, in their eagerness to reduce, have not stopped to consider whether it was wise or safe to take off the "pound of flesh".... Women have pounded and rolled, dieted and drugged themselves, and submitted to tortures rivaling those of the Inquisition—all in the search for beauty.[30]

An essay later in the same volume notes that the people who tend to engage in the reducing craze are "young girls, older women who wish to be considered young, and middle-aged men who want to increase their business efficiency."[31] The same article asks, "Would young girls work so zealously, I wonder, for boyish figures if they realized that by doing so they were endangering their chances of motherhood? Would middle-aged business men, anxious to reduce their bay windows, turn themselves over so blindly to physical trainers ... if they realized that too violent exercise at their time of life often leads to irreparable injuries?"[32]

Despite its criticisms of extreme reducing methods, the AMA accepted the undesirable nature of fat: "Abhorrence of undue fat is today a characteristic American vogue.... Whether obesity is due to laziness and overnutrition or to some obscure derangement of the endocrine glands ... the American of today is likely to reject its advances as far as he comfortably can."[33] Indeed, according to the *New York Times,* some doctors even considered reducing a praiseworthy activity, especially for females:

> The girls who really try to reduce to attain an ideal of physical beauty were praised by Dr. Lewellys F. Barker, Emeritus Professor of Medicine at Johns Hopkins University. "They are praiseworthy because they desire social

approval," he said, "and social approval in their set is given to people who are undernourished. And I am going to praise them because they are exhibiting a willingness to curb their natural appetites for food and candy and for the fattening things of life for the sake of an ideal."[34]

The proliferation of ads that promoted physical culture, particularly in motion picture fan magazines, also provides evidence of a trend. The number of such ads in fan magazines increased tenfold between 1915 and 1925. To reduce, such ads offered pills (often containing thyroid extract), eating plans, cream, soap, bath salts, foam, gum, tea, and various machines (including vibrating belts, suction cups, and rolling pins designed to massage fat away). (See figure 1.) To build muscles, ads offered development systems (usually consisting of several booklets) and various machines designed to augment and shape the chest and arms. (See figure 2.) The form and content of physical culture advertising also evolved rather dramatically during this period.

Figure 1: Ads for passive products such as pills, tea, and soap were usually aimed at women. *(Motion Picture Magazine,* July 1925)

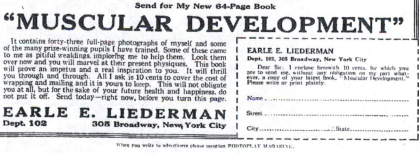

Figure 2: Men were urged to develop muscles to increase their self-worth. (*Photoplay Magazine*, February 1924)

9

Until the mid- to late 1910s, advertisements that recommended heathful eating plans or programs of exercise were simply informative, making no attempt to humiliate readers or to persuade them to lose weight. By 1920, advertisers were urging consumers to shed useless fat in order to live happier, more productive lives. Such ads routinely bludgeoned readers not only with the notion that fat was disgusting, but also with the idea that they had a *responsibility* to lose weight.[35]

The reducing wave crested in the mid- to late 1920s, at about the time *Photoplay Magazine* ran its "reduceomania" series. Physical culture advertising in *Photoplay* declined sharply in 1926 and 1927, though such advertising began to rise again in 1928 and 1929. In the early 1930s, the Great Depression made it less attractive for people to starve themselves for "fashion" when so many were facing real hunger. By the middle of the decade, says historian Frederick Lewis Allen, "No longer was it the American woman's dearest ambition to simulate a flat-breasted, spindle-legged, carefree, knowing adolescent in a long-waisted child's frock. The red-hot baby had gone out of style."[36] Seid also notes that dieting dropped beneath the radar of most Americans in the 1930s and 1940s: "In a nation gripped by depression and then war, with threats of food shortages and with rationing, overweight could hardly loom as a serious problem."[37] Widespread interest in weight loss did not re-emerge until after World War II.

POSSIBLE CAUSES OF THE CRAZE

Why did physical culture activities, especially reducing, become popular in the World War I and post-World War I era? A number of forces were at work, including wartime sentiment, industrialization, consumerism, sexuality, fashion, feminism, science, and Hollywood.

World War I

In 1931, historian Frederick Lewis Allen tried to document and analyze the trends that had characterized the 1920s. He concluded that World War I had had an enormous impact on American thought. Because of the war, the nation "formed the habit of summary action, and it was not soon unlearned.... The war ... brought with it a mood of Spartan idealism.... Everything was sacrificed to efficiency, production, and health.... In 1917 and 1918, whatever was worth doing at all was worth doing at once, regardless of red tape, counter-arguments, comfort, or convenience."[38] Allen claims that these war-generated attitudes paved the way for dry political leaders to pass the Eighteenth Amendment (prohibiting the production or consumption of alcohol) with surprisingly little opposition. This "Spartan idealism" was probably a factor in the birth of the reducing craze, as well. During the war, reducing one's weight became part of civil defense; it was considered unpatriotic to carry around extra calories that someone else—such as a soldier—might need.[39] A popular diet book of the period took overweight Americans to task for their selfishness:

> In war time it is a crime to hoard food.... Yet there are hundreds of thousands of individuals all over America who are hoarding food.... *They have vast amounts of this valuable commodity stored away in their own anatomy....* Instead of being looked upon with friendly tolerance and amusement, you [fat individuals] are now viewed with distrust, suspicion, and even aversion! How dare you hoard fat when our nation needs it?[40]

Susanna Cocroft, a dieting expert whom Schwartz describes as the most influential of the war era, considered physical culture a part of "preparedness"[41] and ran ads that claimed readers could "Have the Vitality & Good Figure of a Soldier" if they purchased her course of instruction.[42]

As Allen points out, however, the bubble of Spartan idealism surrounding the war burst soon after its conclusion in late 1918:

> Human nature, the world over, was beginning to show a new side, as it has shown at the end of every war in history. The compulsion for unity was gone, and division was taking its place. The compulsion for idealism was gone, and realism was in the ascendant.... The temper of the aftermath of war was at last giving way to the temper of peace. Like an overworked businessman beginning his vacation, the country had to go through a period of restlessness and irritability, but was finally learning to relax and amuse itself once more.[43]

Disillusioned, tired of war, and ready for play, Americans were no longer interested in making sacrifices to make the world safe for democracy. Prohibition, which had seemed like a good idea during the war, suddenly faced a tidal wave of resistance. Woodrow Wilson's pleas for a strong League of Nations fell on deaf ears and were repeatedly rejected by the Senate. Furthermore, the nation experienced what Allen describes as a "revolution in manners and morals," wherein young people set aside the traditional moral code. Women began to wear short skirts, smoke cigarettes, and drink alcohol, and the sexes fraternized in automobiles, speakeasies, and movie theaters.

If Spartan idealism dissipated so obviously in these areas, it would be logical to assume that the fat which had seemed unpatriotic during the war would be welcomed in the post-war celebration of excess. That, however, was not the case. Although Americans loosened their manners and morals, they tightened their control over their body size. During the war, fat was merely unpatriotic; after the war, it became inexcusable. This demonization of fat may have been generated by the consumerism of the post-war decade and by a new aesthetic of movement that was part of the Industrial Age.

Industrialization and Consumerism

In the late 1800s and early 1900s, America evolved into an industrialized nation. Mechanization became a fact of life, allowing manufacturing to become ever more efficient and fostering an aesthetic of pure movement: "Between 1880 and 1920 life in America and western Europe was revolutionized, propelling society into the modern age. Industrialization, mechanization, and mass production produced the systems, the perceptions, the mentality, and the artifacts of the present: the bicycle, the streetcar, the automobile, the airplane, the phonograph, moving pictures, and the telephone. . . ."[44] In this era of constant motion, efficiency experts, and dynamic balance, fat, which had once been considered benign tissue indicating wealth, jolly disposition, or protection against wasting diseases, became dead weight that marred the essential human form. It was an impediment to the optimal functioning of the human body. "Fatness was awkward, imbalanced, inefficient, uneconomical," says Schwartz. "Fatness meant overnutrition, the center of the body out of control."[45]

Michael S. Kimmel, Gaylyn Studlar, and others have argued that the Industrial Age also contributed to a feminization of American culture that prompted men to participate in physical culture in order to prove their manhood.[46] As factories and large corporations became commonplace, many men were no longer employed as artisans or farmers who engaged in rugged outdoor activities. Instead, they spent their days doing repetitive factory tasks or sedentary office work. Furthermore, as the spheres of home and work became more and more separate, women took over the socialization of young boys. Consequently, men turned to physical culture, especially sports such as boxing and baseball, to recuperate their masculinity. According to Kimmel, men "compulsively attempted to develop manly physiques as a way of demonstrating that they possessed the virtues of manhood."[47]

Perhaps the most significant way in which the Industrial Age impacted physical culture, however, was through its facilitation of a new culture based on consumption—a culture that, in turn, had its own effects on attitudes toward fat. The 1920s has been identified as the first decade of consumer culture,[48] the first decade in which consumerism became a dominant ideology. Robert Bocock defines consumerism as ". . . the active ideology that the meaning of life is to be found in buying things and pre-packaged experiences."[49] Consumerism is a particular *kind* or *degree* of consumption; it is consumption based upon perceived (psychological) need rather than actual (physical) need. This kind of consumption is prompted by an excess of production. Manufacturers seek consumers to absorb this excess; they use advertisements to urge consumers to buy. Such advertisements attempt to convince consumers of the satisfaction that consumption brings: happiness, success, youth, and beauty. In *Land of Desire*, a book that traces the rise of consumerism in America, William Leach suggests that the primary features of a consumer culture are "acquisition and consumption as the means of achieving happiness; the cult of the new; the democratization of desire; and money value as the predominant measure of all value in society."[50] Innovation spurs the production of more and different goods, and consumers are free to covet and pursue the lavish lifestyle prominently featured in department store displays, advertisements, and motion pictures.

Prior to the late 1910s, America did not have a full-fledged consumer culture. This is not to say that goods were not produced and consumed or that ads were not printed before World War I, but rather to suggest that consumerism was not a prevailing ideology in pre—World War I America, where the Puritan values of hard work and thrift tended to predominate and a relative scarcity of goods, as well as limited leisure time and disposable income, made immoderate consumption difficult. After the war, a new atmosphere of production and consumption emerged. The advent of scientific management in the 1910s, pioneered by such figures as Frederick W. Taylor, allowed manufacturing to be done more efficiently and America became a land of excess. In *Our Master's Voice: Advertising*, a 1934 book about the nature and development of American advertising, James Rorty cites statistics which indicate that per capita production advanced twice as fast in the post– vs. the pre–World War I era.[51] This created a new pressure to sell goods, and advertising increased dramatically. Rorty notes that in 1909, advertisers spent $54,000,000 placing ads in periodicals; in 1929, the figure was $320,000,000.[52] Stuart Ewen, in the more recent *Captains of Consciousness*, offers the following figures: "In 1918, total gross advertising revenues in general and farm magazines was $58.5 million. By 1920 the gross had reached $129.5 million; and by 1929, $196.3 million."[53] (Though Rorty's and Ewen's figures differ somewhat, the trend they highlight is clear.)

Ewen identifies the 1920s as the crucial period for the advent of consumer culture. Of that period, he says:

> With a burgeoning productive capacity, industry now required an equivalent increase in potential consumers of its goods.... In response to the exigencies of the productive system of the twentieth century, excessiveness replaced thrift as a social value. It became imperative to invest the laborer with a financial power and a psychic desire to consume.... Foresighted businessmen began to see the necessity of organizing their businesses not merely around the production of goods, but around the creation of a buying public.[54]

Industry's new productive capacity prompted a re-evaluation of the role of workers. Instead of being viewed simply as producers, they were now seen as potential consumers of the goods they created. Factory owners began to be less resistant to shorter hours and higher wages, since such apparent concessions to workers offered them the time and the financial means to be better consumers. In their quest to manufacture consumers, industry leaders also turned to advertisers, who promised to wear down Victorian notions of

thrift and to habituate the public to buying. "Modern advertising must be
seen as a direct response to the needs of mass industrial capitalism," claims
Ewen. "In the 1920s, advertising played a role of growing significance in
industry's attempt to develop a continually responsive consumer market."[55]
According to Frederick Lewis Allen, "Business had learned as never before
the immense importance to it of the ultimate consumer. Unless he could be
persuaded to buy and buy lavishly, the whole stream of six-cylinder cars,
superheterodynes, cigarettes, rouge compacts, and electric ice-boxes would
be dammed at its outlet."[56]

A new breed of advertisements emerged in the 1910s and 1920s. Prior to
World War I, advertisements had extolled the individual merits of products,
noting such attributes as usefulness or sturdiness. But in the 1910s that began
to change. Instead of talking about *products*, ads began to talk about
consumers, fostering and preying upon their fears and insecurities. Robert
and Helen Lynd, who in 1925 conducted their field investigation to "study
synchronously the interwoven trends that are the life of a small American city
[Muncie, Indiana],"[57] recognized this trend:

> In place of the relatively mild, scattered, something-for-nothing, sample-
> free, I-tell-you-this-is-a-good-article copy seen in Middletown a generation
> ago, advertising is concentrating increasingly upon a type of copy aiming to
> make the reader emotionally uneasy, to bludgeon him with the fact that
> decent people don't live the way *he* does.... This copy points an accusing
> finger at the stenographer as she reads her *Motion Picture Magazine* and
> makes her acutely conscious of her unpolished finger nails.[58]

Historians disagree about how and why such pressures to buy may have
impacted physical culture during this period. A public that indulged itself in
the consumption of manufactured goods may have turned to weight loss as
a way of demonstrating personal control. Schwartz, Seid, and especially
Stearns argue that a society that indulges in excess in one or more areas of
life seeks compensatory discipline in others. In the 1920s, "excess" became
the watchword in several previously restrictive avenues of public and private
life. Advertisements urged consumers to buy, buy, buy; Freudian psychology
revealed the importance of satisfying the sexual drive; alcohol consumption
was a way of protesting an amendment now considered ill conceived; and
religion became a "debatable subject instead of being accepted without question among the traditions of the community."[59] "New areas of discipline to
compensate for those that were crumbling" had to be invented, says
Stearns.[60] As Americans indulged themselves in the purchase of new
consumer goods, the loosening of sexual mores and religious discipline, and
the use of alcohol, they may have demonstrated their morality and self-
control by more strictly regulating their body size. Dieting was moral ballast
against growing consumerism and other perceived extravagances:

People could indulge their taste for fashion and other products with [the] realization that, if they disciplined their bodies through an attack on fat, they could preserve or even enhance their health and also establish their moral credentials. The widespread association of fat with laziness, so vivid in fashion and medical commentary alike, directly translated the desire to use disciplined eating as a moral tool in a society where growing consumer tastes and more abundant leisure time seemed to contradict the work ethic of the Victorian middle class.[61]

Other scholars have argued that dieting is a product of rather than a reaction to consumer culture. Mike Featherstone, in an article that focuses specifically on the 1920s,[62] claims that physical culture supports consumer culture rather than serving as redress for its existence. According to Featherstone, consumer culture uses advertising to generate continual dissatisfaction and self-consciousness, especially in such areas as physical appearance, in order to convince the public to buy exercise courses, diet pills, make-up, and so on. Yet Stearns disputes this position. Pursuant to his claim that dieting was (and is) moral compensation for consumerism, he asserts that "commerce in this area [dieting] seems to have imitated life at first, rather than the other way around. . . . Commercialization exploited the nervousness about weight, but it did not create it."[63] Stearns claims that dieting became a part of consumerism only in later decades: "[It] was ironic, to be sure . . . [that] a hostility to fat that was intended to compensate for consumer passions increasingly pushed people to buy new things [to improve their bodies]."[64] Whether dieting and other physical culture activities were a reaction to consumer culture or an integral part of its operation, it clearly played a significant role in their development.

Sexuality

The new ideology of consumerism also encouraged physical display and self-gratification, raising interest in matters of sex and signaling the decline of the restrictive Victorian moral code. This code, which had promoted modesty, hard work, and the sublimation of sexual urges in Western culture for well over half a century, was gradually rejected in favor of more visceral pleasures. Victorian sexual morality was born in Europe in the early nineteenth century, when an emerging bourgeoisie wanted to "protect its new power . . . [and] to dissociate [itself] from the violence and sexual promiscuity associated with the lower classes," and so transformed the human body "from an instrument of pleasure into an instrument of production. . . . [There was an emphasis on] self-reliance, self-control, and the love of work—all of which inhibited a sexuality involving mutuality, abandon, and playfulness."[65] This austere paradigm dovetailed with the Puritan values then prominent in the United States, values that humorist H. L. Mencken argued amounted to "the haunting fear that someone, somewhere may be happy." What emerged was a brand of American Victorianism that accentuated thrift, decency, decorum, productivity, and the utilitarian aspects of sexuality.

With the advent of consumer culture, the body became an instrument of pleasure whose value was closely connected to its approximation of the idealized images of youth and beauty promoted in advertisements and mass media. "Consumer culture permits the unashamed display of the human body," says Featherstone. "The body ceases to be a vessel of sin and the secularised body is found more and more contexts for display both inside and outside the bedroom."[66] In the post—World War I era, this aspect of sexual display was particularly apparent in physical culture advertisements. A 1930 pamphlet promoting the George F. Jowett Institute of Physical Culture, for example, features dozens of images of muscular, nearly naked male bodies in bold, erotic poses. (See figure 3.) These images foreground the notion that sexuality could be *bought*; for the price of a correspondence course, readers were assured that the bodies highlighted in the pamphlet could be theirs. Such images also suggest the contradictory associations forming around the notion of manhood during the early decades of the twentieth century. As Kimmel argues, physical culture did serve to recuperate masculinity, but ironically it also objectified the male body, placing it in a more passive, feminine, potentially homoerotic position. Such contradictions were evident in the screen careers of male matinee idols, who had to fight accusations that they owed their celebrity not to talent or skill, but to an attractive physical appearance and to the female fans who supported them. Rudolph Valentino, especially, found himself using physical culture to quash accusations that he was a "pink powder puff" whose career was "woman made." (See chapter 4.)

Popularization of the work of Sigmund Freud, growing awareness of the existence of birth control, and the post-war mood also served to make the 1920s a decade marked by a "widely pervasive obsession with sex."[67] Freud had published his first book before the end of the nineteenth century and had lectured in the United States prior to World War I, but it was not until after the war that "Freudian gospel began to circulate to a marked extent among the American lay public."[68] This gospel suggested that mental health depended on a satisfying sex life. "Sex, it appeared, was the central and pervasive force which moved mankind. . . . If you would be well and happy, you must obey your libido."[69] Sexual pleasure—or the lack of it—could set the tone for one's entire existence, and Americans considered how they might secure happiness through physical gratification. Greater knowledge of birth control methods made sex for pleasure a more practical proposition, at least for the upper classes. In 1929, Robert and Helen Lynd noted that the "prohibition [against] voluntary control of parenthood . . . is beginning to be somewhat lifted"; their researches in "Middletown" showed that women of the business (white collar) class tended to take efficacious birth control methods "for granted," while women in the working classes used hit-or-

Former Pupils of George F. Jowett
Who Have Become Successful Teachers of Physical Culture!

The men whose splendid physiques are shown on these two pages are all former students of George F. Jowett, whose exceptional achievements have made them foremost teachers of physical culture. They are all strong exponents of the Jowett System of teaching.

George Dembinski, Albany, N. Y. *George Dembinski is one of the smallest-boned of body builders I have ever seen. His constant persistence in following my methods has rewarded him with one of the most perfectly developed bodies it is possible to get. He is the last word in physical grace and perfection. His body is a challenge to the question, "Can a small-boned man get a perfectly-developed body?" Just do what Dembinski did—Enroll with George F. Jowett.*

Dembinski says, "Your course is by far the best on the market."

LARRY CAMPBELL

Larry Campbell, New York. *Larry Campbell came to George Jowett for training when he was 20 years old and weighed only 110 pounds. Today he is a perfect physical specimen .... a strong man who has won many strength competitions. He is now actively engaged in teaching Physical Culture in a prominent New York Health Institute.*

GEORGE DEMBINSKI

J. CANDLER WEAVER, M. P. E., Atlanta, Ga.

So enthusiastic was Mr. Weaver, he determined not only would he have a magnificent body but he would also teach others and impress them by his superb physical development. He writes:

Dear Friend Jowett:
At your request I have tried your Scientific Course in Body Building, using Dumbbells, and find it to be all you claim for the development of the entire body from head to heel. After having tried it on a number of students and myself, why, I unhesitatingly endorse it.

J. CANDLER WEAVER

18

Figure 3: Sexual display in a physical culture pamphlet (1930)

17

miss approaches or were unaware of the possibility of birth control altogether.[70] Allen also claims that the "state of mind brought about by the war
and its conclusion" was one that emphasized the dramatic and transient
nature of life, encouraging young adults to ignore "traditional restraints and
reticences and taboos" against sexual contact, especially pre-marital sexual
contact.[71]

Post—World War I sexuality, whether it prompted reactive physical discipline in response to sexual excesses (as Stearns argues) or simply emphasized
sexual pleasure and display, became a cornerstone of the physical culture
movement. Indeed, the sex act itself functioned as a form of physical culture,
an intimate exercise in which people bared their bodies for mutual aesthetic
evaluation and, hopefully, approval, so that the act could be consummated
and both parties could advance toward the personal contentment brought by
a satisfied libido. The forces of consumer culture and the theories of Freud
created a nexus within which the body became a secularized object of physical display whose value as a sex object was directly related to the degree to
which it achieved the standards of physical perfection promoted in the mass
media. Those without attractive bodies would be unable to draw the interest
of potential sexual partners and thus would be debarred from the personal
fulfillment available to individuals with active sex lives; thus, happiness
depended upon sexual satisfaction which itself depended upon sexual display.
The power of sexual display was great, and as a strategy employed in physical culture ads, it served as both a promise and a warning: For those willing
to pay for the product and do the "body work," personal and sexual gratification awaited. For those not willing, social isolation and mental
dysfunction were the possible results. (See figure 4.)

Fashion

Interest in sexual display did, of course, have effects on fashion, which in turn
may have affected participation in physical culture. Indeed, when any shift
in the popular bodily ideal takes place, fashion is one of the usual suspects.
(This term is often used in a general sense to signify "popular attitudes" or
"cultural fads." In order to pinpoint the relationship of clothing styles to the
reducing craze, I use it to refer to the "prevailing style of dress.") In the
1920s, popular magazines repeatedly attributed the new slim standard to
the dictates of fashion:

> Even the great of the earth cannot afford altogether to disregard the
> dictates of the fashion which decrees that all men and all women shall
> present to the world the outlines of spare severity.[72]
>
> But of late, Fashion ... has ... decreed that henceforth slimness and lean-
> ness and flatness are to be the order of the day in youth as well as in middle
> life; that our girls and boys, our youths and maidens, are to be rid of all

No Excuse for Fat

Millions now grow slender in an easy, pleasant way. No abnormal exercise or diet. A method your own druggist guarantees after 18 years of proving

There was a time when fat reduction was hard and slow and risky. It called for strenuous exercise, restricted diet. It often overtaxed the heart or led to malnutrition.

That day is past. Modern research has found that the cause of this excess usually lies in a certain gland. It has found a way to correct that condition—an easy and pleasant way.

Now that method is employed by millions. The results are seen in every circle. Excess fat is not one-tenth so common as it was. Users have told others, until people are now using 100,-000 boxes of these tablets every month.

No over-fat person has any excuse when people all about are now reducing in this easy, scientific way.

The New-Day Method

This modern method is Marmola Prescription Tablets. It combats the cause of the trouble, which usually lies in a gland.

One simply takes four tablets daily. No abnormal exercise or diet is required. Reduction is prompt, but not too rapid. It rarely exceeds one pound per day. Thus the body adjusts itself to the new conditions. Wrinkles are avoided.

The method is not secret. Our books state every ingredient. All users know just what they are taking, how it acts and why. They know why results come without any ill effects. Marmola improves one's health and vitality.

Marmola has been used for 18 years. Its use has now spread the world over. In every circle everywhere you can see

what it is doing. Probably many of your friends have used it.

It has proved so reliable that results are now guaranteed. Your own druggist signs a warrant that within 45 days you'll be satisfied.

You owe to yourself an investigation of a method which has done so much for millions, and for 18 years. It must be right.

Beauty Is Slender
Fat is today an offense

Slenderness is now the vogue. All ideas of style and beauty, health and fitness now demand it.

Fat does more than make one conspicuous. It crowds the heart, checks the circulation, reduces length of life. No one can be either attractive or fit, who carries this extra load.

Now it has no excuse. Multitudes control their weight in an easy way. Learn about it, for your own sake. The coupon will bring you free samples, our books and our guarantee. Investigate. Clip coupon now.

MARMOLA
Prescription Tablets
The Pleasant Way to Reduce

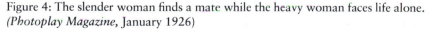

Figure 4: The slender woman finds a mate while the heavy woman faces life alone. *(Photoplay Magazine*, January 1926)

roundness and plumpness of figure ... that the figures of our flappers and subdebs shall be slender and slinky and lathlike, and the line of grace no longer the curve, but the prolonged parallelogram.[73]

The evolution of fashion during this period was two-pronged. First, corsets were gradually abandoned in favor of slim, straight gowns. According to Seid, the voluptuous hourglass figure that had been the hallmark of the Victorian Age fell out of general favor around 1908: "Paul Poiret, an up-and-coming Paris designer, proudly took credit for this transformation, which he believed was liberating for women. In 1908 he introduced his sleek, 'natural' look, soon called neo-Empire, and by 1910 it had become the fashionable silhouette. Poiret banished the S-curve, the exaggerated hips, and the voluminous skirts and petticoats of the past."[74] Seid claims that the impulse for this new, slim ideal came from the imperatives of the Industrial Age: "In setting up this ideal, fashion was again responding to larger aesthetic trends that made curves and fleshiness hopelessly passé.... Painters were ... engaged in a bold search for what they thought of as essential forms. In the hands of Picasso, Mondrian, and Modigliani, the female nude became a series of lines, angles, or curves."[75] Influenced by a new economy of form, European arbiters of fashion replaced corsets and petticoats with light, "golf bag"-style gowns requiring slim, straight bodies to inhabit them. "Who dares to dream of being plump in a tubular gown, designed to cling close to a figure which has no more need for a corset than a bamboo fishing pole?" the author of 1924 article in the *Saturday Evening Post* asked pointedly.[76] Around 1920, perhaps as a consequence of an increased interest in sexual display, clothes became less conservative, especially for women. Hems on skirts rose and bathing suits shrank (though both were still modest by today's standards); women rolled their stockings to reveal bare knees; and diaphanous dress materials enjoyed greater vogue.

Despite a strong anecdotal association with the reducing craze, however, fashion in all probability played only a secondary role in its genesis. Whatever effects fashion had on reducing were produced only when fashion was itself influenced by larger cultural trends such as industrialization and consumerism, feminism, and more open sexuality. Furthermore, the reducing craze emerged well *after* fashion had shifted in favor of slimmer, straighter styles. Even as early as 1926, the medical community was doubtful about fashion's effects on the "fad for slenderization." Morris Fishbein, M.D., the editor of the *Journal of the American Medical Association*, commented,

It is interesting to speculate whether the change in dress is responsible for the craze in weight reduction or vice versa. Unquestionably the fad for slenderization is not wholly dependent on the change in fashions. By 1890 or 1900 women were beginning to seek release from the absurd fashions of the time. The corset was a terrible armor, planned to produce unnatural constrictions of the body.... One must realize that the fashions had advanced greatly ... long before the mania for thinness disturbed the nation.[77]

Feminism

The rise of feminism in the first decades of this century affected body size as well as fashion. The 1910s and 1920s were a period when women's roles underwent radical changes; women won the right to vote, moved into the workplace in greater numbers, stayed single longer, smoked cigarettes, and drank. For example, as Allen noted in 1931,

> No topic was so furiously discussed at luncheon tables from one end of the country to the other [in the 1920s] as the question of whether the married woman should take a job, and whether the mother had a right to. And as for the unmarried woman, she no longer had to explain why she worked in a shop or an office; it was idleness, nowadays, that had to be defended.[78]

Feminist scholars have argued that periods of female liberation tend to produce a diminutive feminine ideal, and clearly the model female of the 1920s was slighter and leaner than in preceding decades. A *Photoplay Magazine* article of 1922 describes this "New American Beauty":

> The statuesque and fulsome pulchritude of a generation ago has given way to the fragile, girlish type.... In spite of the 19th Amendment [women's suffrage], the last ten years have seen the American beauty softened, feminized, and reduced to an amazing extent.... The American beauty was big, athletic, stately.... Today we find beyond question that the new and reigning American beauty is small—the tiny, childish, girlish type [for example, Mary Pickford and Lillian and Dorothy Gish].[79]

Susan Bordo claims that "female hunger is especially problematized during periods of disruption and change in the position of women.... Dominant constructions of the female body become more sylphlike—unlike the body of a fully developed woman, more like that of an adolescent or boy (images that might be called female desire unborn)."[80] Bordo's description of such periods of "problematization" of female hunger, though not intended to refer specifically to the 1920s, closely echoes the 1922 *Photoplay* article cited above and Frederick Lewis Allen's characterization of the 1920s' feminine ideal: "The quest for slenderness, the flattening of the breasts, the vogue of short skirts ... the juvenile effect of the long waist—all were signs that, consciously or unconsciously, the women of this decade worshipped not merely youth, but unripened youth: they wanted to be—or thought men wanted them to be—men's casual and light-hearted companions; not broad-hipped mothers of the race, but irresponsible playmates."[81]

While Bordo views the slender feminine ideal as a backlash against female power, however, others scholars and journalists have considered the boyish figure an indication of female freedom, either in a practical or a symbolic sense. Dr. Morris Fishbein noted the practical value of the boyish figure in 1926:

> Many observers are inclined to urge that the fad for slenderization is the result of the rise of feminism and the passing of some eleven million women out of the home and into industries and occupations which were formerly the prerogatives of men. The binding of the breasts, the bobbing of the hair, and the attempt to reduce the figure to malelike slenderness are perhaps the result of a desire for a greater ease of movement required by a change in the nature of women's work.[82]

Seid came to similar conclusions more than sixty years later: "Dress reformers and feminists ... encouraged the emergence of a new woman whose beauty would be characterized by health, naturalness, and athleticism.... In part, the banishment of corsets and petticoats was a response to the new need for more practical ... clothing. Voluminous petticoats could be cumbersome in small working spaces, and they projected an image of domestic femininity that didn't seem to fit in the workplace."[83]

In terms of symbolic significance, Allen characterizes the slim female ideal of the 1920s as an outgrowth of war-weariness and women's search for a freedom wholly different from that sought by suffragists in the previous decade:

> Women [in the 1920s] were bent on freedom—freedom to work and to play without the trummels that had bound them heretofore to lives of comparative inactivity. But what they sought was not the freedom from man and his desires which had put the suffragists of an earlier day into hard straw hats and mannish suits and low-heeled shoes. The woman of the nineteen-twenties wanted to be able to allure man even on the golf links and in the office.... In effect, the woman of the Post-war Decade [*sic*] said to man, "You are tired and disillusioned, you do not want the cares of a family or the companionship of mature wisdom, you want exciting play, you want the thrills of sex without their fruition, and I will give them to you." And to herself she added, "But I will be free."[84]

Though Allen casts women as agents of action in the construction of the slender feminine ideal, as individuals who *chose* to pursue boyish figures, the distinction he draws between suffragists and women of the 1920s inadvertently lends support to Susan Bordo's backlash theory. As soon as the Nineteenth Amendment had passed, women suddenly had to prove that they could still be feminine. They adopted a diminutive, youthful ideal that was distinctly non-threatening to male power. "Dieting and thinness began to be female preoccupations when Western women received the vote around 1920," notes feminist Naomi Wolf.[85] It is likely that the slender feminine ideal of the 1920s did not develop "in spite of" the Nineteenth Amendment and other new female freedoms, but rather because of them.

Science

Feminism alone cannot account for the broad scope of the reducing craze of the 1920s, however. Though it did center on women, it was not devoted exclusively to them; men were urged also to become fit and shed excess fat. A 1924 *Saturday Evening Post* article that lamented the pressures on women to slim down also declared that "of recent years little less than a regular propaganda of slander has been directed against fat. The charges are that it overloads our muscles, clogs our heart action, packs our livers, spoils our figures—and nobody loves a fat man."[86] A 1925 article in *The American Magazine* paints a discouraging picture of the fat man's existence:

> A fat man is a series of unnecessary and unsightly bulges, located where they will produce the most comic relief. He is a combination of flesh, discomfort, and slow motion. He is simply a good prospect gone to waist. And, contrary to a long-nourished idea, he is not jolly, happy, and care-free. As a matter of fact, pound for pound, he is very miserable. Deep under his skin—or deep under his fat tissues—he is a sad, sore, peeved, dissatisfied, envious, and greatly disturbed person.[87]

Interestingly, overweight men were usually described as objects of ridicule who had lost their ability to inspire respect and garner power, while overweight women were tragic, pathetic figures whose potential beauty had been marred by "avoirdupois" (corpulence).

Perhaps one reason that men failed to escape the net of the reducing craze lies in reducing's association with science, including principles of nutrition and life insurance statistics indicating that overweight shortened life expectancy. As members of the gender traditionally associated with reason and logic, men may have been more likely to face mockery or self-doubt if they disregarded the pronouncements of science, especially in the 1920s, when science, along with business, enjoyed incredible prestige. Allen claims that "the one great intellectual force which had not suffered disrepute as a result of the war was science.... The word science had become a shibboleth. To preface a statement with 'Science teaches us' was enough to silence argument.... The prestige of science was colossal."[88] This was certainly true in the realm of physical culture, where science helped establish the "how" and "why" of weight loss.

The science of nutrition developed in the late 1800s and early 1900s. By the 1920s, the field was accorded significant respect, as evidenced by a 1923 book called *What to Eat in Disease and Health*. Sprinkled throughout the book are photographs of scientists who have contributed significantly to the discipline, beginning with Russell Chittenden of Yale, who appears at the start of chapter one. The caption claims that Chittenden's nutritional studies "are counted among the scientific classics."[89] Early research on nutrition took place primarily in Europe; in the 1880s, German scientist Max Rubner showed that one gram of fat had twice as much energy as a gram of protein or carbohydrate. Around this time, the world "calorie," which had served as a general heat measurement, began to be used to describe the energy capacity in food. American scientist Wilbur Atwater replicated Rubner's work in the 1890s, as well as conducting new experiments which demonstrated that the average person should consume 3,000 to 3,600 calories each day (an amount that was soon ratcheted downward). At the turn of the century, Russell Chittenden formulated specific recommendations for "calorie counting" in order to ensure a healthy diet. "Why not govern [food] intake by energy rather than by instinct or appetite?" asked Chittenden.[90] Avoiding excess food consumption and maintaining health seemed merely a matter of ingesting the appropriate number of calories. Initially, scientists in the field of nutrition were interested not in weight reduction, but in determining the precise amount of energy humans needed to function effectively. The applicability of their work to reducing was soon apparent, however. "Here," says Peter Stearns, "was a scientific means of developing a pattern of weight control, or if necessary of weight reduction, in a period when fashion as well as health considerations were beginning to dictate restraint."[91]

Popular literature reinforced the notion that weight control was simply a matter of following scientific principles of energy storage and energy consumption. A 1925 article in *Sunset Magazine* describes the straightforward nature of weight regulation:

> The body gains flesh from two causes, overnourishment and lack of exercise. The food that is eaten supplies energy for the daily activities of life. If there is more food than these activities demand it is stored in the body as fat.... There is no secret about reducing. Any amount of flesh can be taken off if you have the courage and strength of purpose to be persistent and unfailing in your effort.[92]

By the 1920s, diet books were routinely using calorie counting as a framework for weight control. *Diet and Health—with Key to the Calories*, a 1918 diet book that was reprinted several times during the 1920s, included a detailed definition of the word "calorie" as well as charts listing the caloric values of various foods. In addition, Dr. Lulu Hunt Peters offered the following blandishments to her readers:

> You should know and also use the word calorie as frequently, or more frequently, than you use the words food, yard, quart, gallon, and so forth.... Hereafter you are going to eat calories of food. Instead of saying one slice

of bread, or a piece of pie, you will say 100 calories of bread, 350 calories of pie.... Remember this point: *Any food eaten beyond what your system requires for its energy, growth, and repair, is fattening, or an irritant.*[93]

Some diet books focused on other nutritional principles in lieu of counting calories. Vitamins (or "vitamines," as it was spelled then) and minerals were newly identified players on the nutritional scene, and their ability to provide vital substances to the body without adding calories made them particularly interesting to dieters. In his 1923 book *Girth Control*, Henry Finck criticizes the calorie method of reduction: "Possibly, under the daily guidance of an expert physician who knows you and your habits from toe to top, the calorie method *might* be of *some* use, but with the amateur it must always be guess-work and worse."[94] Instead of calorie-counting, Finck emphasizes the importance of mineral salts: "... a fat man on a demineralized diet—as most Americans are—keeps on eating and eating because his subconscious mind tells him he *needs more* of something.... Dr. J. H. Kellogg [brother of W. K. Kellogg] was one of the first medical men to recognize the dietetic importance of iron and lime and other food salts."[95]

A significant number of reducing products of this period did not specifically discuss nutrition. One of the most popular alternative appeals was to the new field of endocrinology, which had revealed a possible link between obesity and an underactive thyroid gland. "Endocrinology was just coming into its own at the turn of the century," says Seid, "and researchers discovered that thyroid extract, mixed with iodine, could cause weight loss."[96] According to Schwartz,

> There were, most everyone agreed, two kinds of obesity, the exogenous and the endogenous. The first resulted from a misguided appetite; fat accumulated because so much was taken in from outside. The second resulted from an "unhealthy" metabolism; fat accumulated because the internal fires burned so low.... Thyroid extract could be introduced into the body to turn up the metabolic furnace and burn off the unwanted fat.[97]

Though the medical community downplayed the thyroid method of weight loss, it did endorse the scientific principles upon which it rested. "If you are excessively thin or excessively fat the fault may lie with your glands. Certain drugs will reduce weight because they stimulate or supplement the activity of the thyroid gland, but to take them without a doctor's advice is extremely dangerous," reads the introduction to "How Glands Affect Weight," a 1927 article by Lewellys F. Barker, M.D., in *Your Weight and How to Control It*.[98] Dr. Barker notes that in most cases the thyroid gland is not a factor in weight control: "Even when there is a marked natural tendency to be either a skinny débutante or an over-ample matron, you can usually bring yourself to your normal weight, provided you are strong-minded enough to obey the rules for food, exercise, and rest."[99]

Scores of dieters hoping to achieve the new standard of slenderness without suffering through strict reducing diets or exercise plans purchased thyroid pills, which were available without prescription either over the counter or through the mail. These pills usually contained thyroid extract from sheep glands. One full-page 1923 ad for "Rid-O-Fat" declares,

> Scientists have discovered that excess fat is often caused by the subnormal action of a small gland. Once this gland is healthy and functioning properly, your weight should reduce naturally and without effort on your part.... Rid-O-Fat, the scientific compound, comes in convenient tablet form, and is practically tasteless. You simply take one at each meal and bedtime. Results often surprising in their rapidity.[100]

Unfortunately, over-eager reducers often downed sizeable amounts of thyroid extract, leading to reports of heart complications. A 1926 article in the *Journal of the American Medical Association* cited a case in which a 33-year-old Detroit woman died of heart disease brought on by excessive use of thyroid tablets.[101] In that same year, *Photoplay Magazine* warned readers of the dangers of thyroid medication, quoting the American Medical Association: "That the prolonged administration of thyroid gland will sometimes bring about a marked reduction in weight is true, but its use, even under skilled medical supervision, is fraught with danger."[102]

Calorie-counting and the use of thyroid medication had the endorsement of "legitimate" science, but nearly all weight reduction methods tried to invoke science in some manner. For instance, many of the products contained the word "doctor" in their title, like Dr. Folts' Soap (for dissolving fat through skin); Dr. Lawton's Fat Reducer (a suction cup for massaging fat away); and Dr. Jeanne Walter's Rubber Reducing Garments for Men and Women. Quack science ran rampant. In 1923, Dr. R. L. Graham explained in a *Photoplay* advertisement that "the fat in your body is caused by a simple chemical process. Yeast cells in your stomach combine with starch and sugar and form alcohol. When alcohol gets in the blood, fatty tissue is made instead of healthy, lean muscle.... Destroy this excess of yeast cells and you immediately destroy Fat at its source! ... [This] marvelous prescription, known as NEUTROIDS, destroys the yeast cells."[103] Offering similar scientific deception, a 1924 ad claimed, "Scientist discovers fat solvent.... I, M. J. McGowan, after five years of tireless research, have made the discovery you have all been waiting for.... Reducine is a pleasant Cream that you can apply in the privacy of your own room.... A harmless chemical reaction takes place, during which the excess fat is literally dissolved away."[104] "Real" scientists worked to expose the pseudo-scientists; the *Journal of the American Medical Association* offered a regular feature called "The Propaganda for Reform," in which quack weight-loss methods (and other deceptive uses of science) were debunked.

In addition to providing several "hows" for weight loss, science also offered Americans several compelling "whys." First were the health considerations; the obese were found to be at higher risk for heart disease and diabetes. By 1927, such associations were commonly acknowledged in reducing literature. "I know that serious organic diseases, such as diabetes, impaired heart action, and so on are often associated with fat; and I know that, even with organic heart disease absent, the fat man or woman doesn't ... have half the comfort, fun, ease or health he would have if he were not so fat," noted a diet article in *The Saturday Evening Post*.[105] The medical community itself was careful to advise individuals to be neither too fat *nor* too thin, citing the potential side effects of either condition:

> Pulmonary tuberculosis and certain other infections claim many of their victims among persons who have long remained too thin. In such persons, too, nervous breakdowns are relatively common. So are disturbances of digestion due to sagging of the abdominal organs because of insufficient support by normal pads of fat. On the other hand, among those who long remain very obese, the serious disease known as diabetes mellitus is much more common than in those of normal weight. Furthermore, the excessive indulgence in food and the lazy bodily habits that so often cause obesity are also conducive to the origin of disorders like hardening of the arteries and certain forms of Bright's disease in which high blood pressure, heart failure or apoplexy may occur.[106]

Such conservative admonitions should have perhaps had a dampening effect on the reducing craze, persuading potential dieters that radical weight loss had dangers which rivaled those of weight gain. But this was not what occurred.

A complicating factor was that it was becoming increasingly unclear what "too thin" meant, since newly circulated life insurance statistics indicated that thinness, particularly after middle age, could prolong life. Schwartz summarizes the conclusions that were reached after scientists analyzed over two decades' worth of life insurance statistics: "Between 1912 and 1914, the Actuarial Society of America and the Association of Life Insurance Medical Directors published five volumes of studies summing up insurance experience, 1885–1908. On the basis of more than 700,000 insured male lives, they found that the more overweight a man was, the shorter his life, and that overweight was deadlier than a corresponding degree of underweight."[107] Though these data were later criticized because they were collected in a haphazard, retrospective fashion and focused only on white males, the results of these studies were cited repeatedly in popular literature and generated the first tables of "average" or "normal" weights. These tables soon began to refer to "ideal" or "desirable" weights in lieu of average weights, and their recommendations were slowly adjusted downward.

"What are the insurance companies' figures?" asks a 1923 diet book. "They show that when you are fifty years old every pound of overweight means 1 per cent taken from your life expectancy."[108] In a similar fashion, an article by Dr. Eugene Lyman Fisk asks, "Where is the proof that the middle-aged American is overfed? It is found in the following analysis of life insurance experience.... The death-rate increase[s] in regular proportion to the increase of overweight."[109] A 1921 magazine article includes a table of normal weights for men and women used by insurance companies and notes, "In judging whether your own weight is ideal, remember that, especially after you pass the age of thirty, you should try to keep *under* the average weight for your height.... Middle-aged or elderly persons who are *under* normal weight have proved to be much better 'risks.'"[110]

Most sources that quoted life insurance figures recommended remaining at or slightly above normal weight up to the age of thirty, since persons of such weight were statistically at a lower risk of contracting tuberculosis. (In the early 1920s, normal weight for a 5'8" thirty-year-old man was 152 pounds; for a 5'5" woman of thirty, normal weight was 134 pounds.[111]) The fact that the reducing craze primarily affected young women, however, suggests that they ignored such warnings in favor of other cultural forces which influenced them to reduce. However, such statistics may have lent the practice of reducing new urgency and importance for middle-aged men or women who respected the institution of science and feared their own mortality. In addition, men were admonished to be fit as part of their responsibility to succeed in business and support a family—since a fat man would get ill more frequently and would be more likely to die at an early age. For example, one particularly strident ad that urged men to purchase the Lionel Strongfort course of physical instruction declared that "marriage is a crime" when a man who is "not 100 percent [physically] perfect ... deliberately marries a good, wholesome woman.... He abuses the love and confidence of the woman he pretends to love."[112] (See figure 5.)

Hollywood

Clearly, a number of cultural forces were nudging Americans toward weight-consciousness during the 1910s and 1920s, so Hollywood's influence was not operating in isolation. Yet Hollywood, through the promotional vehicle of its fan magazines, typically blamed itself for the country's compulsion to reduce, perhaps as a backhanded attempt to highlight its power to influence the masses. A 1925 article in *Motion Picture Classic* baldly asserted that Hollywood was behind the diet craze: "'Oh, that this too, too solid flesh would melt, thaw, and resolve itself into a dew.' This is the cry which is heard round the world.... The eighth industry of the world, viz. the movies, is directly responsible for this state of affairs."[113] *Photoplay* offered melodramatic pronouncements about Hollywood's impact on dieting throughout the 1920s, including this one from 1929:

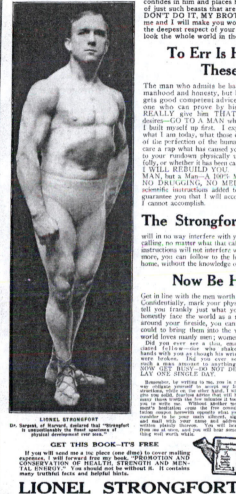

Figure 5: Men are told that it is their *duty* to be fit. (*Motion Picture Magazine*, March 1921)

29

Diet! It has put the one world famous star in her grave [Barbara La Marr], has caused the illness of many others, has wrecked careers and has become, largely through its practice in Hollywood, the Great American Menace! For as Hollywood does so does the rest of the world.... The stars have set the styles in slim figures. The correct weight for a girl five feet two inches tall is 119 pounds. The average screen player of this height weighs only 108 pounds.[114]

Whether Hollywood actually played so central a role in the craze is, of course, debatable. The logic of asserting Hollywood's responsibility is straightforward. By the late 1920s, Hollywood had become the major purveyor of society's standards of physical attractiveness. The vertically integrated studio system had been established, and Hollywood was able to exhibit several hundred films a year in theaters across the United States—and indeed across the world, especially after World War I left Europe's once-vital film industries in disarray. One-reel productions and nickelodeons were abandoned in favor of bigger-budget, feature-length films and increasingly opulent picture palaces. The establishment of the star system in the 1910s helped generate screen idols who enjoyed unprecedented public fame. (The rise of the star system is considered in detail in chapter 3.) Tens of millions of people sat in the dark each week, exposed to larger-than-life images of glamorous, young, attractive, slender and/or muscular motion picture stars. By the early 1920s Hollywood's perceived importance as a source of cultural influence had many social critics calling for censorship of film content. (To help protect itself from this eventuality, the film industry established the Motion Picture Producers and Distributors Association and placed renowned conservative William H. Hays at its helm, hoping that he might be able to ward off attempts at censorship while serving as an apt public relations man.)

In such a context Hollywood's impact upon physical culture may seem self-evident. Surely motion picture audiences *must* have been influenced by the thousands of images they consumed; surely seeing Clara Bow, Gloria Swanson, or Douglas Fairbanks again and again must have prompted viewers to wonder how they might improve their own bodies or to look more critically at the bodies of potential mates. Yet, as mentioned earlier in this chapter, such self-evident assumptions provide an imprecise and incomplete picture of Hollywood's relationship to physical culture. Instead of analyzing 1920s' film content, this study assesses Hollywood's involvement in the reducing craze of the 1920s primarily through the scrutiny of secondary sources, such as fan magazine articles, advertisements, and stars' contracts, in four rich subject areas: First, as Lary May discusses in *Screening Out the Past: The Birth of Mass Culture and the Motion Picture Industry*, the region in and around Hollywood, California emerged as a land of physical culture, a place with a warm climate that was symbolically free of the conservative rules against bodily display which existed in the eastern part of the country.[115] Second, advertisements for physical culture products appeared most prominently and frequently in motion picture fan magazines, where a dozen such ads per issue was not uncommon at the height of the craze in the 1920s. Third, the camera itself may have necessitated weight loss. During that period, the camera's apparent ability to add weight to the body was widely acknowledged. Stars dieted simply to appear normal on screen. Fourth, motion picture stars became the public exemplars of successful reducing. Articles detailing stars' weight loss plans commonly appeared in fan magazines. Theirs was a career predicated upon physical attractiveness; unlucky starlets who were injured or gained weight could have their contracts summarily canceled. Star autobiographies of the period revealed that slenderness was a prerequisite to success in the industry, potentially influencing fans who had their own dreams of motion picture fame. These areas are examined in detail in the body of this work; their relative importance to the reducing craze is addressed in the final chapter, which attempts to draw broad(er) theoretical conclusions about the relationship between Hollywood and physical culture.

CHAPTER 2

The Drama-Canning Industry Heads West
Hollywood Emerges

No romance has ever unfolded on the silver screen, no fantastic tale from the pen of a Jules Verne has ever depicted the glamorous drama of Hollywood, America's real, live Fairyland—the dreamer's dream come true. Brilliant as the eternal California sunshine, soft and languid as the California moon, the beauty of Hollywood is the glorious envy of the artist, the never-to-be-obtained goal of the poet.

—Charles Donald Fox, *Mirrors of Hollywood*, 1925

Hollywood has become the Enchanted City; it is not far-fetched to suggest that Mohammedans have their Mecca, Communists have their Moscow, and movie fans have Hollywood. The astonishing interest of the public in Hollywood is too obvious to call for elaboration; but it is important ... to understand the place and the people with which the world's populace is so intensely concerned....

—Leo C. Rosten, *Hollywood:*
The Movie Colony, the Movie Makers, 1941

For the vast public out there H-O-L-L-Y-W-O-O-D [in the 1920s] was a magic three syllables invoking the Wonder World of Make Believe. To the faithful it was more than a dream factory where one young hopeful out of a million got a break. It was *Dreamland*, Somewhere Else; it was the Home of the Heavenly Bodies....

—Kenneth Anger, *Hollywood Babylon*, 1975

HOLLYWOOD AS PRODUCTION CENTER
Filmmakers Arrive

In the early 1900s, filmmaking in southern California was an unknown activity; New York and New Jersey were the production centers of the nascent American cinema. Turn-of-the-century Hollywood was a small suburb of Los Angeles, with "a population of about 500 who lived in [a] beautiful residential community of sparsely scattered two-story homes on wide dirt avenues that skirted the foothills. Tilting gently away to the south was farmland ... and a few copses of trees planted and nurtured to shade

33

the farmyards from the hot, semitropical sun."[1] Los Angeles, with a population of 100,000, lay approximately seven miles to the east, and Mexico lay a hundred miles to the south.

Hollywood had gotten its name from a Kansas couple, the Wilcoxes. In 1883, Harvey Wilcox came to Los Angeles and opened a real estate office. In 1886, he bought a 120-acre tract west of the city in Cahuenga Valley. On a trip to the East, Wilcox's wife, Daeida, met a woman whose summer home was named "Hollywood." According to legend, "the sound of the name so pleased Mrs. Wilcox that upon her return from the East she christened her Cahuenga Valley ranch with the name."[2] Hollywood was incorporated as a city in 1903, and in 1910 was annexed by Los Angeles, retaining an area of roughly twenty-four square miles.

In 1907, bad weather in Chicago prompted Colonel William Selig of the Selig Polyscope Company to send a film company to the Southwest to film scenes for *The Count of Monte Cristo*. They shot footage in Los Angeles and on the beach at Santa Monica, then departed for Colorado. When the weather there proved unpredictable, they returned to Los Angeles, where they rented a Chinese laundry. Here, director Francis Boggs shot *The Heart of a Race Tout*, the first film made entirely in California. It was released in July 1909. Soon after, Colonel Selig built a permanent studio in Edendale, and other motion picture companies, following his example, began to migrate West.[3]

The first studio in Hollywood was built in 1911. This exclusive community had recently passed a liquor ban, so a Sunset Boulevard saloon was only too happy to lease its premises to the Centaur Film Company. Their western operation was called "Nestor" and the Nestor Studio became the first in Hollywood.[4] As silent film historian Kevin Brownlow notes, this was followed by a rapid proliferation of film factories in the Hollywood area. Some studios, including the Universal, Eclair, and Lasky, were built in Hollywood itself, prompting the Hollywood Board of Trade to establish a zoning ordinance. "Hollywood was thus spared the fate of becoming the true centre of film production, but it was still the most attractive of all the suburbs around Los Angeles, and it boasted a fine hotel, the Hollywood Hotel. For this reason, the picture people gravitated to Hollywood, rented rooms at the hotel and began to buy homes in the town."[5]

Here, Brownlow highlights one of the great ironies of Hollywood. Though the term "Hollywood" has been synonymous with the production of American films for decades, most filmmaking in southern California has actually been *near* Hollywood rather than within its borders. In addition to referring to a specific district of Los Angeles, by the early 1920s "Hollywood" had become a generic name for the film colony in southern California. This may have been because, as a 1924 article in *The Saturday Evening Post* noted, motion picture stars often resided in Hollywood: "Owing to the fact that ... many prominent movie folk live in the neighborhood of Hollywood, the great newspaper-reading public of America thinks of Hollywood as a place where the streets are cluttered with movie stars from morning to night."[6] Historian Lary May explains, "Hollywood had been nothing more than a sleepy community of orange groves. But after the [motion picture] industry moved west, it came to symbolize the fruits of the screen and the Los Angeles paradise. It was not the locale of the studios; rather it was an almost mythic place where the movie folk spent money on personal expression."[7]

Why Hollywood?

Los Angeles and southern California experienced phenomenal growth in the early part of this century, much of it due to the motion picture industry. By 1924, Hollywood had increased its turn-of-the-century population of 500 to over 100,000.[8] The author of an article on Hollywood was moved to comment, "The only historical precedent that compares with the growth of Los Angeles is the growth of the bean stalk originally planted by one Jack. The component parts of Los Angeles have grown with the same vigor that has characterized the growth of the parent organism, and chief among the component parts is the flourishing suburb of Hollywood, home of the movies...."[9] By 1915, the West Coast studios were producing sixty to seventy percent of American films, and by 1922, the proportion had reached nearly eighty-five percent.[10]

Why was southern California such an ideal home for motion pictures? Chief among the reasons cited by historians are climate and landscape. "The constancy of the sunshine was a vital economic factor, for manufacturers could depend on making films without lights.... [Also,] the variety of scenery in Southern California was unmatched anywhere in the world," claims Kevin Brownlow.[11] Historian Bruce Torrence explains that Colonel Selig, the first man to move his film company to southern California, "realized that the predictable weather and variety of landscapes immediately available made the Los Angeles area ideal for the making of moving pictures."[12] In addition to sunshine and varied scenery (which included the extremes of snow, ocean coast, and desert), filmmakers in southern California could usually count on mild temperatures and low humidity. Land was cheap and plentiful as well. For example, Carl Laemmle was able to buy a huge tract of land in the San Fernando Valley that he dubbed Universal City and incorporated as a town.[13] Labor costs were also low, coming in at virtually half what they were on the East Coast. "Los Angeles was well-known for being a non-union town, and there were plentiful supplies of Mexican and Oriental workers. Extras were cheap, and sometimes free, local people being willing to act for the fun of it."[14] As the popularity of motion pictures grew, there was a steady influx of new residents, which helped to keep labor costs down.

It has also been argued that independent producers, eager to escape the strong-arm tactics of Thomas Edison's Motion Picture Patents Company (which held the rights to most motion picture equipment), set up shop in southern California so that they could go across the Mexican border when and if agents of the MPPC came to serve subpoenas. Historian Robert Sklar considers this highly unlikely, however:

> A moment's reflection reveals the absurdity of this [scenario]. Mexico was a five-hour drive from Los Angeles in those days; to make the trip would have cost at least a day's production, while the legal papers could be served at the business offices in New York. The independents, in fact, stood their ground to fight the Trust [Motion Picture Patents Company]. There is evidence of only one occasion when a film company retreated below the border, and that was to escape a possible morals charge. Actually, the first motion pictures produced in Southern California were made by members of the Trust.[15]

Clearly, a pleasant climate, varied topography, ample labor, and cheap land were among the major factors that made southern California an ideal permanent home for the movies. A 1924 book with comments by industry insiders asked, "What future has Hollywood as a moving picture producing center?" and concluded:

> Speaking from a business standpoint, Hollywood is more efficient for us. New York—and when I say New York I mean every other city—is entirely unadaptable to our purpose.... If you want a thousand people in Hollywood you can depend on getting them and also know that they will report punctually on location. In New York the weather is always an uncertainty and often it is necessary to wait until the very morning of the day's work before ordering the crowd to report.... Hollywood will always remain the film producing center of the country.[16]

The industry took full advantage of the opportunities available in the Hollywood area, and by the 1920s filmmaking dominated not only the landscape of southern California, but also the leisure time of most Americans. By 1928, attendance at movie theaters had reached 65 million people per week,[17] and motion pictures were consistently ranked as one of America's top industries.[18] The industry itself moved steadily toward consolidation and standardization as it shifted from one-reel to feature film production. As early as 1915, most films were made under the "producer" system, wherein all scripts were cast into continuity form, allowing careful preplanning of shooting. A central producer could monitor production without having to attend the filming of each scene. In the hopes of stabilizing an unpredictable business, film companies began to churn out genre films headlined by well-known stars. By the end of the 1920s, the motion picture industry had evolved into a vertically integrated oligopoly dominated by a few major studios. According Lary May, "... from 60 firms making over 2,000 movies in 1912, the 'Big Eight' [MGM, Paramount, Warner Brothers, Twentieth-Century Fox, RKO, Universal, Columbia, and United Artists] made 90 percent of the 800 films made yearly in the 1920s."[19]

HOLLYWOOD AS A LAND OF PHYSICAL CULTURE

Historical Evidence

As Hollywood's association with the film industry gained momentum, so too did its status as a land of physical culture. Words like "beauty," "health," "exercise," "athleticism," and "outdoor life" became a routine feature of commentary on Hollywood. It was a place where rigorous physical standards were accepted almost without question as a necessity of the filmmaking profession. A 1921 article in *The Literary Digest* that summarizes the opinions of Benjamin B. Hampton, one of the early chroniclers of the motion picture industry, declares:

> To say "beauty fades like a flower" is not poetry in movie language. It is hard, practical sense. The camera demands the beauty of freshness and sweetness. The movie magnate pays high prices for these qualities, and once the freshness has faded or the sweetness has started to sour—the icy-hearted movie magnate moves the girl downward into lower-priced roles.... You can accept it as a fact, says the writer [Benjamin B. Hampton], that as a general rule, "If you are very tall or very short, or very heavy or very lean, your chances for success in pictures are very remote."[20]

A *Photoplay Magazine* article published in 1926 quoted Dr. Nathan O. Reynolds, who claimed, " 'Keeping fit ... is a religion with them [stars]. With both men and women their faces and figures are a great part of their fortune and constant exercise keeps them young-looking and prevents those few extra pounds which might prove fatal. I know many stars who work harder at keeping "in the pink" than do some of our champion fighters.' "[21]

Essentially, the American motion picture industry, synonymous with Hollywood, became the first industry where success not only seemed to come quickly and effortlessly, but also seemed to depend (at least for stars) largely on physical appearance: "In the strange place which is Hollywood ... when success does come, it comes swiftly and almost without effort. Youngsters, without any preparation, receive immense contracts for a trick of smiling, a tilt of a nose, the curve of a cheek."[22] Speaking disparagingly of motion picture stardom, another writer declared, "Hollywood is complete proof that you have only to be pretty in a way that the camera likes, in order not only to be rich and beautifully dressed, but to be called a genius and to be mobbed out of sheer public adoration."[23]

What is significant about this and other period commentary is not that a *particular* standard of attractiveness was desired and/or demanded of motion picture stars, but that *physical appearance* was perceived—both by the public and by industry insiders—as one of the key factors in screen success. Although it was generally agreed that slenderness was an important prerequisite, other standards were in fact somewhat variable, since it was not easy to know what made a star. "No one, you see, until he or she has been filmed, knows whether or not he or she will film well," author Katharine Fullerton Gerould commented in 1923.[24] But what *was* clear was that motion picture stardom was dependent upon an attractive physical appearance. Defining and identifying attractiveness thus became an important part of the Hollywood mystique. Fan magazine articles regularly attempted to define standards of beauty and to identify the most beautiful women in Hollywood. "After all," said one article, "Hollywood is the Mecca of the world's beauty—and to be pronounced one of the beauties of Celluloidia is to be named as one of the world's most favored of pulchritude."[25] Personal attractiveness thus became one of the hallmarks of Hollywood success and of the Hollywood lifestyle.

This state of affairs conspired with southern California's warm, sunny climate and ample land to promote outdoor recreation as a way for stars to keep fit and attractive. A 1925 book about Hollywood described the sporting and outdoor life in southern California:

> Sports and outdoor life feature the daily round of social activity in Hollywood.... Splendid tennis courts are always alive with players—the swish of the racket making a pleasant sound as the tiny ball is volleyed back and forth in the dazzling sunlight, while the spectators applaud skilled players. Bridal paths always are the scene of much activity, [with] cantering horses bearing riders to and fro, all adding to the scene of athletic activity which marks Hollywood as an outdoor city. Swimming, too, is very popular— many homes have their own open-air pools, which are always populated with swimmers of all ages.[26]

Swimming pools became part of the "signature" of the Hollywood landscape. "They build the swimming pool first out here," said star Aileen Pringle, "and then if there's still room on the lot, they build a house!"[27] In 1922, a two-page photo spread on "The Swimming Pools of Hollywood" in *Photoplay Magazine* featured pictures of Norma Talmadge, Harold Lloyd, Douglas Fairbanks, and Mary Pickford enjoying their private swimming pools.[28] Stars regularly spent time at the beach, as well; another 1920s' feature entitled "Health—Hollywood's Greatest Asset" pictured Ramon Novarro doing gymnastics in the sand: "Every star exercises regularly. Ramon Novarro likes to do his on the Santa Monica Beach. He likes swimming best of all and he goes through his beach gymnastics every morning before breakfast."[29] Of course, any kind of swimming was an opportunity for stars' bodies to be displayed. Tennis, riding, golf, and archery were also popular—all performed outdoors during stars' leisure time and all helping to associate Hollywood with physical culture.

Such associations surfaced repeatedly in references to Hollywood's lifestyle. "You see," explained one author, "there's so darn much outdoors. Consequently you find a reckless, buoyant, sun-warmed '*joie de vivre*' that separates it entirely from any real 'daughter of the pavements' like Greenwich Village or the Latin Quarter."[30] Hollywood's initial lack of cultural life may have been one of the factors contributing to the interest in outdoor recreation. When Norma and Constance Talmadge arrived in New York City in 1922, they told the *New York Times* of the "delightful outdoor life" in Hollywood and minimized the importance of the recent William Desmond Taylor scandal. (Taylor was a motion picture director who had died under mysterious circumstances.) "'The publicity given the Taylor case has been most distressing,' said Norma. 'The midnight parties and the wild life there is greatly exaggerated. Since there are no theatres, few restaurants, and other indoor diversions, we find our recreation out of doors. We give tennis parties, golf parties, and spend hours swimming.'"[31]

By the 1920s, Hollywood's emphasis on physical appearance and the outdoor life had helped to make it a popular symbol of physical culture, especially in connection with reducing. In Hollywood "there is one topic of unfailing interest and charm, suitable to any place, any company, both sexes, ever fresh, ever thrilling—and that is 'diet,'" commented an article in *Motion Picture Magazine*. "There is probably no [other] place in the world where so many diet experiments are tried.... Diet in Hollywood has passed beyond the experimental stage and has become a fairly exact science."[32] Reducing diets popularized in Hollywood were copied across the country. One of these was the "eighteen-day diet," which featured eighteen days of various combinations of grapefruit, oranges, toast, vegetables, and eggs, each totaling approximately 500 calories. No one was sure exactly where the diet had originated, but "someone somewhere started the rumor that Miss [Ethel] Barrymore, alarmed by what her mirror told her and her scales corroborated, had paid the Mayo brothers five hundred dollars to create a special diet for her," claimed an article in *Photoplay Magazine*.[33] "On her return to Broadway, svelte and slim," continued an article in *Motion Picture Magazine*, "she gave the diet to a friend, and the friend came to Hollywood to work in a talkie, and passed it on. Now half the stars are eating celery and grapefruit."[34] The diet quickly spread from its Hollywood epicenter and became a popular fad. "Restaurants all over the country have bowed their heads before the Mayo-Hollywood 18-day diet.... It is running neck and neck with Lindbergh—and Lindbergh had better look to his laurels," concluded Harriet Parsons in *Photoplay Magazine*.[35] Robert Pollack Seid claims that the eighteen-day diet was all the rage: "It apparently had the same wild popularity as the Scarsdale diet in its day."[36]

Another well-known Hollywood diet consisted of lamb chops and pineapples. This diet was endorsed by a doctor in a 1924 article in *Photoplay*: "These beauties of Hollywood and other favored cities who have adopted the pineapple and lamb chop diet have done well.... The lamb chop provides the

lean meat necessary for maintaining the strength. It supplies sufficient protein
to repair the waste of body. Yet it contributes no fat. The pineapple supplies
enough of sugar to keep the fires of strength burning."[37] Of this diet, actress
Nita Naldi said, "'Yep, I have adopted the lamb chop and pineapple diet. Up
to now I've been taking it for a month.... The old saying that one must
suffer to be beautiful is true, but it doesn't tell all the truth. One must suffer
Hades to be thin.'"[38] When Hungarian actress Vilma Banky arrived in
America in 1925, "lamb shops und pineappfel" was reportedly one of the
first English phrases she learned.[39] Like most fad diets, this one enjoyed a
brief day in the sun. In 1925, an article in *Motion Picture Classic* tried to
account for the waning popularity of the lamb-chop-and-pineapple method:
"This was the popular combination for all ladies who desired to be as slender
as a screen star must be. It seemed to work, too. But the poor unfortunates
told me that they finally got so that they couldn't look at a piece of pineapple
reposing in the proximity of a lamb chop without having a nervous chill."[40]

Most of the material that promoted or otherwise discussed reducing either
appeared in motion picture fan magazines and/or cited Hollywood in some
fashion. In 1920, a fan magazine article's comic exaggeration of the reducing
craze provided a sense of just how widespread it had become. "There are
61,789,576 women in the United States according to the very latest returns
from the Census Bureau. Of this number, 60,889,546 want to reduce."[41]
Corliss Palmer, the 1920 winner of *Motion Picture Magazine*'s Fame and
Fortune Contest, published a series of advice articles in *Motion Picture
Magazine* in 1921. "If you are one of those persons whose food is readily
assimilated and quickly turned into fat, you will have to control your
appetites [sic] and learn the proper diet, and do it now," Palmer told her
readers.[42] *Photoplay Magazine* became a resource for those wishing to lose
weight. In 1926, Carolyn Van Wyck, who wrote a regular personal advice
column in *Photoplay*, announced that she would send diet and beauty
instructions to any interested reader. "I have been so deluged with requests
that as yet it has been absolutely impossible to comply with all of them," she
declared in a subsequent column. "The majority of the letters have asked
for instructions on diet and reducing. To comply with these I have had
printed a new, eight-page pamphlet illustrated with exercises that help you
reduce in a sane manner."[43] Later in the decade, *Photoplay* announced that
Dr. H. B. K. Willis, "one of the foremost physicians of Los Angeles," responsible for treating "leading film stars," would offer regular diet advice in
response to readers' letters.

Many physical culturists were eager to associate their names with Hollywood, even if their messages did not appear in fan magazines. In "You Can
Keep a Youthful Figure If You Treat Your Muscles Right," an advice article
in *The American Magazine*, a physical fitness expert explains how to prolong
the endurance of youth and lose fat by exercising the muscles. There is no
reference to Hollywood in the article itself, but beneath a photo of the fitness
expert, the caption reads: "For over twenty-five years Milton H. Berry, of

Hollywood, California, has been studying the muscles of the body. He is not a physician nor a physical culturist. He terms himself a physical re-educator."[44] Here, the mention of Hollywood lends credibility to Mr. Berry, making him a more "authentic" expert. In a similar but more explicit fashion, Sylvia, a popular physical culturist of the period, also had a Hollywood pedigree. *Photoplay Magazine* refers to her as "Sylvia Ulbeck, masseuse extraordinaire of Hollywood, the flesh sculptor who pounds, beats and curses the stars into shape."[45] Ms. Ulbeck published a series of reducing articles in *Photoplay* in the early 1930s. In these articles and in a book she published in 1934, Ms. Ulbeck bases her authority and reputation on the fact that she has worked in Hollywood. "The list of stars who have Sylvia to thank for miraculous aid is too long to mention here," reads the introduction her book. "Gloria Swanson, Constance Bennett, Norma Shearer, Ruth Chatterton, Ronald Colman and Ramon Novarro are but a few of the hundreds of Hollywood players who swear by Sylvia."[46]

In addition, "Hollywood" may have been coupled with "weight control" in the mind of the public partly because coin-operated scales were often placed in the lobbies of movie theaters. Personal weighing was a relatively new activity in the early 1900s. In the late 1800s, the Fairbanks and Howe companies, which both produced commercial scales, "encouraged personal weighing at fairs as good publicity for the accuracy and convenience of plat-form scales in stores, farms and factories."[47] By the 1890s, platform scales had been redesigned for humans of 300 pounds or less, and scales began to appear in high-traffic public areas. Movie theaters were popular locations for so-called "penny scales" because of the large crowds that passed through them each day. By the 1920s, scales had become icons of health and physical culture; "not even the stethoscope approached in power or glory the role of the scale."[48] Also by that period, penny scales often featured ". . . the portrait of an aviator or a movie star: *what you could be*. . . . As the scales departed in shape from the grandfather clock, stolid and paternal, they departed from the active present tense and entered the realm of the active ideal: the sleek silhouette of a woman in an evening dress, the streamlined thrust of a skyscraper."[49] The physical placement of scales in movie theaters may have led the public to associate Hollywood with ideal weights: A scale adorned with the image of a svelte star not only provided patrons with a physical standard to emulate but also gave them a sense of how far they had to go (or how much they had to "lose") to achieve that standard.

Perhaps the most telling evidence of Hollywood's association with phys-ical culture can be found in advertisements from the 1910s through the 1930s. Ads promoting physical culture appeared as much as ten to twenty times more frequently in motion picture fan magazines than in other popular magazines. I have examined the advertising that appeared during this period in general popular magazines such as *The American Magazine, The Ladies' Home Journal,* and *Good Housekeeping,* as well as in motion picture fan magazines like *Photoplay Magazine, Motion Picture Magazine,* and *Motion*

Picture Classic (which began as a supplement to *Motion Picture Magazine*). These magazines were some of the most popular of their era. For example, both *The Ladies' Home Journal* and *The American Magazine* had circulations of over two million throughout most of the 1920s, and *Photoplay Magazine,* a leading motion picture periodical, had a circulation of over 200,000 by 1918 and over 600,000 by the early 1930s.[50] Because the reducing craze of the 1910s and 1920s primarily targeted women, I have focused chiefly on women's magazines. (Men did represent a significant secondary target, so I have included *The American Magazine,* which addressed men and "male" interests, such as business. Furthermore, though motion picture fan magazines were assumed to have a predominantly female readership, ads that addressed men often did appear.)

Before 1915, advertisements for physical culture products appeared sporadically in all of these publications. Around 1915, the number of physical culture advertisements in motion picture magazines began to increase significantly. In 1915, for example, *Photoplay Magazine* averaged one physical culture ad per monthly issue; in 1920, it carried over three physical culture ads per issue, or more than thirty-five per year, and in 1925, the peak of the reducing craze, *Photoplay* averaged eleven physical culture ads per issue, or over 135 physical culture ads per year.[51] *Motion Picture Magazine* and *Motion Picture Classic* echoed this trend.[52] *The American Magazine, Good Housekeeping,* and *The Ladies' Home Journal* showed no such increase in physical culture advertising. In 1915, *The American Magazine* carried eight physical culture ads; in 1920, eleven; and in 1925, five. *Good Housekeeping* had no physical culture ads in 1915, ten physical culture ads in 1920, and seven physical culture ads in 1925. *The Ladies' Home Journal* carried ten physical culture ads in 1915, ten in 1920, and only three in 1925.

One might argue that these data are deceptive. Movies became longer and more elaborate during this period, and it is reasonable to assume that fan magazines also grew longer and more elaborate as they became more popular and more adept at promoting Hollywood. Physical culture advertisements in *Photoplay Magazine, Motion Picture Magazine,* and *Motion Picture Classic* may have increased in number simply because more advertisements of all types were being published in fan magazines. This, however, was not the case. In *Photoplay Magazine,* for example, it is true that advertising sections prior to 1919 or so were confined to the range of twenty to thirty pages. By 1919, however, advertising sections that totalled sixty to seventy pages per issue had become the norm. This figure remained relatively constant throughout the 1920s, even as the number of physical culture ads per issue skyrocketed.

If, as authorities of the period suggested, women were the principal participants in the reducing craze, women's magazines would have been an ideal place for physical culture ads to reach a female audience. But clearly, advertisers promoted their physical culture products more heavily in motion picture fan magazines than in popular women's magazines. Reaching women was not enough; the ads had to reach a particular audience of women. It would seem that the readers of motion picture fan magazines were more receptive to the arguments offered in physical culture ads, perhaps because they had absorbed the standards of physical perfection offered in Hollywood films and maintained by Hollywood stars. Such readers may have also been younger than the readers of popular women's magazines and therefore more attentive to advertisements that promised to make them more attractive.

In terms of ad prominence, motion picture fan magazines also led the way. At this time, magazines usually presented a few pages of advertisements at the beginning of an issue, followed by the body of the magazine. Ads again appeared toward the end of the publication, interspersed with feature items. In general popular magazines, no physical culture ads appeared in front advertising sections, while in motion picture magazines full-page physical culture ads appeared in front advertising sections as early as 1915. Beginning in 1920, one or more physical culture ads routinely appeared in the beginning of *Photoplay.* In *The American Magazine, Good Housekeeping,* and *The Ladies' Home Journal,* physical culture ads, when they appeared at all, were always published in the rear advertising sections.[53]

Furthermore, a number of physical culture ads explicitly cited Hollywood standards of physical perfection or specific Hollywood stars to establish an appeal for their products. Hollywood stars provided examples of physical perfection that readers could admire and/or attempt to emulate. In 1915, swimmer and motion picture star Annette Kellerman advertised her physical culture system in *Photoplay Magazine,* declaring, "My motion picture, *Neptune's Daughter,* and my own exhibitions on the stage, show what my course of Physical Culture has done for me.... Devote but fifteen minutes daily to my system and you can weigh what nature intended."[54] In 1925, an ad for Sangrina Reducing Tablets announced, "Famous Movie Actress Once More Slender."[55] Though the actress is not identified by name, the appeal to Hollywood is clear. Later in 1925, an ad for Form-O-Youth Reducing Foam informed readers, "From Hollywood Comes This Wonderful Reducing Foam! In this famous community of beauty has been discovered a remarkable REDUCING FOAM."[56] (See figure 6.) A 1928 ad for Marmola Prescription Reducing Tablets offers an endorsement by Constance Talmadge:

> Constance Talmadge says: "The demand for slender figures is so universal that movie stars must have them. Not only beauty, but good health and vitality argue against excess fat".... This is to women— and to men—who admire and desire the slender figures shown by movie stars.... Note how slenderness prevails wherever you look today.... Anyone can see that overweight is generally inexcusable.... Anyone who suffers excess fat, in any part, should try Marmola.... Start now. Order a box before you forget it. You cannot afford to stay fat. Beauty, health and vitality forbid it. Learn how easily Marmola corrects this ill condition.[57]

Figure 6: Hollywood's physical culture is already "famous." *(Motion Picture Magazine,* November 1925)

A 1929 ad for the Battle Creek Health Builder (a machine with a belt to vibrate fat away) advises readers: "Keep Fit the Battle Creek Way. For radiant health, alluring beauty—[try] this easy new method that famous screen stars use and recommend. Screen favorites must keep trim and vigorous. Back-breaking exercises are too exhausting. 'Starvation' diets are inadvisable, often dangerous. How, then, do they solve this important problem? Easily. They use the Battle Creek Health Builder."[58] This ad includes endorsements by Edmund Lowe of Fox, Joan Crawford of MGM, Reginald Denny of Universal, Renée Adorée of MGM, and Sue Carol of MGM. Later in 1929, an advertisement for the "Hollywood Method of Reducing," a three-week course of diet instructions, appeared. "Now the famous Hollywood Method of Reducing is offered to the public at nominal cost.... Being used with remarkable success by actors, actresses, producers, business men."[59] In 1930, Kellogg's began an advertising campaign for All-Bran cereal, promoting it as an aid to reducing. The initial ad includes a picture of Laura LaPlante of Universal. "The most envied women today. You know them—the women who wear fashion's latest clothes with stunning effects.... By including Kellogg's All-Bran in a reducing diet, you keep fit as you take off weight."[60] (See figure 7.) Later ads for All-Bran offered endorsements by Joan Crawford and Loretta Young.

In addition to urging ordinary readers to lose weight, physical culture ads also assured screen hopefuls that physical culture was a legitimate route to stardom. A 1930 ad for Bonomo's Physical Culture Course tried to persuade readers that having the perfect body was a necessary and sufficient condition of stardom:

> Like you, I wanted to get into the Movies. I wanted fame—fortune. I was under-developed. [I] knew the directors would not accept me. But Physical Culture got me into moving pictures. It can do the same for you.... Many stars such as Milton Sills, Reginald Denny, Herbert Rawlinson, Laura LaPlante, Barbara Worth and Patsy Ruth Miller have been my pupils.... MEN—I'll make a real HE-man out of you. Give you big muscles, massive strength. WOMEN—my special course for women will give you a beautiful figure, grace, charm, health.[61]

The connection between Hollywood and physical culture was usually not an explicit one, however. Physical culture advertisements that specifically cited Hollywood were actually rather rare, comprising less than one percent of all physical culture advertising. Most ads for reducing or muscle-building products included an image of the lean and/or well-sculpted body of the product's creator or "before and after" pictures of satisfied, "ordinary" customers. It may be that the cost of securing endorsements by Hollywood stars discouraged most physical culture advertisers from pursuing them. Or perhaps such explicit endorsements were not necessary. Merely placing the ads in motion picture fan magazines was enough to implicitly invoke Hollywood standards of attractiveness. Motion picture fan magazines were closely linked with Hollywood, providing moviegoers with star interviews, star photos, and sometimes even articles written by stars. Such magazines served as extensions of star personas and general discourse about Hollywood. As readers associated the information in these magazines with Hollywood, so they would associate the advertisements with Hollywood. By placing their advertisements primarily in fan magazines, marketers of body shaping products took advantage of—and strengthened—Hollywood's budding ties to physical culture. Further, the pronounced frequency with which physical culture advertisements were placed in fan magazines suggests that they proved to be a singularly profitable venue for such products.

Figure 7: Hollywood stars as objects of envy *(Motion Picture Classic,* January 1930)

46

Here, I should note that some caution must be exercised in applying this conclusion to Americans of color. Judging by the images they present, physical culture advertisements of this period, as well as related articles and books, addressed a white audience. Americans of color may also have been affected by the reducing craze, but further investigation is necessary before any conclusions about the nature or extent of their involvement may be reached.

Contributing Factors

Physical Culture in Hollywood

An intricate pattern of synergistic circumstances contributed to Hollywood's rise as a symbol of physical culture, chief among them California's warm, sunny climate, coupled with its dependence on a popular industry whose success seemed predicated upon the personal attractiveness of its stars. Other areas of the country were warm (Florida, Texas) and other areas of the country had been centers of film production (the East Coast), but none became symbols of physical culture as Hollywood did. Historians have emphasized Hollywood's separation from the rest of the country as a key factor in its development of a unique perspective. Richard Koszarski claims that there was "an emotional and intellectual distance between Hollywood and the traditional centers of American culture. The physical isolation of the place—five days by rail from the corporate home offices [in New York]— very quickly inculcated a special 'Hollywood' way of looking at life that generations of audiences would instantly recognize."[62] Located in the West and offering apparently unlimited economic opportunity, southern California became America's new frontier: "Los Angeles offered the vision of a new West. This was crucial for the image the movies were to create. For ever since the mid-nineteenth century the frontier symbolized freedom from the hierarchical, industrial East."[63] As early as 1941, Hollywood was described as "the last frontier": "In the movie colony, as in the content of the movies themselves, romantic individualism, the most compelling idea in American history, has reached the apogee of its glory,"[64] claimed sociologist Leo C. Rosten. Such comments recall Theodore Roosevelt's "rugged individualism" and its implied link to physical culture.

Hollywood's frontier associations helped establish a sense of social freedom. As historians have explained, Hollywood's location in the West predisposed it to be a new frontier. But it was also that community's association with a phenomenally successful, previously unknown industry that created a frontier atmosphere. Those who worked in the motion picture industry were breaking new ground. Here was an industry that produced not cars, oil, textiles, or even food, but "dreams." "[It was] probably the first time a great industry was ever set up to grind out a dream a week," observes Manley Halliday, the faded 1920s writer of Budd Schulberg's novel *The Disenchanted.*[65] Never had such an intangible, unpredictable product reaped such rich monetary rewards.

Hollywood was therefore a frontier on several levels. Like the western frontier of pioneer days, the Hollywood frontier was a place where everyone worked, including women. "Few people realize," explained a 1923 fan magazine article that detailed the careers of screenwriters June Mathis, Jeanie McPherson, Anita Loos, and Frances Marion, "what a gigantic factor women are in motion pictures.... In no other great commercial industry in the world has woman become so valuable and indispensable an element."[66] In the 1920s, the women in Hollywood were career women—writers, actresses, and secretaries—a circumstance that afforded them greater social equality than they typically enjoyed. A 1921 article on Hollywood claimed, "The freedom between men and women is very great. Conversations in mixed crowds are no different to those when it isn't mixed. Women can—and do—what they like. They work, play, love and draw their pay checks on exactly the same basis as men."[67]

This extensively publicized freedom between men and women soon faced condemnation by the general public when, beginning in 1921, a series of Hollywood scandals erupted, the most famous of which involved comedian Fatty Arbuckle. At a long party held in San Francisco, Arbuckle was accused of contributing to the death of actress Virginia Rappe. A horrified (yet fascinated) public believed Arbuckle had crushed Ms. Rappe as he forced his attentions on her, though he was later cleared of wrongdoing. Such scandals prompted one U.S. senator to denounce Hollywood as a place where "debauchery, drunkenness, ribaldry, dissipation and free love seem to be conspicuous."[68] "Movie morals" were increasingly called into question by the more "civilized" areas of the country.

Hollywood's social freedom extended to the body, which could be displayed much more informally (and completely) than in the East. As Rosten noted, "Hollywood, which is given to extremes in most things, is characterized by either very elegant or very informal dress; there are no hard and fast rules governing the decorum of clothes.... The distaste for formal dress in the movie colony has further logic if one considers the climate and the informality it encourages. There is an infectious freedom in Hollywood's attire."[69] Stars, weary of formal dress often required during production work, frequently showed up for social events dressed casually and revealingly. (On "swanky" occasions, however, stars were required to display all their glamour.) In addition, the popularity of outdoor recreation, especially swimming, offered southern Californians the opportunity to bare their bodies.

The legend of Hollywood's social freedom and wild atmosphere quickly exceeded the reality, and the early 1920s were punctuated by a spate of articles that attempted to debunk the myths about Hollywood's lifestyle. One author who spent two months in Hollywood commented, "I was expecting to find myself caught up in the mad whirl of an outdoor carnival—fifty comics in loose clothes negotiating headspins on an elevated platform, while an army of bathing beauties cavorted in the foreground...."[70] He found no evidence of licentiousness or a "carnival" atmosphere, however. "I assure you that Hollywood is just about as frolicsome as Evanston, Illinois; or Asheville, North Carolina; or Clearwater, Florida—namely, three of the best-behaved towns with which I am familiar."[71] A later article that described Hollywood as a "homelike" city declared, "William Faversham, actor, who has spent the last three months in Hollywood, has returned to New York with a startling picture of the community where vice is supposed to be rampant. He found it a sanitarium where the motion picture workers are on the "lot" ready to work at 7 a.m. and where barber shops are opened at 5 o'clock to accommodate these thousands. . . ."[72]

This article addresses one of the core tensions of Hollywood life—and one that relates specifically to the body. Though Hollywood was, as has been discussed, a place of symbolic freedom located in the West, it was also a place whose major industry depended upon physical discipline. Everyone in the industry, including those who did not have to appear in front of the camera, still had to have the stamina to endure long, exhausting days that began at sunrise and often lasted until well after sunset. Stars offering advice to Hollywood hopefuls recommended physical culture courses to build up health and strength. Screen star George Walsh explained the need for athleticism in a 1927 book called *Breaking into the Movies*:

> General athletic ability is health insurance, and, as such, is the greatest possible boon to an aspirant to screen honors. Only those who have long been engaged in motion picture making can know that there is, perhaps, no more strenuous work that one can undertake. The working hours of the screen actor are long and most uncertain. Much of the work is tedious and of such a nature that the physical and mental strain would soon sap the vitality of one who is not in well-nigh perfect condition.[73]

In the same book, screen star Billie Dove declares, "Screen acting is no sinecure. It is hard, hard work." For women trying to start a screen career, she counsels "a careful system of physical culture. Plenty of outdoor sports, such as tennis, swimming, riding, and hiking—within reason. Next I would suggest a course in dancing—interpretive as well as modern. Of course, in addition to all these things, are the essentials of proper diet and sleep, dressing and so on."[74]

Articles about Hollywood often used the hard work associated with the production of motion pictures as a way to illustrate the morality of the industry—to prove that members of the industry would have neither the time nor the inclination to engage in immoral activities. "All hands work hard while an important picture is being made," declared one 1922 article. "Anybody who knows the game from the inside will tell you that the big stars cannot and do not work like dogs all day in the studios, then raise Cain all night."[75] Physical conditioning was touted as an adjunct to a successful motion picture career; it provided the necessary stamina, and it tended to purify one's mind. When describing the outdoor life available in Hollywood, Norma Taldmadge commented, "Such a life is sure to make one healthy and clean-minded."[76] A 1926 article explicitly linked morals, physical conditioning, and Hollywood success: "The community [Hollywood] is made up largely of actors, writers, artists, successful men of business and other persons of high artistic and moral ideals who must keep in physical condition to hold their places in competition. They cannot afford to dissipate if they would be successful."[77] Such commentary attempted to elevate the industry and perhaps to derail the frequent cries for censorship that loomed at every turn in the scandal-ridden 1920s.

Emphasizing the difficult physical labor that went into motion pictures and the conditioning necessary to endure it may also been a way of proving that Hollywood deserved the wealth that appeared too easily won. Members of the industry were dismayed and discomfited by the fact that no one seemed to understand the intense labor that went into producing motion pictures. Even those authors who acknowledged the hard work involved still emphasized the quick success the industry offered: "I am not so ignorant as to suppose that motion-picture actors do not work very hard while they are producing a picture; and it must, too, be work of a nerve-racking kind," said writer Katharine Fullerton Gerould. "But I can think of no other career that comes so near to offering the great American desideratum of earning big money without serving a long and arduous apprenticeship."[78] Stars were the particular targets of such commentary, since their fame seemed to rest upon an activity that *any* attractive person could emulate, if given the opportunity: "The visual evidence of the films offers the waitress a chance to compare herself to the movie queen; it gives the shoe clerk a chance to match himself against the matinée idols. It provokes the thought, 'Say, I could do that. . . .'"[79]

There is evidence that Hollywood embarked on what might be termed a crusade to dispel the notions that screen success was either (1) easy or (2) rapid, producing commentary that was usually couched in kindly maternal or paternal terms as guidance for Hollywood aspirants. Such commentary served to legitimate the motion picture industry as one requiring skill, perseverance, and hard physical labor. Since stars were the usual examples of the "effortlessness" of industry success, they tended to be the most vocal defenders of that success. Subject to traditional human frailties, stars did not want only adulation; they wanted *respect* for their specialized labor, and they wanted to prove that their labor was difficult enough to warrant the generous monetary rewards associated with it. A short advice article written by screen star Betty Compson in 1924 is a good example of this phenomenon and worth citing in its entirety:

> The life of an actress is often held up as a model of ease. I think that every girl who aspires to be an actress because "it is an easy life," should know the truth. The working day of the average actress—and there are six

working days in every week, and often seven—begins at 7:30 a.m. By that hour she must be at the studio and in her dressing room, and beginning the long and tedious process of "making-up" with the assortment of creams and cosmetics required for the proper photographic effect.

By 9 A.M. she must have reported to her director, and from then until noon she appears steadily before the camera, depicting emotions which, in many cases, are extremely trying.

Often during the noon hour she has only a hastily procured sandwich because she must pose for "still" pictures.

From 1 until 5 o'clock she continues to work before the camera, and many times this is prolonged far into the night.

On days when she is not appearing before a motion picture camera every hour is occupied. Scenarios must be studied, gowns fitted, "still" photographs taken, mail must be answered, besides appearing at necessary social functions.

If that constitutes a "life of ease" I apologize.[80]

The petulant tone that emerges in the last line effectively eliminates the argument that this piece exists merely for the lofty purpose of assisting potential stars.

A 1922 booklet published by the Photoplay Research Society was enthusiastic about Hollywood opportunities, yet warned, "It *looks* so easy! But the fact is, the easier it looks—the simpler and more natural the actions—the more headaches lie behind the making of the scene. There is a popular superstition that most of our great stars appeared over night [*sic*]. Soulful Sadie, plus opportunity, and presto! —Stardom. Such, however, is far from the truth. The cases of instantaneous success are so few as to be negligible."[81] Stars were keen on publicizing the complexity and subtlety of motion picture acting, but clearly they also felt that the physical stamina required of them— and the good health and conditioning necessary to maintain it—served to prove that they had labored hard to earn their wealth. Stars also had to work simply to maintain their attractiveness, a fact that was emphasized in publicity articles about their lifestyles. For example, a rather melodramatic 1929 article entitled "They Must Suffer to Be Beautiful" described the beauty routine of female stars: "Massages, facials, diets, manicures, marcels. Ever demanding. Ever constant. A star must be lovely every day, every hour. She must face the continual grind and give to it money, courage and time."[82] A piece specifically about dieting declared, "Slender stars are easy to look at, but their slimness was not easy to acquire! Diet! Exercise! Honest-to-goodness hard work!—these are the weapons used to make the scales behave!"[83]

Indeed, though important as a tool for legitimating fantastic earnings, physical conditioning's central role in Hollywood probably rests primarily upon the fact that the motion picture industry depended for its survival on the continued popularity of stars whose personalities and appearance could engage the interest (and money) of the public. Such stars had to deal with the simple truth that their faces and physiques were a key part of screen success. Discussing requirements for female stardom, a casting director for Universal commented,

> I believe that some time ago someone said that beauty did not count as much as brains. I think most picture people will agree with me when I say that beauty comes first, especially in the case of ingenues and leading women. Given beauty—we are very often able to develop ability. And, as a matter of fact, I believe that the majority of people would rather look at a beautiful girl who is not a clever actress, than one who is tremendously clever but who is not good to look at.[84]

Since motion picture stardom promised not only extravagant financial rewards but also wide-reaching fame, the stakes were considerable. Most motion picture performers became very concerned about their physical appearance, devoting as much attention to their looks as "a glassblower to his respiration."[85]

In this context, the exhibitionism characteristic of Hollywood may be seen not only as an outgrowth of frontier freedoms or of the physical conditioning necessary to maintain endurance, but also as stars' attempt to publicize their assets and to elicit reassurances about their continued attractiveness. Rosten argues that Hollywood's bodily display is simply a consequence of the nature of motion picture acting: "Exhibitionism is to be expected among actors, who earn their living in an occupation which maximizes vanity and is devoted to the exploitation of the self.... Their careers rest upon either pulchritude or a talent in simulation; both require constant attention to the self by the self."[86] The motion picture industry was predicated upon the display of bodies onscreen, and this celluloid display affected stars' offscreen lives. Whether stars wished to promote their own attractiveness (and subsequently boost their fame and their income), to participate in Hollywood's symbolic freedom, or merely to continue the bodily display in which they engaged during daily production work, developing and keeping attractive bodies became a significant part of their workloads.

In addition to the motion picture industry's dependence on physical attractiveness, its elusive, volatile nature may have magnified stars' insecurities. "The motion picture industry cannot be cornered because it does not deal in stable products such as wheat and beef. It deals in ideas and personalities. There is no absolute way of gauging what the market will demand next year," a *Photoplay Magazine* article commented in 1925.[87] Quickly changing public demands and tastes could snuff out a promising career virtually overnight. "So moves the phantasmagoria that is Hollywood, a magic lantern show of passing shadows, as fascinating as roulette, as gay or tragic, it's all according to you."[88] The future of the industry as a whole seemed uncertain, as well. In 1941, Rosten described Hollywood as an "anxious place" with a "vague, restless fear that 'it can't go on,' that the mighty structure is impermanent, that its foundations are unsound.... Optimism and insecurity run through the movie colony side by side."[89] According to a 1931 fan magazine article, movie stars, especially the most successful ones, faced the constant fear of having that success wrenched away from them: "Hollywood's Age of Fear is the Age of Success. It is when the stars have reached the summit that the horrors of a terrific nightmare harass them and fright of the future becomes an obsession."[90] Stars worried about losing their colossal salaries, about potential marriages affecting their popularity, and about their friends revealing too many of their personal secrets to the press. They had "fear of [facial] lines, [deteriorating] beauty, fat, heart trouble from over strenuous work, illness from wrong foods ... and always the fear of unlooked for [sic] circumstances."[91] In an atmosphere where one's own career—and indeed the very industry upon which it was based—might face extinction seemingly without warning, it is not surprising that stars used every available tool to preserve their status. Physical culture, as a means of achieving and maintaining a "winning" appearance, was a popular and, indeed, pragmatic choice.

Hollywood's emphasis on youth also pushed stars to keep in condition. Any signs of aging were taboo, and avoirdupois was considered one of the chief signs of being over the hill. The authors of a 1930 memoir about Hollywood remarked,

> There is a character in a tale by Conan Doyle who continually calls out: 'Youth will be served, my masters.' The very lamp-posts of Hollywood often shout advertising matter through loud-speakers, but surely over every studio gate should be set a trumpet intoning this most pregnant sentence.... Hollywood stars work 'under the constant threat of time.'[92]

Everyone in Hollywood seemed to agree that youth was at a premium. Novelist and screenwriter Elinor Glyn declared, "The motion pictures call for youth and beauty, and I am a champion of youth."[93] Some bemoaned the fact that the motion picture industry was composed of such youthful personnel. "In all the history of the world there was never a place where youth was so lavished with fame and fortune," lamented Herbert Howe. "That's the chief trouble."[94] Whatever the results of young people having access to wealth, Hollywood still sought them out—and rewarded them only as long as they were able to maintain their youthful appearance.

Hollywood's Slender Ideal

"Youth" and "beauty": these became Hollywood's watchwords. Although the cinema's status as a visual medium may have predisposed it to seek attractive onscreen performers, why did youthful, slender and/or muscular bodies become the embodiment of attractiveness? On a fundamental level it is reasonable to claim that youth and slenderness became prized in Hollywood simply because the presence of those attributes in screen performers resulted in profitable motion pictures. In the end, it is likely that both the

motion picture industry and the culture at large participated in the emergence of the young, thin screen idol. However, it is also possible to identify
circumstances specific to Hollywood that may have contributed to the forma-
tion of this ideal body type, described by actor Bert Lytell in 1922 as one of
"rounded slenderness that typifies youth" for women and "slender[ness],"
with the possibility of big bones, exemplifying virility, for men.[95]

First, as noted earlier in this chapter, Hollywood was a place of women's
liberation, relative to many other areas of the country. It was a place where
women could be respected as motion picture professionals—not just as
actresses, but also as writers and, on some occasions, as directors. Hollywood's status as a frontier town and its dependence on a medium of fantasy
tended to make male-female sexual relations at least marginally freer than in
other regions of America. In chapter 1, I argued that the female figure tends
to become more youthful and sylphlike when women's power and/or liberty
expands. "Perpetual youth ha[s] significant consequences in a time of
women's newly found freedom. . . ." says Lary May. "It signal[s] subordina-
tion."[96] Slenderness is a marker of physical frailty, while youth is a marker
of inexperience and dependence. Given the passage of Women's Suffrage in
1920, a waif-like, youthful feminine ideal may have been likely to emerge
nationally, but Hollywood was a community where female freedom was
manifest to an unusual degree. Consequently, it may have been even more
inclined than the country at large to pursue a young, slender feminine ideal—
an ideal that quickly became the celluloid standard.

Second, Hollywood may have been plagued by consumer guilt. Social
historians have argued that consumer culture first emerged in the post—
World War I period, when scientific management allowed manufacturing to
be done more efficiently and an excess of goods began to be produced.[97]
Hollywood played a key role in the emergence of this new consumer culture.
Essentially, it was (or at least seemed to be) the fulfillment of everything that
consumer culture promised. Films of the 1920s tended to present extravagant
lifestyles with expensive homes, cars, clothes, and accessories. Hollywood
itself became a place of conspicuous consumption, a place for the *nouveau
riche*—the young, suddenly wealthy producers, directors, and stars of the
motion picture industry—to flaunt their affluence. Consumption emerged as
a marker of success, especially in an industry where the product itself was
insubstantial. "As huge sums of money rolled in," explains May, "the stars—
who after all did not make a tangible product—used spending to validate
their almost magical success."[98] And most stars had abundant leisure time to
consume their wealth, despite their protests to the contrary; contracts of the
period usually provided for two six-week "lay off" periods each year, with
an additional two-week rest period after every film.[99]

The rampant consumerism of the Hollywood community may have
predisposed its members to dislike fat. Social historian Peter N. Stearns,
whose work was mentioned in chapter 1, has argued that as early twentieth-
century Americans indulged themselves with more and more consumer

products, they began to discipline their bodies as a kind of penance for consumerist excess. If consumerist excess *can* be a catalyst for physical discipline, then such a catalyst probably existed in greater concentration in post—World War I Hollywood than in other areas of the country. In addition, as Rosten suggests, the *way* that Hollywood personnel earned their wealth may have predisposed them to guilt:

> There seems to be an unconscious *need* for anxiety in the movie colony, and anxiety is provoked, nursed, and kept alive in a manner which suggests self-punishment for obscure and disturbing guilts. . . . The movie makers are paid to dream their dreams and exploit their reveries. They are paid for doing things that other people would like to do without being paid. Is it any wonder that [they] are plagued by ambiguous guilts?[100]

The extravagant consumerism of Hollywood, coupled with the apparently easy way in which it generated its wealth, may have elicited an interest in reducing amongst its denizens. An attack on fat could have been one way to demonstrate self-discipline and moral worthiness, traits that members of the film industry were eager to have associated not only with themselves, but also with the community as a whole.

Hollywood's slender bodies may have also been, at least in part, an attempt at assimilation. Lary May argues that motion picture performers of the 1920s lost weight in order to disguise their ethnic, working class origins. "The twenties saw a much higher degree of personal cultivation as players took on what can only be called a slim, pasted down look. The effect was to stylize even further the playful and erotic appearance of the stars, in order to legitimize what was seen as the potential anarchy in their foreign and formerly low-class activities."[101] As Gaylyn Studlar has noted, the 1920s was a xenophobic decade. Anglo-Saxon social critics feared that women who mated with dark immigrants arriving from southern and eastern Europe were committing "race suicide."[102] To calm such fears, foreign movie stars adopted the refined appearance May describes and publicized their (usually fabricated) aristocratic backgrounds.

A major participant in the establishment of a diminutive bodily ideal for female screen performers was D. W. Griffith, one of the most prolific and influential American film directors of the 1910s and 1920s. Griffith's predilection for petite, youthful stars was well known, and his status in the industry gave him the opportunity to promote that preference regularly. According to Walker,

> [The new woman of cinema was] small, very feminine, soulful or child-like, yet vigorous, energetic, resilient, and above all, young. The reigning beauties of the American stage had been Junoesque types like Lillian Russell, the Floradora sextet and the Irene Brent chorus girls. . . . With the movies one seems to be among a totally new brand of feminine charm—certainly a

new dietary ideal—typified by Mary Pickford, Mae Marsh, Blanche Sweet
... and Lillian and Dorothy Gish....

Credit for establishing the strain rightly goes to D. W. Griffith.... For
such girls existed in Griffith's imagination long before he ever met them
and was able to offer them work.[103]

We must be careful not to ascribe too much historical agency to one man,
however. Griffith's power was significant but not dictatorial; no individual
was in a position to exert absolute authority over so large and unwieldy a
venture as the motion picture industry. Furthermore, Griffith's preference
for slight, young women was not forged in a vacuum, but in the culture at
large (see chapter 1 for more on this point).

Ultimately, early Hollywood's slender physical ideal is arguably most
directly attributable not to D. W. Griffith, women's liberation, consumer
guilt, or attempts at assimilation, but to the operation of the motion picture
camera itself. Though exacerbated by the former factors, stars' struggles with
weight probably *began* at the behest of this stern taskmaster whose collection of lenses and gears demanded a slender, youthful figure from those who
appeared before it seeking celluloid fame.

A Cruel Eye: The Motion Picture Camera and the Body

It didn't take people long to discover that, for some reason, distances in
the human form divine are much exaggerated when thrown on the
screen.
                          —Harriette Underhill, *Motion Picture Classic*, 1925

Bodies recorded by the camera are in a sense no longer *human bodies* but
camera bodies, saddled with all the distortions, real or imagined, of the film
medium. In relation to Hollywood of the 1910s and 1920s, it is likely that
the rigorous physical regimens adopted by motion picture stars were largely
the result of widespread beliefs about the camera's tendency to highlight or
exaggerate imperfections in the human body. "It is just as necessary for the
motion picture player to keep in condition as it is for the athlete. Perhaps
more so, for the camera is very exacting and to appear before it in poor physical shape is ruinous to the actor," declared Rudolph Valentino in 1924.[104]
Potential distortions included the addition of weight, the emphasis of facial
imperfections, and the reduction of appeal sometimes visited upon apparently attractive people when they were photographed.

The last of these—more recently known as the phenomenon of photo-
geneity—was the most mysterious and the most frustrating effect, since it
seemed to make stardom almost a random event, or certainly one that was
often removed from the control of screen aspirants. "The camera ... sometimes ... fails to recognize the beauty of a face that is ravishing to the eye, and

sometimes makes a beautiful girl out of some homely little thing," observed a fan magazine article of the period.[105] Potential stars had to have not only acting talent and an attractive body, but also an ability to screen well. "I know actresses in Los Angeles who would not be considered raving beauties but who on the screen photograph wonderfully," declared Norma Talmadge in 1924. "Girls with ravishing complexions and figures apply daily at the studios for work, but fail because they do not 'register' well photographically. The camera is a fickle creature, and some girls with light-blue eyes photograph imperfectly while other blue-eyed girls get good parts when the camera tests show that they will 'screen.' "[106] Indeed, Hollywood cinematographer James Wong Howe recalled in a 1970 interview that his ability to darken the blue eyes of actress Mary Miles Minter gave him his start as a cameraman:

> "Mr. DeMille let me make some stills of her; she liked them; she asked me, in fact, to be her personal cameraman. What attracted her to my work was that I made her eyes dark. There were in fact a pale blue; orthochromatic film [a black and white film stock sensitive only to the green and blue thirds of the spectrum] lightened them too much and made them expressionless. I wondered what made the eyes dark, and I suddenly realized that the darkness was caused by the reflection of light off black velvet which happened to be lying in the stills-room. So I had a big frame of black velvet made and a hole cut in the centre; putting the lens through, I did all her close-ups that way."[107]

The camera became the arbiter of screen success, its "cruel eye" ferreting out or magnifying physical flaws. "A round firm face is essential [for motion picture stars] since the camera really lies," commented a 1929 fan magazine article. "The average close-up magnifies the subject fifty times. That means every tiny wrinkle appears on the screen fifty times deeper than it is!"[108] An editor's note in a 1921 *Photoplay Magazine* explained that motion picture stars have to "keep in perfect condition always—for if [they] don't, the camera's cruel eye calls attention to their shortcomings."[109] D. W. Griffith also emphasized the camera's propensity to age screen performers and the subsequent need for youth in cinema:

> The older stage did not need in its plays young actors. Yet it needed youth. But, on the older stage, a woman of forty or more could play the part of youth—Sarah Bernhardt plays such parts to this day. But before the camera the woman of forty is—the woman of forty. Truly, the camera is a horrible weapon! On the older stage, with deft make-up and lights dimmed a little, one could play the youthful part, but not before the camera. We have seen them try!.... No artist has yet been discovered who can at forty imitate youth successfully before the camera, which exaggerates age amazingly. So we need youth![110]

Griffith does not explain how or why the camera has this effect; it is possible that he was simply promoting his personal preference for small, child-like female stars. Griffith, as well as most directors, producers, and cinematographers working in Hollywood in the 1910s and 1920s, agreed that screen performers, especially women, had to constantly battle any signs of aging that might be picked up by the camera's probing lens. Such battles were significant enough to warrant the attention of professional cinematography journals. In 1927, for example, the *American Cinematographer* explained how lighting might be used to "subdue blemishes" and "favor the signs of age." Techniques for appearing youthful before the camera, argued the author of the article,

> ... would seem a matter of supreme importance, especially to our feminine stars, for the question becomes more serious as the years roll by. It becomes almost tragic when they have reached that glorious age which combines the fullness of womanhood, maturity of character, compelling personality and dramatic experience, all of which combine to make them great artists ... [and] they find all this pitted against the smooth, youthful faces of the ingenues.[111]

Though the magnification of facial wrinkles or blemishes was of considerable concern, camera distortion involving body weight seems to have been even more worrisome. Indeed, the call for "youth" in films could also be interpreted as a call for slim bodies, since adolescence was associated with slenderness and middle age with gradually accumulated fat. " 'There are, to my mind,' " declared a doctor warning women against the health risks of pursuing an adolescent figure, " 'three ideal figures. First, there is the slim and somewhat undeveloped figure of the adolescent. Then there is the young matron. And then there is the mother. These figures should under no circumstances be the same.' "[112] Screen performers, largely due to beliefs about the camera's ability to add weight to the body, pursued the lean figure of youth. Indeed, by the early 1920s, the desirability of such a shape was accepted without question, at least among Hollywood journalists and screen stars. According to one fan magazine article,

> It is probably well known to readers of *Photoplay*—it has been told in these columns many times—that an actress photographs ten pounds heavier than she actually weighs. That's just one of those nasty little tricks of the camera.... It has become almost [a requirement] among the actresses in Hollywood that they ... keep their weight below the health line. That, in more cases than one, has led to starvation diets, rapid decline, tuberculosis and other forms of ill-health.[113]

As a 1924 article wryly observed, fat was considered unacceptable onscreen, except for comic actors and actresses:

Grand-dad used to like 'em hefty. That was before the days of the motion picture and the Ford car. . . . Two hundred pounds didn't mean anything to the stout springs of a side-bar buggy or the stouter horse that pulled it. It takes more elbow room to drive a Ford, and a fat girl does spill over the side so! And imagine fat motion picture stars! Fat's only function on the screen today is to provide comic relief. The fat woman, in short, is out of it.[114]

The reason cited for the fat woman being "out of it" was not a change in public taste, but the camera's tendency to magnify the human body. A 1925 article in *Motion Picture Classic* explained, "Any girl who weighs more than 120 pounds and persists in such folly, must realize that she is headed straight for the slapstick comedies. The world has been made safe for the slim silhouette only. . . . If the stars wish to look like normal human beings instead of elephants on the screen, they must face the world with figures which are reed-like.[115]

People who met stars in person were surprised by their diminutive size. For example, a "famous dramatic critic" was shocked when he saw screen actress Dorothy Dalton performing on the stage: "I imagined her to be a huge, cowlike person," he wrote, "And here I find her petite and alluring—almost fairylike. It's a cruel industry!"[116] And screen actress Nita Naldi moaned, " 'Everyone is always shouting at me that I must get thin and will you please look at me! I weigh 118 pounds and my arms are not much bigger than slate pencils!' "[117] In 1931, *Photoplay Magazine* noted that the stately, fleshy beauties of old were not acceptable for the screen:

Compare the measurements of the Venus de Milo with those of the average film star. Venus was a pretty big gal, wasn't she? Recall the description of Helen of Troy—tall, statuesque, queenly. She couldn't get a job in the movies today. Diedre, the Celtic goddess, had a powerful frame. The Amazons were great, muscular women. So were the Valkyrie of German legend. Ziegfeld's famous beauties are long limbed, broad shouldered. For the first time in the history of the world the small woman occupies the pedestal. Screen stars must be small because the one-eyed camera enlarges. . . . The model for beauty that is Hollywood's . . . is a figure five feet tall [with a] weight less than a hundred [pounds].[118]

What is significant is that all of these articles differentiate between what they consider the traditional standard of female beauty (tall, fleshy) and the new "screen" standard demanded by the camera (petite, slender). One article points out that even Miss America, because of her large size, is not screen material. At five feet, six inches in height with a twenty-seven inch waist and thirty-three inch hips, Fay Lamphier, Miss America of 1926,

. . . was called ideal at the Atlantic City pageant. She is nearest the measurements of Venus, the ideal of the ancients. And yet Fay Lamphier is too big to become a movie star. Jesse Lasky states that she has great dramatic talent. There is no doubting her beauty. But before the camera, with its tendency to heighten and broaden everything, she becomes positively husky, she appears too fat, though actually she hasn't an ounce of superfluous weight *in proportion to her height and body structure.*[119]

In 1922, the Photoplay Research Society published an advice book entitled *Opportunities in the Motion Picture Industry—and How to Qualify for Positions in Its Many Branches* that explicitly described the physical qualifications necessary for screen performers. Two lists—one for women, and one for men—were included:

> The ideal woman of the motion pictures has these physical qualifications:
>
> *Features.*—They need not be classic but they must be regular. The retrousse nose, if not too broad, gives a piquant expression to the face. The mouth can be made up and its size it not of great importance.
>
> *Complexion.*—We are looking for blondes. Most men in the films today photograph dark and the contrast provided by the blonde woman is effective. The girl with light golden hair will photograph as a true blonde. Therefore, blonde women are given the preference. The good looking brunette, of course, is always desirable.
>
> *Stature.*—The small girl is preferably the screen type. Many leading men are not tall and they appear to disadvantage unless they are surrounded with small women. The dainty Mary Pickford—Marguerite Clark type has always been very popular, perhaps because it is easier for the little girl to win sympathy. These actresses are exceptions; they are less than five feet, but the slightly taller girl, between five feet and five-feet-three, will be the most readily chosen by the casting directors.
>
> *Weight.*—Any figure is acceptable if it's slender. I do not mean that a 'skinny' figure is desirable, but just that rounded slenderness that typifies youth. Fat is the worst enemy of film actresses. The star must watch her diet carefully, for the first double chin would endanger her popularity.
>
> *Age.*—I need scarcely mention this. The careful eye of the camera detects every little line, every wrinkle and crow's foot. Girls should start in young so that they gain their preliminary experience and achieve stardom before they begin to fade. I would not advise any woman past twenty-six to start unless she wants to develop into a character actress. . . .
>
> [Male physical qualifications are as follows:]
>
> *Features.*—Regular, but not necessarily classic. The virile type of he-man is more popular than the very handsome hero. Strong features are better than small features.
>
> *Complexion.*—Men usually photograph dark, so that the medium blonde makes the best type. But the attractive brunette who has a reputation for being 'romantic' certainly pleases the women.

Stature.—Not too short. A man has to be over five feet four. Occasionally a comedian or a juvenile will get away with less, but the hero must tower above his lady love. Rich Barthelmess is not tall; neither is Charles Ray. The ideal man of the movies is a little over that vague standard known as 'average height.'

Weight.—A man can be heavy if he wants to be funny, but if he expects to be taken seriously, he must be slender. The long lines are better than the broad, although fans are apt to classify the large-framed, big boned man as 'virile.'[120]

Motion picture performing was thus a profession with specific *physical* qualifications; the "careful eye of the camera," it was believed, demanded youth and slenderness. A fan magazine article written along similar lines even went so far as to recommend the ideal physical dimensions for screen stardom: 5 feet 4 inches and a weight of 120 pounds for women, and 5 feet 10 inches and 165 pounds for men.[121]

When analyzing the reason(s) for the camera's distortion of body weight, such sources typically cited the camera's conversion of three-dimensional objects into two-dimensional objects. One fan magazine article claimed,

If a practical stereoscopic camera lens were perfected these all too rigid diets would be unnecessary.... The camera photographs but two dimensions. This tends to flatten a round object. Look at a pipe. Then shut one eye. The pipe immediately widens and appears several inches broader than it really is. A skillful cameraman may arrange his lights so that this condition is helped, but only the three dimensional lens will alleviate the necessity of the stars being underweight.[122]

Of course, fan magazines of the period were not renowned for their factual accuracy. A survey of other 1920s' sources yields little relevant information in this area, however. The *American Cinematographer,* which was published throughout the decade, makes no mention of weight distortion caused by the camera. A 1927 article in the *Cinematographer* referred to earlier in this chapter does discuss how different lighting may "change the character of the subject; destroy or preserve beauty, exaggerate or subdue blemishes, aggravate or favor the signs of age" but never specifically addresses the subject of weight.[123] The journal of the Society of Motion Picture Engineers, known as *Transactions of the Society of Motion Picture Engineers*, also makes no mention of weight distortion associated with the camera. Interestingly, both the *American Cinematographer* and the *Transactions of the Society of the Motion Picture Engineers* printed several 1920s' articles on the development of a stereoscopic camera, suggesting that the topic was one of general interest during this period, and perhaps explaining its use in the technical explanation offered in the fan magazine (cited above).

The question then remains: Did (and does) the motion picture camera actually add weight to the body? This query is a contentious one without an immediately apparent answer, largely because the subject has never been adequately explored in print materials, which either equivocate or offer a definite opinion on the subject without a supporting technical explanation. Though 1920s' sources appear to agree that the camera *did* add weight, current film industry professionals tend to dismiss this notion (with varying degrees of certainty). Carl Girod, the Director of Engineering for the Society of Motion Picture and Television Engineers, offers a cautious assessment of the camera's effect on body weight: "From a technical standpoint, assuming the equipment is all aligned correctly, the system should reproduce what the eye sees—almost. Aside from a few three-dimensional experiments, all film and television are two-dimensional images, [and are] not exactly what the eye sees. There may be psychophysical effects that 'add weight.' SMPTE does not have any more information on this subject." Girod *does* agree that the addition of body weight is not a given the minute a performer steps in front of a camera, however.[124] Steven Poster, a member of the American Society of Cinematographers who has served as Director of Photography on such films as *Someone to Watch Over Me*, *Life Stinks*, and *The Boy Who Could Fly*, claims, "Today's lenses are designed with state-of-the-art optical science. There is no visible distortion in the high quality lenses that are used for motion pictures.... So I'm sure that the true size of actors is shown on the screen."[125] Iain Neil, an Executive Vice President at Panavision who specializes in optical design, is also convinced that modern high-quality lenses do *not* distort the body's size to any appreciable degree. Further, he explains that the shift from three dimensions to two dimensions that occurs when three-dimensional objects are photographed does not "stretch" the resulting images, as the fan magazine article cited earlier in this chapter suggested. Lighting, focal length (length of lens), and camera angle can affect the body's appearance, but they are as likely to *slenderize* the body as they are to *fatten* it.[126]

As far as modern cinematography is concerned, then, the notion that the camera always adds weight to the body appears to be a myth. This was *not* true for 1920s' cinematography, however, since lens elements could not be corrected for optical distortion as easily as they can be today. As a result, lenses of the 1920s were relatively crude. "It was equivalent to taking a Coca-Cola bottle and using it to make lenses," says Neil. Consequently, it is extremely likely, according to Neil, that such early lenses produced what is known as "barrel distortion," where imperfections in the lens elements would have caused objects on screen to appear slightly bowed out, like a rectangle stretched to resemble a barrel. Steven Poster, the director of photography cited above, also acknowledges this possibility: "In those days [the 1920s] the quality of optical design wasn't developed to the fine point we have today. So there might have been some barrel distortion ... in lenses that made the subjects look a bit heavier."[127] Thus it seems that there may be a scientific basis for the claim that screen performers of the 1920s had to reduce in order to, as one fan magazine described it, "look like normal human beings instead of elephants."

On a more speculative note, there are other production factors specific to the 1920s that may have made screen performers more conscious of bodily imperfections. One was the development of the close-up, which came into wide use in the late 1910s and early 1920s. Close-up shots, when presented on movie theater screens, magnified faces and other body parts to many times their normal size, exaggerating wrinkles, crooked teeth, receding chins, and other so-called "imperfections." Such shots allowed audiences to examine performers' faces in great detail; fat may have suddenly seemed less desirable simply because it was more visible. Also, as David Stenn, author of the Clara Bow biography *Runnin' Wild*, has pointed out, screen stars of the silent era quickly realized that thinner faces seemed to have larger, more expressive eyes. In order to emote more effectively and memorably in close-ups, stars kept their weights as low as possible.[128]

Orthochromatic film, the standard stock of this period, may have appeared to add weight to the body, particularly the face, because it did not record the entire color spectrum. Black and white orthochromatic film was sensitive only to the blue and green thirds of the visible spectrum; red did not register. Because of this, the pinkness or rosiness that added shape and depth to the face was not recorded by the camera, resulting in a flatter appearance. Of course, such effects were minimized by the use of make-up appropriate to the film stock in question. For orthochromatic film, performers used make-up with bluish and/or greenish tints. In the late 1920s, panchromatic film, which was sensitive to the entire visible spectrum, came into general use, and a series of articles in the *American Cinematographer* addressed the adjustment in screen performers' make-up that ought to be occasioned by such a shift:

> The panchromatic film, now being widely used, is sensitive to a wide range of colors, compared to the ordinary film [orthochromatic stock], and for this reason the make-up may assume the more natural flesh tints. . . . Flatness is often greatly relieved, even under highly diffused light. . . . Although some cameramen are very enthusiastic as to [the] powers of panchromatic film, we suggest caution among the stars and principals in relinquishing make-up entirely.[129]

Max Factor, the era's acknowledged authority on screen make-up (and its chief source of make-up products), echoed this sentiment: "No matter how fine the quality of photography may be . . . or the finesse of the lenses used for panchromatic filming, without the correct application of make-up there is no method of covering up the defects of nature, and [of] bring[ing] out the true characterizations needed."[130]

Though Hollywood journalists and even industry professionals of the period failed to produce an accurate technical explanation for the camera's addition of weight to the body, they acknowledged the existence of this phenomenon and took steps to address its effects. The first line of defense was to use various camera and make-up tricks to counterbalance any distortions of the body. "'Anyone can be photographed—and, if the cameraman is expert—practically anyone can appear to advantage,'" commented Los Angeles photographer Biddle Keyes in a 1925 *Photoplay* article. "There are a thousand and one tricks of photography," the article continued. "[For example], lowering the camera has the effect of making a player appear thinner."[131] (No explanation is offered for this phenomemon.) Carefully arranged lighting was considered a prime weapon in the arsenal against physical defects and a prime culprit in the exaggeration of any distortions of the camera. "The stronger the light the harsher the shadows and the harsher the shadows the more prominent the imperfections," declared author Louis Physioc in the *American Cinematographer.*[132] A Hollywood writer who spent some time as a "juicer," a "meek and lowly worm who turns on the lights by which the stars radiate their expensive egos," commented, "Of course there are many stars, like Mary [Pickford], who are beautiful on and off the screen, but most of them have certain defects (even Mary has her good side) that must be overcome by lighting, and such results are achieved only after years of experiment."[133] Physioc explains that close-ups can be specially lit to "burn out a little fullness under the chin that seems not to have worried Venus, but annoys some of the present beauties."[134] Make-up was also considered a key factor in enhancing screen appearance: "Imperfections of contour and features, disfiguring marks undetectable by the eye in normal conditions, but emphasized by the camera and by the tense attention paid by an audience to the greatly enlarged picture on the screen, [can] be corrected and rendered invisible."[135] Such tricks were designed to make the body appear thinner or better looking without actually changing its size or shape.

The second line of defense against camera distortion was to permanently modify the body, usually through diet or exercise. Indeed, though there may have been other reasons for members of the Hollywood motion picture community to participate in physical culture (see chapter 1 and previous discussions in this chapter), the camera's propensity to enlarge the human form was the most frequently cited motivation for such activities. One 1930 fan magazine article commented, "In Hollywood, if you take care of the pounds, the pence will take care of themselves. The camera has a way of exaggerating size without mercy. One potato, recklessly indulged in, may cost a contract."[136]

While established stars had to avoid such "reckless potatoes" to continue enjoying the largesse Hollywood offered them, aspiring stars had to slim down in order to improve their chances of achieving screen fame, and no method was too drastic. In 1929, a Hollywood physician related the story of a young starlet:

I noticed that she was losing weight rapidly and asked her what trick diet she was following.

She smiled and said, "I am a Roman."

Not understanding, I pressed her for further information.

"Oh," she said, "all of us girls are doing it now. We eat whatever we want and after the meal is over, we get rid of it by simply sticking a finger down the throat."

This young miss had her history, as well as her digestive apparatus, slightly messed up. The Roman epicure regurgitated after a banquet so that he could eat more. The movie maid "snaps her cookies" so she can eat less.

It is hardly necessary for me to condemn such a repulsive practice. It merely shows to what lengths girl will go to get the figures that the hard-hearted producers seem to favor because the camera lies, at least in so far as the matter of curves goes.[137]

Losing weight became part of the magical process of transformation that forged stars from ordinary human beings. In *Photoplay Magazine*, for instance, readers were treated to the story of Clara Bow, who rolled around her room in order to become a celluloid beauty: "Clara Bow ... beat the Brooklyn department stores out of another tubby ribbon clerk and gave to Hollywood a rollicking gaiety that has stirred the pulse of its languid social realm."[138] ("Rolling" was a popular method of exercise during this period; see the Clara Bow section in chapter 4 for a more complete discussion.) Joan Crawford also lost weight before she became a star:

> When Lucille Le Sueur changed her name to 'Joan Crawford,' she changed something else as well—her figure. While Lucille was a big buxom girl weighing a hundred and forty-nine pounds, 'Joan' became the slim hipless flapper whose ability to wear scanty clothes has made a world of women sigh for vanished waistlines. And the amazing thing was that she decided definitely to reduce all in a minute, did actually reduce in three weeks, and has never varied since then more than a pound or two from her present weight of a hundred and eighteen![139]

Years later, one of Joan Crawford's biographers claimed that her weight loss was occasioned by a cameraman's advice:

> A special friend was Johnny Arnold, the cameraman on *Sally, Irene and Mary* [1925]. "Your face is built," Arnold told Joan.
>
> "What do you mean?" she asked.
>
> "It isn't like any other actress's. The bones are made just right for the camera. There's only one trouble.... The camera can't see them. You have to lose weight."
>
> Immediately Joan gave up starches and sweets and existed on steak and grapefruit for breakfast, steak and tomatoes for lunch, steak and tomatoes

for dinner. Within weeks she dropped twenty pounds, and the change was dramatic. Her eyes seemed immense, leading to rumors that she had undergone an operation in which the skin was slit to make them bigger. No longer was she apple-cheeked; her flesh became elegantly molded to the bone.[140]

In 1927, Universal star Laura LaPlante described some of the hurdles that "Eloise," a typical young woman in pursuit of stardom, might face. Looking "heavy" on screen is one of them:

> At last ... some studio may decide that Eloise has possibilities. An individual screen test is arranged....
>
> In the event ... that Eloise's screen test is a good one, and, so, she is launched on a screen career, her next work is the most important and hardest test. If she is physically well and strong, the long hours will not wear so much on her. The chances, however, are that Eloise has been a dainty, delicate sort of girl and the long hours tax her. If she accepts invitations to dinners and to dances occasionally, she may be all worn out in a short time. And the result—she looks dull in the 'rushes,' the daily screening of the previous day's work at the studio. Even her lovely profile displays lines and looks older than her eighteen summers.
>
> *If she is inclined to be the least bit fat, she may look heavy on the screen. The director will shrug his shoulders and she will be ordered to reduce* [my emphasis].[141]

A slender body was repeatedly touted as one of the necessary ingredients of screen stardom. For successful Hollywood stars, dieting became a way of life—one of the guarantors of continued screen fame.

By the end of the decade, some writers were declaring the slender screen figure passé. "Don't diet! Curves are coming back!" exclaimed Dorothy Calhoun, a fan magazine writer who had authored several articles offering reducing advice. "That's the word that's going around Hollywood these days—and the screen beauties are heeding it.... There is even room for dimples in elbows and cheeks these days! Several of the best-known reducing parlors in Hollywood have recently closed for lack of business."[142] Despite a spate of articles that trumpeted this "return of curves," concerns about the camera's propensity for adding weight remained ever present. One author claimed that although fad diets were no longer popular, the camera would always require slenderness:

> The trick diets are gone from Hollywood! They're as dead as last year's sparrow. Sanity once more rules the film colony.
>
> It is not because voluptuous Turkish curves are coming in. The need for reduction is as great as it ever was. By a strange optical illusion the camera still adds ten to fifteen pounds to the human subject being photographed.

The necessity for being slender is as vital now to the screen actress as it was a year ago or five years ago.[143]

CONCLUSIONS

Hollywood was a new animal; it was not only evolutionary, but also revolutionary—or at least exotic. It basked in sun-warmed, open land, thousands of miles from traditional centers of civilization. It was a community of contradictions, producing a product and a lifestyle that offered extravagant intangibility, disciplined freedom, and adoration that frequently devolved into moral criticism. Both Hollywood and the industry that was its lifeblood grew up together, creating a land with a distinctive signature of beauty, luck, romance, and tragedy—a land whose activities were monitored with great interest by the rest of the nation and the world. Part of Hollywood's signature was written across the body, which was a crucial portion of the film industry's raw material, and, subsequently, of the Hollywood mystique. As stars of the 1910s and 1920s struggled to maintain attractive bodies that would garner box office success, they and a variety of interrelated factors, including climate, location, and lens distortion(s), helped Hollywood become our nation's first land of physical culture—a land where dieting and exercise played an the integral role in the lives of movie stars, those rarified beings whose extensively publicized lifestyles both catalyzed and intensified the reducing craze of the 1920s.

CHAPTER 3

Capitalizing Their Charms
Cinema Stars and Reducing

Any actress of course is obliged to watch her diet day by day in every way, if she cares anything about her figure and complexion. I never allow myself to eat all I want at any meal and I never eat candy or potatoes or fattening things.

—Viola Dana (motion picture actress), 1924

Don't hitch your scales to a movie star in your hope for an ideal figure. Almost every star has to diet herself nearly ill to retain a good movie figure. Yet the figure of the movie star ... [is] actually the figure sought after by the mass of women attacked by reduceomania.

—Catherine Brody, *Photoplay Magazine*, 1926

Herewith we offer you Hollywood's famous eighteen-day diet, on which the stars lose a pound a day.... Faithful movie fans, tempted almost beyond bearing by a chocolate éclair or a box of candy, may buoy up their resolution by whispering the magic formula, "What the stars can do, I can do."

—Dorothy Calhoun, *Motion Picture Magazine*, 1929

If any one category of individuals became synonymous with the reducing craze of the 1920s, it was "motion picture stars." Idols of the silver screen, both male and female, became the exemplars of successful diet and exercise programs. Their trials and tribulations with the "battle of the bulge" received regular coverage in fan magazines and other press outlets, as did their fabulous lifestyles, which featured elegant and expensive homes, cars, clothing, and hobbies. And the latter seemed to flow from the former in a manner that was altogether novel. Movie stars were a new order of being; they were in the vanguard of a profession that seemed insubstantial, chimerical, and mysterious—a profession that meted out fantastic monetary rewards and adulation for good looks. Certainly stardom was not synonymous with an attractive body. But there was also no denying the fact that Hollywood had commodified attractiveness in ways that were not possible before the age of mechanical reproduction. As their images were replicated thousands of times for millions of fans, motion picture stars became public figures whose success, though ostensibly predicated upon acting skill, seemed to depend to a large extent upon *appearance*. Indeed, early stars' physical caretaking rituals quickly became an indispensable part of their professional duties. Stars were frequently featured as experts in diet and/or beauty articles; star contracts featured weight clauses requiring slenderness; being either an athlete or a bathing beauty was a potential route to stardom; and star biographies claimed that losing weight was a key part of the frequently inexplicable process whereby ordinary human beings became celluloid luminaries.

THE EMERGENCE OF MOTION PICTURE STARDOM

The label "motion picture star" is bestowed upon a scant number of motion picture performers who appear in major roles and have great box-office appeal. Performing on the silver screen is no guarantee of stardom; one can be an extra, a bit player, a featured player, or even the principal player in a film and still not be accorded the status of "star." Perhaps the most succinct and straightforward definition of motion picture stardom was published in *Motion Picture Classic* in 1930: "Stardom is generally conferred upon an actor only when his popularity and prominence are deemed more important to the box-office than the title of his current picture."[1] Stars are those performers *whose name alone* is sufficient to draw audiences to the theater. Motion picture stars are a monopoly unto themselves. They have some unique quality or set of qualities—a "personality"—for which audiences are willing to pay. This personality is something that exists apart from any particular film, and, indeed, is influenced by all of the sources that work to construct a star's image.

Motion picture stars appeared with the establishment of the star system circa 1913–14. The term "star system" is not synonymous with the "studio system" that emerged in the mid-1920s when the motion picture industry became vertically integrated. The star system to which I refer is more an *orientation* or an *approach* than a specific film production, distribution, or exhibition system, yet it is vital to the existence of stars. Ira Konigsberg, in his *Complete Film Dictionary*, describes the star system as "the method and manner of exploiting the on- and off-screen existence of specific performers to sell motion pictures to the industry." In *Picture Personalities: The Emergence of the Star System in America*, Richard deCordova refers to the star system as "the full range of practices that constitute movie stars."[2] The star system assumes that motion picture stars are *the* currency of the industry. Stars are the main "subjects" of films. They are what audiences pay to see—and what viewers remember when they leave the theater.

Today, such assumptions are commonplace. In the early years of motion pictures, they were unheard of. "Moving pictures existed for over a decade before anything resembling a star system appeared," says deCordova.[3] When motion pictures were introduced to the public in the 1890s, many films were simply "documentary views" of ordinary life or newsworthy events. No stars were needed. When short narrative films began to be produced, the performers who appeared were not named, either in the films themselves or in any promotional materials that accompanied them. Some films did feature well-known public personalities such as vaudeville performers or actors from the stage, but these figures were not movie stars. Their fame came from achievements in other arenas. Most film histories claim that motion picture stars began to emerge in 1910. Until that point, performers were content to remain anonymous, since appearing in the disreputable "movies" was considered a step down from the legitimate stage. Production companies were not anxious to promote performers, either, lest they develop larger egos and demand greater remuneration for their cinematic efforts. But the public was clamoring for more information about their favorite performers, and in 1910 independent producer Carl Laemmle (who founded Universal in 1912) minted the first "star" by releasing the name of popular player Florence Lawrence to the public. DeCordova summarizes the accepted history of motion picture stardom:

> The explanation [of the rise of the star system] offered by the classic film histories remains fundamentally unchallenged. This explanation basically proposes a series of four 'events': 1. The public wanted to know the names of the performers. 2. The producers resisted revealing the performers' names for two reasons. First, they did not want to pay higher salaries to performers, and second, the performers were in reality legitimate actors who would risk their reputations by appearing by name in films. 3. Carl Laemmle, in a move designed to gain an ascendancy over the Motion Picture Patents Company [known as "the Trust" and initiated by Thomas Edison, this company tried to monopolize the industry by denying competitors the use of their patented film equipment], introduced the first star, Florence Lawrence. The star system thus emerged out of a struggle between Trust members and Independents. 4. The Independents and the public finally won and the star system was born.[4]

In reality, claims deCordova, the development of motion picture stardom was a complex event that cannot simply be attributed to the desire of the public to know more about the performers or to the actions of a man who attempted to satisfy that desire. If the public *did* wish to know more about its favorite performers, what source motivated that desire?

According to deCordova, the public's curiosity about motion picture performers was cultivated by discourse about motion picture "acting" that began to be published around 1907 in newspapers and industry trade papers. Prior to that time, there was no agreement, even among industry insiders, that motion picture performers actually *performed*; rather, they seemed simply to *pose*. Indeed, in that first decade of motion picture technology, there was an emphasis on the *machine*, on the equipment that *recorded* and *exhibited* the image. There was no discussion or acknowledgment of the labor that *produced* the image. "The activity behind a particular representation was relegated to the workings of the machine, not to the 'creative' labor of humans," explains deCordova.[5] But as more nickelodeons began to open (at least 2,500 by 1907), the industry could no longer depend upon documentary films, which were subject to the unpredictable ebb and flow of newsworthy events, and production of fictional films rose dramatically. Magazine and newspaper articles began to adopt a theatrical model of film performance. "From 1907 on we can see a kind of struggle between the photographic conception of the body and a theatrical one—between posing and acting. The ascendancy of the latter followed in part because it could account for the body as the site of a fictional production."[6] DeCordova also points out that the discourse on acting "did not emerge simply because people acted in films ... [it worked] to assert and establish the 'fact' that people acted in films."[7] This discourse helped film companies to differentiate their films from the hundreds of others on the market. It also solicited the public's desire to "see identifiable figures acting on the screen."[8]

Hence, shortly after 1907 the actor became the primary focus of motion pictures: "In effect, a system of enunciation was put in place that featured the actor as subject. This institutionalized a mode of reception in which the spectator regarded the actor as the primary source of aesthetic effect. It is the identity of the actor as subject that would be elaborated as the star system developed."[9] Alexander Walker, in his well-known history of stardom, claims that the increased use of close-ups during this period was also a key development. "By isolating and concentrating the player's looks and personality ... [the close-up] was to be the decisive break with stage convention, the most potent means of establishing an artist's uniqueness and the beginning of the dynamic psychological interplay of the filmgoers' and the film actors' emotions."[10]

Initially, moviegoers got to know their favorite "picture personalities." Discourse that publicized players' names, their screen personas, and their professional experience revealed interesting bits of information about their backgrounds. "A large percentage of the early discourse on picture personalities presented itself as explicitly posing or revealing a secret," asserts deCordova. "The spectators' sense that they were uncovering secrets with every answer gleaned from the films and fan magazines piqued their will to knowledge and afforded a bonus of pleasure with every 'discovery.'"[11] From the beginning, audiences sought to know *more* about their favorites, to know the "real" story. If, as most film histories claim, motion picture companies and/or players were reluctant to reveal information of this nature, it was not an impediment to the emergence of the star system. "Quite the contrary—the sense that information about the players was being held back was an integral, and often quite consciously utilized, part of the publicity efforts designed to promote personalities."[12]

Until the early 1910s, stories about picture personalities remained within clear boundaries, serving only to reinforce the "truth" of the character types performers played in their films. "Everything written about the players' real personalities would support, amplify, and, in effect, advertise, the representations for sale in the movies themselves," deCordova explains. "Even though the player's 'real life' identity was delineated, it was drawn from his or her appearance in films."[13] Shortly thereafter, however, another layer of secrecy was probed; around 1913–14, there was a significant increase in journalistic discourse about the players' private lives. At first, such articles presented a very conventional view of stars' love lives and family lives, but the scandals of the early 1920s (for example, comedian Fatty Arbuckle's arrest for sexual assault and director William Desmond Taylor's mysterious shooting death) contradicted this picture, and "references to divorce, adultery, and moral transgression [then] became a regular feature of star discourse."[14]

Public interest in the intimate details of a star's "real life" or "true identity" was, according to deCordova, a consequence of the new star system:

> The fascination over the players' identities was a fascination with a concealed truth, one that resided behind or beyond the surface of the film. The actor first appeared as the revelation of the mystery of the labor behind filmmaking; the picture personality appeared as the revelation of the 'real' names and personalities of the actors; and the star appeared as the revelation of the picture personalities' private identities outside of films. Each of these stages introduced a new level of secrecy and truth beneath or beyond the previous one.[15]

Here, deCordova makes one of his most important points. The star system is an apparatus that posits stars as the "truth" of films; it reduces the reality of a film to "a question of the 'true' identity of the actor as the film's source."[16] In short, it is "an orientation of the spectator's attention ... but not essentially a visual orientation. The star system leads us toward that which is behind or beyond the image, hidden from sight."[17] This is the nature of all discourse on stars; it piques our interest in what lies just outside our realm of knowledge. The spectator pays to experience the identity of a star. Because our culture equates identity with the private, the spectator seeks information about the private life of a star to know the truth of the star's identity.

In terms of causality, then, the star system seems to have been precipitated by the exigencies of the motion picture industry, circa 1907. As companies adopted production of fictional films, placing the spotlight on actors proved a convenient way of differentiating their films from the hundreds of others on the market. "Their company name and the genre of the film accomplished this to a degree," argues deCordova, "but not to the degree or with the force that the presence of an actor would."[18] Discourse that helped proved the "fact" that performers acted in films solicited the interest of the public in the men and women who appeared on the silver screen. Very quickly, actors became the central focus of the film industry. By 1916, contract players were the acknowledged lifeline of the studios. And according to Walker, advances in film technique between 1914 and 1917, such as improvements in scripts, cameras, and lighting, "opened the way for the audience to enter into a new relationship with the personality on the screen.... By the last half of the decade all the technical and economic conditions were present for the emergence of the great star prototypes."[19]

THE RELATIONSHIP OF STARDOM TO PUBLIC LIFE

Motion picture stars of the 1910s and 1920s often elicited intense and dramatic public reponse(s) to their personas. Walker describes the moment when Mary Pickford first recognized that cinematic performers wielded a new and different kind of power:

> Ironically it took her brief return to the stage to prove this to [her].... She first had the nature of her fame and future brought ... home to her by the audiences which packed the theatre and thronged the stage door not to see a [David] Belasco leading lady, but the ex-Biograph film star. As an emotional response, it was different in kind and fervour from that which greeted stage celebrities. It was close and personal, yet dissociated and mob-like. It radiated love, yet turned the loved one into an object. It derived from a star's uniqueness, but was diffused by her ubiquity.[20]

Such ubiquity was a critical attribute of motion picture stardom. Unlike theatrical performers, film stars were creatures of the age of mechanical reproduction: "Instead of an advertisement in the local paper and bills outside the theater where she was appearing, the new film publicity multiplied the presence of a player ten thousand times, wherever mechanical reproduction purveyed her film image ... creating a public interest in her personality, earning power, likes and dislikes—things that might have nothing to do with her art."[21] Thus the social role of stars in the 1910s and 1920s has to be considered in terms of the paradoxical position(s) they occupied in the public sphere. Stars were simultaneously ubiquitous yet unique, well known yet ultimately unknowable, and dependent upon the public yet able to exert power over it. Stars of this period functioned in at least four ways: (1) as the "truth" of films (the public sought information about star identities); (2) as ideal figures; (3) as living proof that the fantasy lifestyles of onscreen characters could exist in the real world; and (4) as examples of success for those who wanted to become stars themselves.

After the establishment of the star system, stars became the principal focus of the film-viewing experience. "You recall that picture you saw last night, or last week—or rather how much *do* you remember of it?" asked a fan magazine in 1928. "The title, the producer, the distributor, the author, the director, the cinematographer, the scenarist, the principal player—ah! You recall the name of the star! Surely! Patricia Whoosis, or Rinaldo Wham-sitt, wasn't it?"[22] If, as deCordova suggests, the star system foregrounded star identities as the center or "truth" of films, then any additional information about those identities deepened and enhanced the film-viewing experience. Tidbits about stars' acting backgrounds, personalities, and private lives functioned to reveal layers of "behind-the-screen" truth. In this regard, the body received particular attention, perhaps because physical details had been kept intensely private during the Victorian era. Any information that pierced the veil of secrecy surrounding the body was especially fascinating. Stars' diets, exercise routines, beauty regimens, and fashion choices received extensive publicity in fan magazines of the period, feeding fans' appetite for further morsels and helping to stimulate interest in physical culture.

Stars also functioned as ideal figures. As much as audiences may have appreciated and been titillated by the personal information revealed in fan magazines, they also distanced themselves from their silent screen idols, whom they placed on pedestals. In his now-classic consideration of motion picture stardom, *Stars*, Richard Dyer notes that scholars such as Edgar Morin, Richard Schickel, Alexander Walker, and others have suggested that "in the early period, stars were gods and goddesses, heroes, models—embodiments of *ideal* ways of behaving. In the later period, however, stars are identification figures, people like you and me—embodiments of *typical* ways of behaving."[23] One oft-cited reason for the shift is the transition to sound films circa 1930. According to Walker,

> A "loss of illusion" was certainly one of the first effects that the talkies had on audiences. Richard Schickel defined "silence" as the most valuable attribute of the pre-talkie stars. "A godhead is supposed to be inscrutable. It is enough that his image be present so that we may conveniently worship it." Once they had dialogue on their lips, the once-silent idols suffered a serious loss of divinity.... Their voices made them as real as the audiences watching them.[24]

Stars of the teens and twenties were made mysterious and exceptional through their silence, which clearly separated them from the ranks of mundane mortals. According to historian David Robinson in his book *Hollywood in the Twenties*:

> The Twenties was the age of idols: aeronauts, baseball players, preachers, politicians, but above all—movie stars. It was not just by chance that the greatest of all the gods in the Hollywood pantheon all belonged, pre-eminently, to the post-war decade—Pickford, Fairbanks, Chaplin, Valentino, Garbo. The silent stars had a magic that could never quite be recaptured in days of talking pictures. The lack of voices did not constitute a deficiency in a specific human attribute. On the contrary, distancing them

from ordinary human normality, it added to the mystery and romance and remoteness of the image.[25]

Stars' silence, coupled with the presentation of their images on larger-than-life screens in increasingly opulent theaters ("picture palaces"), helped them to become models of behavior and appearance. Youthful, willowy screen players established a new standard of attractiveness that was disseminated on an unprecedented scale. Of course, whether or not motion picture fans *pursued* this new standard is a complicated question. It is likely that the majority of fans sighed once or twice over the figures of their favorite screen stars and then continued with their lives. For those with an interest in physical culture, however, stars' examples of physical perfection offered a convenient yardstick by which to measure their own physical progress—or the attractiveness of a potential mate.

In addition to functioning as the "truth" of films and as ideal figures, stars also served as living proof that the extravagant lifestyles of their screen characters could be a reality. Though they were celluloid gods and goddesses, silent screen stars ultimately had a terrestrial rather than a celestial existence. When they stepped off the screen they landed not in the heavens but on the earth, providing a crucial realization of their onscreen fantasy lives. According to Dyer, "Because stars have an existence in the world independent of their screen/'fiction' appearances ... the value embodied by a star is as it were harder to reject as 'impossible' or 'false'. . . ."[26] Though this theory is not limited to a particular historical context, Alexander Walker argues that when Hollywood stars of the 1920s stepped off the screen, their lives aped art in a manner that was unique to the period: "It is not simply distance away in time which makes the 1920s seem so exotic a decade in Hollywood. . . . What looks in retrospect like a fantasy existence was more often than not simply the economic and social fact of stardom at this time in Hollywood. 'In those days,' Gloria Swanson later recalled, "the public wanted us to live like kings and queens. So we did—and why not?' "[27]

In the tide of rising consumerism that characterized the years after World War I, says Lary May, "consumption allure" became the key to the Hollywood image and "film idols represented national models as leisure experts."[28] The studio system was not completely established, so stars still had relative freedom to strike lucrative deals with various production companies. They paid little income tax (less than one percent of the first twenty thousand dollars earned each year), leaving them ample funds to lead lives that were "a product of the romantic imagination."[29] "The way the stars behaved on and off screen made them objects of the wish-fulfillment drives of ... society," claims Walker.[30] Perhaps because of the rise in consumerism, film audiences of the 1920s were not interested in making a clear distinction between reel life and real life; consequently, "the most characteristic attribute of stardom in the 1920s was the belief, held by millions in a far more passionate way than in any following decade, that the stars were in real life the same exotic creatures that they appeared to be on the screen."[31] Such a belief allowed audiences to nurse the hope that onscreen fantasy life *could* become a reality. Stars were the personification of consumer culture, offering a "real" fantasy life as well as evidence that happiness might be *bought*. They had reached perfection (or so claimed advertisements and articles in fan magazines) through the careful selection of consumer products: cars, clothes, make-up, shampoo, reducing pills, and exercise machines. Fans had only to buy similar products in order to achieve an analogous state of excellence. "It is all part of our hectic optimism," observed one writer. "We refuse to believe that anything is inaccessible to us; we refuse to believe that there is any intangible good—beauty, or *chic*, or wisdom—which we cannot acquire by paying a little money for a magic formula."[32] (Stars' relationship to consumer culture is considered more fully in chapter 5.)

Finally, stars functioned as examples of success for those who wished to become stars themselves. Young people intent on enjoying a romantic Hollywood lifestyle packed up their belongings and headed to southern California, determined to achieve cinematic glory. The area was flooded with screen aspirants; admonitions to prospective stars began to appear in the popular press as early as 1915. "Just a word of warning here to the aspiring young girls all over the country who may believe that a trip to Los Angeles will put them in pictures," advised *Everybody's Magazine*. "The warning is: *don't come*. The Los Angeles Welfare Committee is kept pretty busy right now taking care of young girls who failed to get work and are stranded."[33] By 1923, 10,000 "movie-mad boys and girls" were streaming into Hollywood each month,[34] all intent on achieving screen fame. Fan magazine writer Gladys Hall describes the zeal of these young men and women:

> They *do* break their hearts, these desperate and determined [individuals]. They resort to extremities so fantastic, so reckless, suicidal, [and] dangerous as to pass credulity.... They traverse the country in *coffins* [train passengers could get a free ticket if they accompanied a corpse being transported for burial]; nice girls deliberately involve themselves in scandals in the forlorn hope that the resultant tabloid notoriety may also be resultant of—a contract. They do themselves actual bodily harm; they starve and die of starvation; they employ blackmail and bribery, fainting fits and stolen identities, spiritualistic means and lies that would send the Baron Munchausen tottering home to mama.[35]

Hall recounts the case of a girl with a "consuming ambition" who had very beautiful legs that were always in demand for close-ups. "One day ... she ... poured acid over her legs, burning them so terribly that they were grooved and seared to the very bone. She was rushed to the receiving hospital and there told reporters that she had disfigured her legs in the hope that directors might hear of her and give her a chance to show her face and her abilities on the screen."[36] Men were no less determined to win screen fame.

A 1929 fan magazine article describes a "handsome, Latin-looking boy of twenty-two or twenty-three" who visited an eminent plastic surgeon in Hollywood when a studio told him he was promising but needed larger eyes. "I could see where each eye had been slit at the corner and Dr. Balsinger was explaining that as soon as the scars healed he would be twice as good as new with large and expressive eyes," writes Dorothy Manners. "A heavy something rose to my throat.... I hope that kid makes good in pictures after all he has gone through."[37]

Even if we allow for the hyperbole characteristic of fan magazine articles, it is clear that the young people who came to Hollywood hoping to achieve stardom were an intense, single-minded lot. Arguably, such screen hopefuls were ardent and enthusiastic not because they dreamt of a life of hard work as they perfected their acting skills and gradually achieved fame, but because they yearned for the glamorous, indulgent lifestyle they believed would be theirs as soon as they were discovered. "To the uninitiated, studio life seems to mean an easy, carefree existence," remarked Reverend Neal Dodd, a rector at a Hollywood church. "In reality it is hard work, and only those putting forth their very best efforts at all times can hope for recognition."[38] A 1921 *Photoplay Magazine* article cited Marion Davies on this subject:

> "It is to laugh!" says Marion Davies, when she reads some of the letters written to her in which the youthful writer sighs for the life of the "movie star" and begs to know how she, too, can get into that enchanted life wherein with a magic wand all worries vanish and life looms forth one golden dream.
>
> "I should like to write a form letter," declared Miss Davies, "which would disperse for all time the popular conception of the tranquillity and ease of the life of my profession....
>
> "The life is one of unremitting work, calling for every resource of mind and body."[39]

Such protestations appeared regularly during the 1920s and give some indication of just how strongly screen hopefuls believed (or wanted to believe) that movie stars led charmed lives. And if they did believe, it is hard to blame them. For every article that attempted to disabuse fans of the notion that screen stars enjoyed an easy life, five others detailed their sumptuous Hollywood lifestyles. The one caveat that echoed throughout these and countless other fan magazine articles was that screen success could not come without a trim figure. When interviewed, stars frequently identified losing weight as a crucial factor in their elevation to stardom and the maintenance of a low weight as one of their ongoing responsibilities. The hundreds of thousands of young men and women who dreamt of a screen career, many of whom, if fan magazine writer Gladys Hall is correct, were willing to resort to "drastic measures" to achieve stardom, would have been unlikely to overlook or ignore such oft-repeated advice.

STARS' LINKS TO PHYSICAL CULTURE

Reducing as a Professional Duty

Much of the evidence for stars' links to physical culture in the 1920s can be found in motion picture fan magazines of the period. These publications, which played an important role in promoting Hollywood, were an unofficial clearinghouse for information about reducing. Far more than other popular periodicals, fan magazines focused on physical culture. Of course, there *were* magazines, such as Bernarr McFadden's *Physical Culture,* whose primary focus was the body. But of the periodicals whose main subject was ostensibly something *other* than physical culture—such as movies, or women's home life, or business—motion picture fan magazines published the most material focused on dieting. Advertisements, articles, and photos trumpeted the benefits of reducing, as well as cautioning against its potential ill effects. When the reducing craze hit its peak in the mid- to late 1920s, it was *Photoplay Magazine*—not *Time,* or *The Women's Home Companion,* or *The American Magazine*—that published a series of detailed and well-researched articles probing its genesis and development, with particular attention to the dangers involved in using quack reducing methods such as thyroid medication (although, of course, *Photoplay* failed to note its own role in promoting such methods). In many ways these magazines *were* the craze, since their articles and advertising defined it more completely than any other source.

As article after article clearly documents, reducing was considered one of the professional duties of motion picture stars, thus making all stars de facto experts in the physical culture arena. Stars were not simply skilled actors and actresses; they were proficient body shapers, as well. For example, *Photoplay Magazine* published a series of articles in 1921 entitled "How I Keep in Condition," with physical culture advice offered by Ruby De Remer, Katharine McDonald, Corinne Griffith, Lila Lee, and Marion Davies. The preface to these articles declares that they are "not beauty articles, but advice on how to keep fit by women who know: famous beauties of the screen. The film star, more than any other woman of any other time, has to guard her greatest asset: her good looks. She has to keep in perfect condition always ...."[40] "I want to eat what I want when I want to eat it," moaned Ruby De Remer in the first article of the series. "However, I can't, and earn an honest living as a motion picture star.... My diet is a great care to me, especially when I'm working, because I keep it strictly. I have to."[41] A 1922 article revealed that "film stardom doesn't entirely consist of electric signs and silversheet closeups. There are trials and tribulations going hand in hand with the glamour.... Physical training is ... essential. One's lines must be svelte and lithe or—cinema oblivion."[42]

Stars were considered diet experts *by virtue of their success as screen players.* No other profession enjoyed such a close association with reducing. There were physical culture "experts," to be sure; Susanna Cocroft and Sylvia Ulbeck worked to get women into shape, while Lionel Strongfort and

Earle E. Liederman promised to make men more "real" by building their muscles and paring their fat. Their professional mission was to make money through physical culture activities. By contrast, motion picture performing had no *direct* relationship to physical culture, yet it quickly became an occupation for which physical culture was an indispensable part. "They say the life of a film star is an easy one!" cried *Photoplay* in 1924. "Easy enough if ... you want a life of work and diet, exercise and starvation; for that's the answer. It's what they all say, what they all have to do."[43] Even doctors seemed to consider screen slenderness a foregone conclusion. In a 1925 article entitled, "The Deuce with Reducing," author Harriet Works Corley explains that screen comics must struggle to keep their weight *up* just as carefully as screen flappers must fight to keep theirs *down*. As she relates, when a physician who was asked how a female screen comic who weighed 240 pounds might regain the 25 pounds she had recently lost, he was aghast: "For this physician had taught many prominent women of society, stage and screen the art of keeping slender, and thus, charming and young. ... He was amazed that any woman, particularly of that profession which usually demands slenderness as the cornerstone of a career, should wish to gain when in her presumably short life she had gained far too much already."[44] In a 1929 article in *Motion Picture Magazine*, an unnamed "health authority" bemoans the fact that actresses are required to be thin: " 'The most tragic thing in Hollywood today,' claims this entity, 'is to see these girls fighting nature in an effort to be thin, and thus conform to the demands of the screen.' "[45] When *Motion Picture* published the particulars of the popular eighteen-day diet later that same year, readers were told, "It may not be as necessary to your profession to keep slender as it is to the picture people, but the day you get into a size smaller gown will one of the most thrilling of your life."[46]

Melodramatic pronouncements about stars' professional dieting obligations continued well into the 1930s. "Beauty!" sighed author Katherine Albert in late 1929. "To you and me the word conjures up a delightful picture of a slim, lovely girl in an organdie frock and a picture hat, seated in a sunlit garden. But to the cinema stars who have capitalized their charms it means vital hours slashed out of their lives, hours of torture, hours of both mental and physical agony!"[47] Sylvia Ulbeck (a.k.a. "Sylvia of Hollywood"), physical culturist to the stars, describes some of her massage treatments in the same article. When Ms. Albert asks if the treatments are painful, Sylvia shrugs. " 'Well, my dear, fat has to be pinched off. There's no other way. But what woman wouldn't suffer a bit for beauty? Yes, you and I would suffer a BIT for beauty. But our suffering is optional. A star MUST suffer for beauty. It is her job.' "[48] In 1930, fan magazine writer Dorothy Calhoun related a question someone had recently put to her: " 'Are the movie stars in earnest about their jobs?' said someone recently. When a person is willing to go without *food* for a cause, that person is in earnest. And half of the women—and men, too—in Hollywood deny themselves food."[49] In that same year, *Photoplay* published a tongue-in-cheek story about dieting in Hollywood called "Weight and Hope" that followed the adventures of screen player Hope Galaday. She is confronted by Abe Zoop, the head of production at her studio, who tells her that, at one hundred and twenty pounds, she is too fat; she must lose twelve pounds before her next picture:

> "What about this last picture?" demanded Miss Galaday, nearer to tears than she dared show. "Wasn't I suitable?"
>
> "Yes, but you was a piece of human flotsam!" shrieked Abe, becoming irritated. "Boxcar Annie could be a trifle plump, because once in a career you can have a part where your costume is an oatsack. From now on only forsaken wives can be plump, and you ain't the type. Roll off the weight or out of the business."[50]

And finally, in August of 1931, Lois Shirley offered a comment that may yet deserve the title of "Most Colorful" of Hollywood's melodramatic dieting similes: "It is vitally necessary for the women of the films to remain beautiful. Their food, clothes and shelter are dependent upon it. Without symmetry of form their screen lives are [as] dead as the gangster who squealed."[51]

It may seem ironic that such a male-oriented comparison should be applied to *women* and not to *men*, but it was also not remarkable, since most reducing commentary in fan magazine articles focused exclusively on female stars. To conclude that men did not face professional pressure to lose their fat is premature, however. Though men's need to keep fit was discussed less frequently than women's, perhaps because of our culture's tendency to highlight women's physical appearance more than men's, the occasions when it was mentioned make it clear that male screen stars, like their female counterparts, participated in physical culture as one of their professional duties. Business metaphors helped establish the need for male stars to keep "in trim." One argument was that male stars managed large sums of money and therefore needed to keep fit to handle their finances wisely. (Interestingly, such conclusions were never drawn where female stars were concerned.) A 1924 article on child star Jackie Coogan declares: "When a fellow's in the millionaire class, and has to bear the weight of grave business responsibilities, like Jackie has, he's got to look out for avoirdupois. That's something Jackie doesn't want to catch, because it sounds terribly formidable. So every day he reports to his gym instructor."[52] A more common argument was that, just as businessmen or athletes needed to keep fit in order to perform well in their respective professions, screen stars also needed to be at the peak of their physical abilities in order to survive the grueling demands of the screen (such as long hours and stunt work).

Both male and female stars may have engaged in physical culture activities to improve their health and stamina as well as their appearance, but any connection between physical culture and attractiveness was noticeably downplayed in articles that mentioned male stars. Reducing to improve one's performance in a manly activity such as business or athletics was perfectly acceptable, but slimming down to improve one's appearance was considered a distinctly feminine pursuit. Discourse about male stars' participation in physical culture emphasized *active* tasks such as weight lifting, riding, and boxing. These activities, in addition to highlighting the goal of enhancing performance (rather than appearance), could also function to recuperate masculinity, especially in the case of romantic stars. (See the "Rudolph Valentino" section of chapter 4 for a more complete discussion of the feminization of American culture and the recovery of masculinity through physical culture.) For example, in 1922, a two-page series of photos in *Photoplay* entitled "How They Keep in Trim" declared, "Motion picture stars have to keep fit. They can't allow themselves to go stale, for it will mean not only a loss of health, but a loss of acting vigor and appeal."[53] Included are photos of Owen Moore playing tennis, Jack Holt playing polo, and Malcolm McGregor getting ready to dive into a pool. Similarly, a series of "Keeping Fit" photos published in 1925 includes shots of Ramon Novarro on the high dive and Rudolph Valentino lifting weights.[54]

The need for male stars to diet does receive mention in a 1930 article by fan magazine writer Dorothy Calhoun, who explains that most stars' favorite reducing method is a low-calorie regimen that "varies with individual cases. Men (oh yes, men players in Hollywood, as well as the women, have to diet) require a somewhat different diet from women; young players in their teens need a different balance of fats and minerals from that of older people."[55] (Here, Calhoun's use of parentheses implies that male dieting *was* a bit of a "guilty secret" in Hollywood.) Silent screen star Francis X. Bushman also admitted that dieting was an important part of weight control for both sexes: "For any excessive weight use a safe and sane method to reduce and keep your figure in trim. If you are too thin make use of a well rounded diet which will induce a more attractive appearance. The rules are simple and apply to men as well as to women."[56] Such explicit links between male stars and dieting were the exception, however. Dieting was considered a relatively passive, "feminine" method of shedding fat.

Whether predicated upon the demands of money management or the demands of the screen, male physical culture in Hollywood received only a fraction of the attention accorded to females. In general, men's body sizes were never scrutinized as closely as women's. Perhaps the most telling example of this dichotomy can be found in the fictional "Weight and Hope" story cited briefly earlier in the chapter. Though the tale is clearly tongue-in-cheek, it presumably mocks generally accepted assumptions about weight loss in Hollywood. The story opens with screen player Hope Galaday being informed by her beau, screen heartthrob Lancelot Leake, that she is too fat: "'Hum!' remarked Mr. Leake in the insinuating tone envied by lesser Lotharios the world over, as Miss Galaday helped herself to five rashers of bacon. 'I dislike to mention it, but it seems to me, Hope, that you're getting fat.'"[57] Miss Galaday takes offense and declares herself exactly the right weight for her height, but Mr. Leake reminds her that "'this is a man's world.... It's up to you to reduce when I ask you like a gentleman.' "[58] At work, Miss Galaday is put on notice that she must lose twelve pounds or jeopardize her contract. Mr. Leake faces no such ultimatum, though we learn that Miss Fairfax, the costar of his current picture, considers him a "hippopotamus." " 'What do you mean, fat? I'm a big, healthy, six-footer,' " counters Mr. Leake, shocked.[59] The story concludes in true fairy tale fashion: Confronted by his own portliness, Mr. Leake modifies his opinions on fat, and no longer pushes Miss Galaday to reduce. Furthermore, the head of production at the studio, having heard that long, curvy skirts are coming into fashion, decides that Miss Galaday's figure will be marketable "as is." This is the ending that female stars no doubt desired, but were usually denied. Far more frequently than their male counterparts, they were required to meet weight guidelines in order to survive in their profession, and the chief route for bringing such pressure to bear was through studio contracts.

Contracts

A contract is an agreement endorsed by law. In the star system that emerged during the 1910s, popular screen players were the capital of the industry, and studios scrambled to sign them to long-term contracts. In these employment agreements struck between stars and studios, each side inevitably jockeyed for more power. Stars negotiated for private dressing rooms, top billing, script approval, and wages commensurate with their box-office appeal, while studios sought well-behaved, reliable moneymakers who could be dropped as soon as their popularity waned. Thus the contracts that resulted were a series of clauses (articles), each detailing the hard-won rights of either the studio or the star. For example, a standard clause of the 1920s, developed after a series of Hollywood star scandals in the early part of the decade, was the "morals clause." It was worded as follows in Clive Brook's 1925 contract with Warner Brothers:

> The Artist agrees to conduct himself with due regard to public convention and morals, and agrees that he will not do or commit any act or thing that will tend to degrade him in society or bring him into public hatred, contempt, scorn or ridicule, or that will tend to shock, insult or offend the community or ridicule public morals or decency or prejudice the Producer or the motion picture industry in general....[60]

Clauses could address any matter that concerned either party to the contract, and ran the gamut from considerations of money to issues of wardrobe, vacation time, or even marital status. They could also address body weight.

Indeed, when it came to contracts, weight was all-important for female screen stars since it could be a contract-maker or a contract-breaker. A plum part, a new contract, the continued validity of a current agreement, or the renewal of an option could all depend upon remaining in the good graces of one's scale. Aspiring stars were frequently told to "lose ten pounds" to win the role or the contract of their dreams, while current stars had to deal with "weight clauses" requiring them to maintain their weight within a particular range. If stars were lucky enough to negotiate a contract without a weight clause, their weight could still be an issue when that contract came up for renewal on "option day." "Options" were clauses giving studios the right to drop a contract at a pre-arranged date. Though contracts were typically good for five to seven years, studios had the option of canceling the agreement at six-month intervals (or sometimes only once a year). If, at the end of an option period, a star's physical appearance had altered in ways the studio felt were unacceptable, the star's contract could be summarily canceled. Thus the absence of an explicit weight clause did not mean the absence of pressure for a star to remain slender, since contract renewal could be jeopardized by excess weight.

Fan magazine articles regularly related stories of the quick weight loss necessitated by the offer of a coveted part. In her 1921 article, "How I Keep in Condition," screen actress Lila Lee describes her encounter with "Opportunity":

> Opportunity was introduced to me by William deMille, who summoned me to his office one day.
> "How much do you weigh, Lila?" he asked.
> Readers, I cannot tell a lie.
> "One hundred and eighteen pounds," I answered, and it sounded like a ton.
> "Hmm," said Mr. deMille. "Eight pounds too much." He pondered a moment. "Could you take off eight pounds in two weeks?" he suddenly inquired.
> I thought perhaps I could.
> "Well, if you can, I want you to play the feminine lead in 'After the Show.' Otherwise—"
> I *knew* I could!
> I had read the story, I love to work with Mr. deMille, and I wanted the part.
> "All right," were his parting words. "But remember—two weeks to the dot. In the opening scenes of the picture, you must seem worn and thin, and you could never do it the way you look now. A hundred and ten pounds is the absolute limit."[61]

This may appear to be a special case, since deMille explains that losing weight is necessary so that Lee will be "worn and thin" in the beginning of the film. But after Lee starves herself (living on nothing but orange juice for an entire week) and loses the eight pounds, deMille tells her, " 'The part is yours. . . . And, if you ask me, Lila, I think you look better than you ever have—thinner, healthier, and livelier.' "[62] Given his earlier request for her to lose weight in order to appear worn and thin, these compliments make little sense; apparently, deMille now feels that the diet has only *improved* Lee's beauty. His attitude echoes the sentiments of many in Hollywood who considered weight loss an automatic boon, particularly in female stars. Lee is so encouraged by deMille's praise that she continues her diet for another three weeks. "By that time I had lost fifteen pounds and decided that my weight was just where I wanted it—one hundred and three."[63] This is slender indeed, considering that a book of the period listed Lee's height as 5 feet 6 inches.[64]

Lee's story of weight loss was not unique. Actresses were not only asked to lose weight for roles in which they could pass as weary and undernourished, but also for standard romantic and/or dramatic leads. It was almost as if women's bodies had become one of the plastic arts; female stars were expected to reshape themselves within a matter of weeks (or even days), usually in order to become more slender. In 1925 actress Gertrude Short declared,

> "I can be any size or shape I choose. Just give me plans and specifications a week in advance! I was fifteen pounds overweight in *The Telephone Girl* series and when I was told I could have a certain role with a big company if I would lose ten pounds in a week, I lost 'em. Prize-fighters have nothing on me. I can weigh in [at] just what I want to at the ring of a gong."[65]

In a 1929 article entitled, "Diet—The Menace of Hollywood," author Katherine Albert questions the practicality of Dr. H. B. K. Willis, a physician who has advised women in Hollywood that it is unwise to lose more than two or three pounds a week:

> That's a nice idea. A physician can sit calmly by and make this truism, but—and this is large and vital—when a producer sits back in his leather chair, looking out across his mahogany desk and says to a girl, "You may have the leading role in my next super-epic if you will lose ten pounds in ten days," what is the girl going to do?
>
> Before her lies fame and fortune, luxury and acclaim. Is she going to think of her health? Is she going to heed a doctor's advice? Not much! She has heard the ultimatum. "Lose ten pounds in ten days." A career against her health. The career always wins.[66]

Just how frequently female stars were required to lose weight for particular roles is uncertain, but the routine nature of the practice is suggested by the fanfare surrounding an apparent *exception* to it: actress Marie Prevost's return to the screen in 1931. "138 Lbs. Ringside!" trumpets the title of the article that relates the details of her comeback. Prevost had been one of producer Mack Sennett's bathing beauties (see "Bathing Girls" section later in this chapter for a discussion of bathing beauties and their relationship to physical culture), but at 100 pounds she was "too curvy" and eventually stopped getting work.

> She'd saved up some money, and decided to rest and live well while she waited for the right part. She gained nearly forty pounds, mostly due to good parties! Of course, diet-crazed Hollywood put her down as *finis*. The hipless, frontless and meatless mode had arrived with a vengeance in the ghostly Garbo and Crawford and the movie catalogues were filled with Eighteen-day diets and other modes of looking like an invalid.[67]

When Frank Capra was casting for his film *Ladies of Leisure*, however, he "wanted a chubby, little comédienne to off-set the drama of Barbara Stan-wyck.... In short, he wanted nobody else but Marie Prevost and her 138 pounds."[68] Prevost's weight, instead of hindering her success, actually made her ideal for the role in question (which, it should be noted, was a *comic* role). The rarity of this situation becomes apparent when Dorothy Manners, the author of the article, concludes, "Somehow I have a hunch that we are going to have at least *one girl* on the screen *who doesn't look as though she was coming down with something.*"[69] Here, Manners exaggerates for the sake of humor, but such a remark would not *be* humorous unless slender stars were the rule in most Hollywood films.

New contracts could also hinge on weight. "I know a stage star who always was what the world calls 'a fine figure of a woman,'" declared fan magazine writer Harriette Underhill in a 1925 article pointing out that many stage stars had to slim down in order to make it in Hollywood. "Well, she decided she'd like to make some pictures and the movie magnate said she could sign a contract with him the day she tipped the scales at 115 pounds. That meant losing twenty-five pounds in six weeks and she had to live on three glasses of milk a day. But she did it!"[70] Similarly, a 1927 article in *Motion Picture Classic* notes that Vilma Banky had to take off fifteen pounds before Samuel Goldwyn would give her a contract, and "if her weight increases over five pounds, it's three strikes and out for Vilma."[71]

Whether such episodes were overstated or simply anecdotal, with no application to the majority of stars, is of course difficult to verify. Other evidence that documents the codification of low to moderate weights as a professional requirement of stardom lends credibility to the tales related above, however. Of paramount importance in this regard are the contracts that set weight limits for stars. "Almost all studios include a 'weight clause' in their contract. If the player passes the prescribed poundage, the contract is void."[72] Such weight clauses were mentioned frequently in fan magazine articles in the most dramatic context the facts would allow. When actress Marietta Milner died in 1929, an article in *Photoplay* speculated about the role her weight clause may have played: "From Vienna came the news that Marietta Milner, Hollywood film actress, was dead as the result of following a starvation diet. It was said she died of tuberculosis as an aftermath of too strenuous dieting. Friends said she reduced to get under the weight limit set by a film contract," noted a fan magazine article in 1929.[73]

Tamer articles simply noted the existence of weight clauses. "It is said that Gloria Swanson's last contract with Famous Players demanded that she retain her slim silhouette at all times," claimed a 1927 article in *Motion Picture Classic*.[74] When possible, such articles revealed the precise poundages stars were legally required to maintain:

> A limitation of one hundred and forty-two pounds is set on Anna Q. Nilsson, who, by the way, now weighs just one hundred and twenty-eight. Joyce Compton may add eighteen to her one hundred and twelve pounds without endangering any contract. Dorothy Seastrom, who weighs some one hundred and eighteen pounds now, may go as high as one hundred and forty, while Blanche Sweet is allowed to add twenty pounds to her present weight of one hundred and eighteen pounds.[75]

An article called "Contracts Is Contracts" published in *Motion Picture Magazine* later that same year also gives the specifics of several weight clauses:

> The freak clause in First National contracts relates to the size of the players, and names a weight limit for each one. If, for example, Anna Q. Nilsson gains eleven pounds over her present 131, her contract may be broken by the company. Dorothy Mackaill now weighs 122, still a safe distance from her specified limit of 130. Billie Dove, at 115, need not start on the lamb chop and pineapple diet for another seven pounds. Milton Sills is dangerously close to his deadline of 190, but there can be 34 more pounds of tiny Colleen Moore before her contract weight is reached.[76]

The word "freak" is used to describe the weight clause in First National contracts, perhaps suggesting how novel it was for a low weight to be a condition of employment. (First National was a major film producing and distributing company formed in 1917 and absorbed by Warner Brothers in the late 1920s.) Of course, it could also mean that First National was the only studio to include weight clauses in its contracts, but other available evidence indicates that this was not the case. For example, in a recurring fan magazine comic strip documenting the adventures of starlet "Cella Lloyd," mention is made of her weight requirements: "Cella's contract with the producers says that she must not weigh over 110 pounds. Money and popularity arrived so quickly that the little minx lost track of her figure. She has strapped herself to the ceiling and dances on air to make her waistline behave."[77] A 1927 *Motion Picture Classic* article cited earlier mentions that Gloria Swanson had a weight clause in a contract with Famous Players, while a 1929 *Photoplay* article tells the sad story of Kathryn Grant and her struggle with Hal Roach Studios:

The "Miss Los Angeles" of a few years ago was Kathryn Grant. A film career was assured when she was given a long term contract with the Hal Roach Studios. Pretty, talented—but overweight!

The order came.

She must lose. Those pounds HAD to come off!

She went on a diet so strenuous that she collapsed and was rushed to a sanatorium. Today you do not see her on the screen. Hollywood has forgotten her.

She has dropped out completely from the film world.[78]

And finally, an advertisement for Borden's Malted Milk from the early 1930s implies that weight clauses were a commonplace measure: "Excess weight carries a terrible price in Hollywood! It can mean not only loss of public popularity, but a *cancelled contract*, too. Is it any wonder screen stars become practical dietitians?" Joan Blondell and Warren William, both Warner Brothers players, explain that " 'keeping slim means keeping our contracts.' " They recommend eating a light "Hollywood lunch" consisting of a sandwich and a glass of Borden's Malted Milk.[79]

This evidence raises two important points. First, most of the contract weights were not shockingly low. According to the fan magazines, Anna Q. Nilsson's, Dorothy Seastrom's, and Blanche Sweet's contracts all allowed them to weigh in the neighborhood of 140 pounds, while Billie Dove and Dorothy Mackaill were limited to the range of 120 to 130 pounds. Though moderate, these weight requirements are significant simply because they *existed*, making the maintenance of a particular weight part of a player's professional responsibilities. And these weight ranges *are* relatively slender, in comparison with the statuesque beauty of the early 1900s, when tipping the scales at 200 pounds was not considered detrimental to a woman's appearance. The second point is that, apparently, most female stars kept their weights well *below* the level mandated by their contracts, suggesting that other factors, such as concern about the camera (see chapter 2), may have prompted them to reduce.

An examination of actual contracts particularizes the claims made in the fan magazines of the period. In the Warner Brothers/First National Archives at the University of Southern California in Los Angeles, California, I was able examine the contracts of eight female and three male screen players from the 1920s and 1930s. I inspected Warner Brothers contracts for Clive Brook, Dolores Costello, Myrna Loy, and Irene Rich. I was able to study First National contracts for Richard Barthelmess, Milton Sills, Mary Astor, Corinne Griffith, Molly O'Day, Colleen Moore, and Anna Q. Nilsson. My sample was limited (due to the paucity of these types of records), but of the stars' contracts I was able to scrutinize, I noted the following: Only First National stars had weight clauses in their contracts; Warner Brothers stars did not. Of the stars who had weight clauses, none were male. Though most stars did *not* have weight clauses in their contracts, the "facial and physical disfigurement clause"—a standard in most contracts—*could* have been used to exert pressure on them to maintain low weights.

Two female stars had weight clauses in their contracts: Colleen Moore and Anna Q. Nilsson. In a contract between Colleen Moore and First National Pictures dated Feb. 28, 1928 that accords Moore $150,000 per picture, a weight clause appears as follows:

> *TWELFTH*: (a) Artist agrees that she will, during the entire term and period of this contract, take diligent care of her health, weight and appearance, so as to render an artistic representation of any roles to which she may be assigned, and will keep her weight at all times below one hundred and forty (140) pounds. . . .

Anna Q. Nilsson's weight clause is more vague. In a contract between Nilsson and First National Productions Corporation dated April 9, 1925, she is given a salary of $1,750 per week, and the following weight clause appears: "15. Artist agrees that she will, during the entire term and period of this contract, take diligent care of her health, weight and appearance so as to render an artistic representation of any roles to which she may be assigned. . . ." The fact that only two of eight women had weight clauses in their contracts, and that these two women were both First National stars, lends credence to the fan magazine's description of the "freak" nature of such provisos. Perhaps First National *was* the only studio to foist such clauses on its players. David Stenn, author of Clara Bow biography *Runnin' Wild* and other highly regarded biographies of screen stars, has also examined studio contracts from the silent period and claims that weight clauses were rare.[80] However, even if First National *was* the only studio to explicitly codify its weight requirements, the use of such clauses at a major studio suggests that weight control had become a "hot button" issue in the industry.

This conclusion is reinforced if we examine the backgrounds of the two stars whose contracts included weight clauses. Neither Nilsson nor Moore were considered "problem" cases in regard to their weights; in all of the fan magazines I examined, I found no mention of either Moore's or Nilsson's need to lose weight. Indeed, in the articles cited earlier, it was noted that Moore's weight was thirty-four pounds *below* her contract weight, while Nilsson's was fourteen pounds below. (The contract cited above has no specific weight limit for Nilsson, but perhaps the fan magazine writer had access to a later version that *did* set a specific limit.) The presence of weight clauses in these stars' contracts when their weights had not been a problem suggests that such clauses may have been a standard contract item. Also, the phrasing of the clause is similar in both contracts, suggesting that it was a commonly used stipulation . At the very least, we know that weight clauses existed in at least *some* 1920s contracts at a major studio, and we can reasonably infer that a clause found in more than one contract was likely to be in others, as well.

In cases where weight clauses were not used, another more general clause regarding physical appearance may have served to keep screen stars' weights in line. The "facial and physical disfigurement" clause was a standard, industry-wide clause predicated upon the notion that stars' physical appearance was a key component of their popularity. Warner Brothers apparently inserted such a clause in every star's contract; of those Warner Bros. contracts I was able to examine, all had facial and physical disfigurement clauses. In a May 1924 contract between screen player Irene Rich and Warner Brothers, this clause is worded as follows:

> 11. In the event that by reason of inability or sickness or otherwise, the artist shall be incapacitated from performing the terms and complying with the covenants and conditions of this agreement on her part to be performed, or in the event that she suffers from any facial or physical disfigurement materially detracting from her appearance as a motion picture actress, or interfering with her ability to properly perform the required services hereunder, then and thereupon this agreement shall be suspended both as to services and compensation....[81]

First National commonly used an "artist's incapacity" clause. A November 1928 contract between First National and screen player Richard Barthelmess offers an example of this clause: "(b) In the event of the ARTIST becoming ill or incapacitated and such illness or incapacity continuing for a period of more than four (4) weeks during the period of this employment, the aforesaid weekly compensation shall be suspended from the end of the fourth week until the ARTIST returns to work...."[82]

These "facial and physical disfigurement" and "artist's incapacity" clauses were vague enough to allow for wide interpretation. Any physical change that translated into lower (or potentially lower) box-office returns for a particular star could be addressed under these umbrella clauses. An artist who packed on additional poundage could be labeled "disfigured" or "incapacitated" and suspended without pay until a satisfactory weight reduction had occurred. The tricky part is uncovering evidence that such legal maneuvering actually took place. Whether the "artist's incapacity" clause was ever used in this regard is unclear. I should note that, of the six players whose contracts used artist's incapacity clauses, some *also* had weight clauses, suggesting that weight control and incapacity were considered separate and unrelated issues. And the "facial and physical disfigurement" clauses used in the contracts of the remaining five players had separate language for disfigurement and incapacity, again implying that the two issues were considered separate problems. Therefore it is likely that language regarding incapacity was not routinely used to address weight gain. This was not the case for the language regarding facial and physical disfigurement, which seems to have been used in exactly this manner to exert pressure on screen player Molly O'Day, who subsequently employed one of the most extreme weight reduction methods of the period in order to continue working.

According to fan magazine articles, Molly O'Day (real name: Suzanne Noonan) began her screen career at First National Pictures in the late 1920s with the film *The Patent Leather Kid*, a "sob-sister" production. She had to fight to keep her weight down, but the production manager, Al Rockett, felt that she had great acting talent, so she was given a chance. By her third picture, the studio found it necessary to hire a dietitian for her in order to get her weight under control, though it apparently did not help:

> Molly didn't dissipate—not, at least, according to accepted standards. She didn't run around with men; she didn't buy Rolls Royces or swimming pools and tie up all her income on down payments.
>
> She just bought ice cream and cream puffs and chocolate candy.
>
> It was while she was on location for *Little Shepherd of Kingdom Come* that she began *her* dissipation, friends tell us. Not in the day time. Oh, no! For there was the dietitian always ready with spinach and lamb chops and pineapple. But at night, on the sly, like a school kid.
>
> When Molly returned, even Al Rockett scarcely knew her. Twenty pounds—well, twenty pounds is enough to ruin even a long-established, ultra-well known, motion-picture lady.[83]

Mr. Rockett puts Ms. O'Day on notice: "'As far as we are concerned, you are through—that is, until you can get down to the right physical size for our pictures,'" and the article concludes on a hopeful note: "She's in Hot Springs Arkansas, when this is written. And she not only has a dietitian but a physical instructor. Hot baths every morning and evening. And three times a day, spinach and lamb chop and pineapple."[84]

I was able to examine the contract Molly O'Day had with First National during this period. In a document dated January 3, 1927 (renewable for up to five years), a facial and physical disfigurement clause appears as follows:

> 8. In the event that by reason of mental or physical disability or otherwise the artist shall be incapacitated from fully performing the terms or complying with each and all of her obligations hereunder, or in the event that she suffer any facial or physical disfigurement materially detracting from her appearance on the screen ... then and thereupon this agreement shall be suspended both as to services and compensation during the period of such disability or incapacity....[85]

Apparently, First National used this clause to suspend O'Day when she gained weight. A First National office memorandum dated July 10th, 1928 makes oblique reference to this action:

> Mr. Rockett advises in Mr. Rothacker's wire of July 9th: MOLLY O'DAY
> HAS BEEN ON IDLE TIME PAST TWELVE WEEKS AND STARTS BACK
> ON SALARY TODAY WE ARE DISCONTINUING HER BONUS UNTIL WE
> FIND OUT WHAT CONDITION SHE IS IN AND JUST WHERE SHE WILL
> FIT INTO THIS YEARS PRODUCTION....[86]

That this "condition" was O'Day's excessive weight is suggested by the fan magazine article discussed above, which was published in the August 1928 issue of *Photoplay Magazine*—meaning that it was written at approximately the same time as the First National memo about O'Day's "idle time." Solidifying the link between the mysterious "condition" and weight is a small article that appeared in the *New York Times* on Sept. 4, 1928:

> Los Angeles, Sept. 3—Molly O'Day, screen actress, was resting in a hospital today after an operation to remove several pounds of flesh from her hips and legs.
> The actress said her excessive weight had been the cause of her idleness while under contract the last year. She resorted to the operation after other methods of reducing failed, she said.[87]

O'Day's contract was not canceled, merely suspended, per the requirements of the facial and physical disfigurement clause. Only extra weight stood between her and a return to the screen. Unable to shed pounds quickly via more traditional reduction methods, O'Day visited Dr. Robert B. Griffith, who performed an operation on her:

> The knife made long incisions on either leg and across the stomach and the fat was removed. Electric needles to melt the fat away were used.... She has suffered acutely, but the doctor assures her that there will be no scars left and that she will be from twelve to fifteen pounds lighter.
> Will there be any ill effects from this? Will the fat return? That remains to be seen.... She is a splendid actress. Her director, her producer, her public know this. But unless she is more sylph-like her art will be wasted. This is the demand of the screen!
> She has high hopes now. Wan and convalescent in the hospital, she smiled and expressed the wish that this drastic measure would allow her to continue her career.[88]

Fat-reducing operations such as this one were rare, though cosmetic surgery itself was not. Dr. W. E. Balsinger, a prominent Hollywood plastic surgeon of the period, explained that his work on stars usually involved nose jobs and facelifts—not flesh reduction, which he considered dangerous as well as futile. "'Fat comes from the inside of the body. It is not a condition on the outside, as so many people suppose. Suppose we do cut off a slice of flesh where we want it least?'" he asked. "'It will grow right back.'"[89] This is apparently what occurred in Ms. O'Day's case. A few months after her operation, a fan magazine article remarked that it had been "dangerous . . . and all in vain."[90] Ms. O'Day did return to the screen in 1929 in a small part in *Show of Shows*, but did not obtain another lead role until 1930. In the early 1930s, her weight remained an issue and she was relegated to supporting roles in most of her films. She retired from motion picture performing in 1936.

Another clause studios could use to pressure stars to keep their weight under control was the "option" clause. This standard clause gave studios the right to drop their contract stars at either semi-annual or annual intervals. A fan magazine article described the practice this way:

> Option Day in Hollywood is the new American holiday. It promises to assume national proportions, considering the constant growth of the drama-canning industry.
>
> . . . . An option is a clause—and sometimes it turns out you should spell it claws—in a movie actor's contract whereby a long-suffering producer may exercise his right to fire his employee if he desires, or to retain that same employee's services for another stated period, generally six months.[91]

Specific discussion of option clauses and/or their relationship to reducing was uncommon, both in fan magazines and other popular literature of the period. A 1931 diet book entitled *Hollywood Undressed: Observations of Sylvia as Noted by Her Secretary* is a rare example of a source that associates the need to reduce with the approach of Option Day. Sylvia of Hollywood, a figure who has received mention several times throughout this work, was a well-known personal trainer to the stars throughout the 1920s and 1930s. In this book, a woman identified only as Sylvia's secretary passes along Sylvia's experiences with the stars: "With amazing frankness Sylvia ruthlessly exposes the foibles and follies of stardom while revealing the inside secrets of the battle for beauty."[92] The author's attitude toward stars is critical and patronizing; her tone is almost gleeful as she describes how a "howling starlet" suffers when Sylvia pounds (massages) her:

> Another talkie star is in there now, laid out face down on the slab, and Sylvia is going to take a pound of ham off her in the next fifteen minutes or know the reason why. . . .
>
> When you see sixteen motion-picture stars a day troop in and strip down to sixteen different kinds of physical results of overeating and other forms of self-indulgence, you get sour on the whole lot of them. . . .
>
> As I figure it, most of them never ate regular until they landed their first Hollywood contracts and now a menu just goes to their heads—their heads and elsewheres. Eat, drink, and be stuffed, for tomorrow we may be fired.[93]

The author's attitude echoes the public persona adopted by Sylvia herself, who was famous for taking out-of-shape stars to task and getting them to "behave."

Here, quite early in the book, Sylvia's secretary comments upon what she sees as the reciprocal relationship between body fat and employment as a screen player: As one increases, the likelihood of the other decreases. Later, Sylvia's secretary unsympathetically declares that the best time for stars to shape up is right before a contract is renewed: "The great time to complete the dietary education of a Hollywood movie girl is during one of those interludes (they all pass through them) when the last picture contract is dead and the new one hasn't been offered. Then, living on credit, running up bills, frightened, chastened, ready to listen to reason, the over-size [sic] babies can be taught something."[94] The reference to "dead" contracts plausibly refers not only to the end of a five- or seven-year contract period, but also to that anxiety-inducing time right before Option Day, when, to all intents and purposes, a contract was "dead" unless the option was renewed by the studio.

Other sources seconded the notion that, during the 1920s at least, fat and option renewal tended to be mutually exclusive. A year after *Hollywood Undressed* was published, when articles declaring that curves were coming back began to appear sporadically in fan magazines, author Dorothy Calhoun emphasized that, traditionally, Option Day had been a time for reducing: "It was only a few months ago that studios were warning their players that unless they kept their weight down or lost weight, their options would not be taken up.... Now, the studios are still keeping a sharp eye on their players' measurements, but their advice has a different tune. They are urging the slim girls to become curved, the thin girls to grow plumper."[95]

Stars may have been less subject to weight requirements in the 1930s as the Depression took hold and curves became more desirable, but even during that period, and certainly for the decade preceding it, achieving and maintaining a relatively low weight was a virtual prerequisite of motion picture stardom, especially for women. Signing or renewing a contract often hinged upon being "the right physical size" for a studio's pictures. And even after a star reached the pinnacle of fame, the spectre of a suspended or canceled contract was ever present. Stars knew that gaining weight was always a risk, and took care to avoid "reckless potatoes" that could jeopardize their careers. In order to survive, each star had to be constantly wary of excess fat. Reporting on such "eternal vigilance" became a cottage industry. Throughout the 1920s, fan magazines were liberally sprinkled with dramatic tales of stars' battles with weight, as well as their helpful advice for readers who might wish to reduce.

Diet Articles

Once fan magazines had publicized the need for stars to diet, they were only too happy to provide the details of stars' reducing. Such reducing stories were packaged in one of two ways: either as "reducing travails"—examples of the great lengths to which stars would go to achieve or maintain their screen status—or as dieting advice offered to interested readers. The travails category was clearly the more titillating, dramatic, and scandalous of the two, since the consequences of extreme dieting behavior could be quite serious, up to and including death. When *Photoplay* began its 1926 exposé of fraudulent, extreme reducing methods, author Catherine Brody first cited the tragic case of Barbara La Marr, an actress who, it was claimed, had perished because of over-zealous dieting:

> Some months ago, the newspaper recorded the death of a young and beautiful and popular motion picture star. The star was Barbara La Marr. She died, specifically, of tuberculosis. This the public knows. What her friends knew at her death, however, was that Miss La Marr had, at a period preceding her collapse, taken a thyroid treatment to lose weight. They knew that her ill-health dated from that time, affecting her lungs and finally causing her death.[96]

Later that year, another article, "The Price They Paid for Stardom," also linked Barbara La Marr's untimely death to her attempts at reducing:

> When Barbara made her first hit, she was a slim young girl. . . . When the money came rolling in, Barbara became a victim of luxury.
>
> She grew plump and prosperous; naturally, because she was carefree and happy. But the public didn't like it. Her "fans" complained; the exhibitors kicked; the critics laughed at her. Barbara's admirers wanted to see her slim and big-eyed. Barbara, alas, looked too healthy for a "vamp."
>
> And Barbara was sensitive and proud, and she hated to be laughed at. And she went on the starvation diet that caused her death.[97]

Known as "the too beautiful girl," La Marr lived a whirlwind life, marrying five times and taking numerous lovers. She became addicted to painkillers after an injury in 1923, and later contracted tuberculosis. Fan magazine articles suggested that her tubercular condition stemmed from her weight loss attempts, a conclusion frequently drawn when stars who contracted the dread disease were known to have dieted. "Tuberculosis, anemia and nervous disorders have been counted among the tolls which voluntary starvation for a slender figure and cinema stardom has exacted," noted Dr. H. B. K. Willis in *Photoplay Magazine*.[98] La Marr collapsed in 1926 and died shortly thereafter, at age twenty-nine. No period sources mention her drug addiction, and though it may have been a factor in her death, there is no reason to conclude it operated in isolation. It is likely that strenuous dieting also contributed. One article, which quoted a doctor, even suggested that La Marr had died because she used the "tapeworm reduction," in which "the head of a tape-worm is swallowed in pill form to eat away the unwanted flesh."[99] Decades removed from the event, there is no means of verifying La Marr's cause of death. What is of importance to this study is the manner in which fan magazines established the link between La Marr's reducing and her death. Mentioning a lady's drug addiction was taboo during this period, so linking a premature death with reducing was an acceptable way to let curious readers in on the "real" story, a way to "reveal" a star's private behavior.

"Death by dieting" was not the only potentially dramatic consequence of stars' need to battle excess weight. Radical reduction methods also generated good copy. Actress Molly O'Day's 1928 operation, during which ten to fifteen pounds of fat was removed from her legs and stomach, was extensively reported (see "Contracts" section of this chapter). In a 1929 article in *Motion Picture Magazine* entitled "The Flesh and Blood Racket," author Dorothy Manners melodramatically describes the lengths to which women in the Hollywood area will go to secure a beautiful face and figure:

> There is no abyss of anxiety, no chasm of fear too deep that women will not cross for beauty.
> Pain is the pass word.
> Admiration is the temporary reward.
> Permanent disfigurement is the grisly risk.
> But there is no hell women will not countenance in the name of Venus.
> This is a part of the philosophy, and a few of the facts I gathered after days of investigation into the beauty farms, rejuvenations palaces and plastic surgery emporiums that have sprung up around the movie center like mushrooms in a shady glen.
> Los Angeles and its boundaries are overrun with these institutions.[100]

Ms. Manners interviews Dr. W. E. Balsinger, a well-known Hollywood plastic surgeon whose respectability had been established by reconstructing the faces of war veterans. He unequivocally denounces fat-reducing operations: " 'I would like to state right here that I am decidedly opposed to operations that resort to freak treatment [to get rid of fat], such as cutting off the flesh from the hips and ankles to reduce the figure.... I have refused many drastic diet cases of the film people. It isn't my business to kill off my patients for the sake of their vanity.' "[101]

Here, in a pattern typical of fan magazine articles on the subject, radical reduction methods are denounced by a respectable authority figure even as they provide lurid copy. This same dynamic is evident in "The Torture Chambers of Hollywood," wherein a "health authority" calls stars' constant fight to be thin a "tragedy." Of course, the details of this tragedy constitute the bulk of the piece:

> In one establishment, much frequented and highly recommended by motion picture people, four machines daily grind flesh away.... These so-

called treadmills can be adjusted to fit certain sections of the body.... As is the case in the mills of the gods, which grind exceedingly slow, so do these, and to a cacophony of clattering machinery....

One much sought-after Hollywood doctor has taken off four pounds in a single treatment. But the treatment was intensive. It consisted of a steam bath, pores oozing perspiration, for from one-half to one hour. Heavy hand-massage for one-half to three-quarters of an hour. A treatment of fifteen minutes with a super-sized vibrator, and then a half hour's intensive massage with the belted reducing machine. Many stars, for quick reduction, go through these rigors every day for a week—or as long as they can stand it.[102]

Such tales of reducing travails, in addition to supplying readers with the sensational details of stars' private battles with fat, served other purposes as well. For example, would-be stars may have reconsidered their plans to immigrate to an already over-crowded Hollywood if they were convinced of the hard work involved in becoming and remaining attractive for the screen. Established stars, well aware that motion picture stardom was considered a carefree, fairy-tale existence, were only too eager to talk about the exhaustive effort required of those in their profession.

These articles were distinguishable from advice articles, which were more moderate in tone and featured dieting tips gleaned from the stars. Both types featured distinct rhetorical strategies, as well. The advice articles assured readers that they, too, could look like the stars, while the travails articles asked readers to pity the stars for their perpetual suffering. In "They Must Suffer to Be Beautiful," author Katherine Albert expounds on the trials and tribulations stars face in their battle to be attractive: "I could go on for pages about the little things, the little constant gestures that you and I do but that you and I may stop doing whenever we choose. A star can't stop. When she gives up minute personal care she might as well tear up her contract."[103] Such stories were thinly veiled consolation prizes for envious readers, affording them a reason to appreciate their lack of celebrity. Stars had a *professional duty* to be thin, while ordinary people could "let themselves go" without facing the severe consequences awaiting wayward (or should I say "weighward"?) motion picture stars.

Yet all reducing articles, even those that highlighted particularly painful or foolhardy methods of weight loss, operated under the tacit assumption that *no one*, ordinary folks included, would wish to "let herself/himself go." Ordinary folks might jump off the reducing wagon on occasion; such was the prerogative of those whose profession was not weight dependent. But in the long run, *everyone* was (or should be) concerned about avoiding or shedding excess fat. Those who wrote and edited reducing articles for fan magazines assumed not only that fans wanted to be thin (relative to the fleshy standard of attractiveness at the turn of the century), but also that they wanted dieting pointers from their favorite stars. Indeed, if fan magazines were the clearinghouses for reducing information, motion picture stars were the reducing experts whose advice was showcased. Dieting recommendations were inevitably refracted through the lens of stardom, as though no reducing plan could be legitimate without the imprimatur of a star. Revelations of stars' dieting methods had a twofold appeal. First, stars' status as professional physical culturists made it seem likely that they had special, inside information about dieting. Second, details about stars' approach to physical culture represented a peek into their private lives.

The cornerstone of stars' dieting advice was its uniqueness. As I argued at the beginning of this chapter, every motion picture star was a monopoly unto him- or herself. Each star had a distinctive set of qualities that audiences were willing to pay to experience. Those qualities emerged from the sum total of discourse that created a star persona—films, stills, newspaper articles, fan magazine articles, and advertisements. Reducing stories were simply a *part* of that discourse, a part of each star's persona. Just as each star had a "How I Became a Star" story, usually of the rags-to-riches variety, each star had a "How I Keep in Condition" story. In many instances, this amounted to a statement of personal philosophy as it regarded health and the body. "I believe in massage more than anything else in the world," explained actress Rubye De Remer in 1921. "I believe in a variation of hot and cold showers every morning. I believe in a strict, thoroughly tested diet.... I believe in walking, lots of walking, whether you like it or not."[104] Later that same year, actress Corinne Griffith explained,

> I believe in keeping fit with as little labor, or strenuous exercise, as possible. My principal form of exercise is dancing.... I like dancing particularly because it seems to be the one form of real and beneficial exercise which can be taken with music....
> It was at a dance that I was "discovered."
> I think, accordingly, that dancing is interwoven with the destiny of my success.[105]

Such "How I Keep in Condition" stories could be framed in either of two ways: as part of an article specifically devoted to the question of physical culture (such articles were usually collections of reducing advice from a variety of stars) or as part of a larger story about a particular star's background and personal life. (I shall reserve discussions of the latter until the following chapter, in which I will offer case studies of Clara Bow and Rudolph Valentino and the role physical culture played in their careers.)

Although there were broad similarities in stars' approaches to weight loss (for example, most stars incorporated fad diets as they came and went), all added their own personal touches to their physical culture programs. "The Stars Tell How They Keep Those Girlish Lines," published in 1924, is a collection of advice from approximately a dozen stars. Here is a sample:

Alice Terry: "I go to a specialist in Hollywood who gives me forty-five minutes of the most violent massage. [Here, she may refer to Sylvia of Hollywood.] I take a series of exercises—and regular setting-up exercises will do—night and morning. And I ride horseback every day—as long as I can find the time. . . ."

Priscilla Dean: "I have taken off a lot of weight in the last few months. I began by taking some very drastic treatments in a rolling machine.

"Then I began a course of exercise and diet, following pretty closely the advice of Annette Kellerman, who is a pal of mine and lives in Hollywood just now. Miss Kellerman disapproves heartily of stringent or unbalanced diet food. I have simply cut down the amount of food I eat and also eliminated from my menu certain articles of food."[106]

"The Right Weigh," a 1925 piece in *Motion Picture Magazine,* offers advice from actress Betty Blythe, who explains,

"There is one subject guaranteed to keep a whole luncheon party of women talking animatedly. It's usually introduced by the question, 'What do *you* do?' 'Heard about the new method?' And then they're off!

"Every woman has her own pet method of keeping thin. One belongs to the lamb-chop-and-pineapple school, another to the hard-boiled-egg-and-tomato-sect, one wears rubber corsets, another takes some special kind of baths, and still another upholds massage.

"I play tennis and swim, primarily because I like to do these things."[107]

Here, Blythe's words capture the spirit of diet revelations among Hollywood stars. Each star had her own "secret," her own method of getting ahead in a game played with good looks. Sharing that dieting secret with other Hollywood women was a way of commiserating and building camaraderie with them, as well as an act of good faith and generosity, since an effective weight control method was part of one's competitive edge in the industry.

There was one group of performers who were in a special category when it came to this competitive edge, however. Unlike their counterparts in dramatic roles, screen comics were often allowed considerable latitude in their weights. As fat became more undesirable and more embarrassing, it also became funnier. Fat comic actors and actresses were not unusual; indeed, if a screen player, particularly a female, *was* fat, it was likely that he/she appeared in comic roles (consider, for example, Fatty Arbuckle or Marie Dressler). (Interestingly, though her girth was no impediment to her stardom, Marie Dressler still tried to lose weight; according to a 1931 book she was Sylvia of Hollywood's first client.[108]) Of course, I do not claim that *all* screen comics were overweight, simply that comedy offered screen opportunities for those whose weights precluded them from pursuing fame in dramatic and/or romantic roles. For example, comedienne Marie Prevost's 1931 comeback was detailed earlier in this chapter. She returned to the screen, despite having gained nearly forty pounds, when director Frank Capra needed a "chubby little comédienne" for *Ladies of Leisure*. In 1925, comedienne Gertrude Short described the effect her comic status had on her approach to weight control:

> "When they want a plump little comédienne—all right. Gertrude eats potatoes and pie and drinks milk. When they want a slim little comédienne, then for a week I live on lamb chops and for a month afterwards I dont [sic] touch anything I like. . . .
>
> "Lamb chops and pineapple three times a day does get awfully monotonous—and they have to be eaten three times a day because it's the combination of acids, or something or other, that does the work. But it's worse not being able to eat at all because you cant [sic] get a job!"[109]

In an article entitled, "The Deuce with Reducing," actress Babe London, described as "one of the screen's high-salaried comediennes," pities the slim actresses who cannot get work:

> "Do you know . . . I used to envy every girl I saw who had a lot of great open space draped around her where the hips ought to be? I used to watch these girls toying with a lamb chop and a piece of pineapple at meal time, and wish that my figure was as easily controlled as theirs. I actually wished that I were thin.
>
> "Then I came to Hollywood.
>
> "Now, Hollywood is as full of girls with slender figures as most towns on the map are of the ordinary kind. . . .
>
> "Fat girls like me don't grow on trees in Hollywood. . . . So—I got into the movies. Pretty soon I saw my salary check grow—just as I was growing—bigger and bigger and bigger. And I had envied the poor little thin girls who came to paralyze the movie world and remained to sling it hash! The deuce, I says, with reducing!"[110]

In a sea of slenderness, London's excess weight made her distinctive and was, or so the article suggests, a key component in her success as a comedienne. Though Ms. London was able to thumb her nose at the pineapple and lamb chop diet, however, the majority of Hollywood actresses were not as lucky. The screen did accommodate a limited number of overweight comediennes, but the vast majority of motion picture roles demanded players with slender figures. This is evident if one examines issues of *The Standard*, a popular casting directory published during this period. Performers of every type advertised their availability in this publication. Each was grouped in one of three main sections: "Principals," "Children," and "Supporting Players" and then further categorized under a subheading within that section. In the May

1923 issue, weight is not specifically cited in the section devoted to "Principals," though "Feature Comedians" and "Feature Comediennes" were in a different category than "Feature Men" and "Feature Women." But among those in the "Supporting Cast" section, overweight was a distinctive feature warranting a subheading for each sex: "Fat Men" and "Fat Women."[111] The need for a special category for fat screen players suggests that slenderness was the standard and overweight the exception.

This was as true for men as it was for women, though men's "How I Keep in Condition" stories were publicized with much less frequency than those of their female counterparts. One of the actors whose diet received such rare publicity (and indeed the only such example I was able to locate) was Jean Hersholt, a character actor born in Denmark whose battle with "avoirdupois" received sporadic attention in the press. In 1928, he appeared in D.W. Griffith's remake of his 1914 film *Battle of the Sexes*, at which time a cartoon titled "Avoirdupois" appeared in the *Los Angeles Record*. The cartoon pictures Hersholt in a vibrating belt trying to melt fat away, while the caption says that there is a "pathetically funny scene" with Hersholt and an "electric exerciser" in Griffith's film. In a photograph probably also published in 1928, Hersholt is again in a vibrating belt, with the caption: "Nobody loves a fat man so Jean Hersholt is doing his best to become a perfect thirty-one. The book of instructions informs him that blondes like 'em with a lean and hungry look."[112] Two years later, in a fan magazine article called "Diet Quickies," or "Three Stars Tell How to Lose Weight Without Fasting," Hersholt and two female stars reveal their weight loss secrets. But while the women face the problem of remaining slender all the time, Hersholt must figure out how to make his weight "elastic" to fit his current role:

> Jean Hersholt ... deliberately changes his size to suit his parts. If they give him three weeks, he can gain or lose thirty-five pounds to order....
>
> He has an inevitable diet which he adheres to without varying a calory [*sic*].
>
> For breakfast: One piece of dry bran toast. One whole grapefruit. One cup of coffee, with milk instead of cream, and saccharine instead of sugar.
>
> For lunch: Fruit salad or cold consommé. Fish or small piece of lamb, chicken or beef. All the vegetables he wants. Fruit.
>
> For dinner: Cold consommé. Fish or small piece of lamb, chicken or beef. All the vegetables he wants. Fruit.
>
> It is a Spartan diet, but it does the work with Jean Hersholt.[113]

Here, Hersholt's status as a character actor is significant. First, it suggests that he changes his weight not because he wishes to be more attractive, but because he wishes to be more convincing in his roles. This article handily converts the point of Hersholt's reducing from becoming more attractive to improving his craft as an actor. Even the cartoon and photograph from 1928 that poke fun at his excess weight allow for the possibility that he gained it specifically to facilitate the comedy in *Battle of the Sexes*. Second, Hersholt's niche as a character actor—especially one who could take on an occasional comic role—put him largely beyond the grasp of Hollywood's "reduction ring." Character roles, like comic roles, admitted players with a greater variation in body weights than leading romantic and/or dramatic roles. Far more than character or comic actors and actresses, romantic and/or dramatic players functioned as ideals—as examples of then-current standards of attractiveness.

It is therefore no accident that the only example of a male player's dieting habits I could locate is that of a character actor. As I suggested earlier in this chapter, reducing in order to become more attractive was considered a distinctly feminine pursuit, and dieting was considered a particularly passive way of shedding excess fat. Consequently, the reducing activities of leading male screen players, especially as they related to specific diets geared to improve their attractiveness, received little press. Men who expected leading romantic and/or dramatic roles *did* need to trim their excess fat, but any details of their activities in this regard tended to focus on their participation in exercises such as sports and weight-lifting. The implication was that men engaged in physical culture to improve their physical functioning, a goal that an industrial society interested in efficiency considered worthy of its male screen idols. Typically, men appeared in articles that were little more than a series of photographs of them "in action." For instance, a 1920 piece on serial star Antonio Moreno (who was later paired with Clara Bow in *It*) features four photos of Moreno exercising—holding a medicine ball, using dumbbells, boxing, and doing leg lifts. "Moreno is an all-around athlete and he loves keeping fit for the pleasure it affords him, rather than as a necessary means to an end," the article comments. "In Los Angeles he lives at the Athletic Club, and scarcely a day passes without his spending an hour in the gym."[114] Similarly, "The Way to Keep Fit" is a 1924 photo series featuring athletic star George Walsh demonstrating various knee-bending and leg-lifting exercises.[115]

Fan magazine articles also featured female stars in physically active poses—swimming, bicycling, and playing tennis—but this was *in addition to* the details of their reducing diets, which were provided either in the same or separate articles. By contrast, fan magazine discourse about male stars uniformly ignored their eating habits in favor of their sporting activities. Indeed, stardom for men was intimately associated with the notion of athletics. (Part of the impetus for this may have been a reclamation of masculinity, especially for romantic stars. See the latter half of chapter 4.) "It must be apparent to all who see on the screen the stunts that picture actors are called upon to do that considerable athletic training is necessary to most of them. So they have a place of their own in Hollywood in which to keep themselves in condition," explained a 1924 fan magazine article. This "place" was the Hollywood Athletic Club, which counted among its members "almost every actor and director of note in the picture world."[116] In an era of prosperity and rising consumerism, male motion picture stars were models of peak physical performance, of what the human body could accomplish if it were in constant, efficient motion.

The "He-Man" Variety: Athletics as a Route to Stardom

Perhaps the man who was the most widely recognized realization of this ideal was screen star Douglas Fairbanks, a man without whom no discussion of physical culture in the 1920s would be complete. Renowned for his athletic grace, Fairbanks advised Hollywood hopefuls, "This system of ours —the universe—is founded on motion.... All men walk, but the man who walks fastest is the one most apt to be noticed. Keep active, be enthusiastic, keep moving in mind and body. Activity is a synonym for health, and with health plus enthusiasm, wealth is just around the corner."[117] An icon of his age who rose to screen fame in the period 1915–1917, Fairbanks was one of the key figures in Hollywood during the 1920s. "[His] importance to Hollywood during the years spanning 1915 to 1934 can hardly be overestimated," claim John C. Tibbetts and James M. Welsh in their 1977 book *His Majesty the American: The Cinema of Douglas Fairbanks, Sr.*[118] In particular, Fairbanks' enormous popularity as an athletic star both exploited and fostered Hollywood's association with physical culture.

Born in 1883, Douglas Fairbanks grew up in Colorado, arriving in New York in 1900, where he began a stage career which he left in 1915 when he was offered $2,000 a week to star in pictures for the Triangle Film Corporation. There, in such films as *Double Trouble* (1915), *His Picture in the Papers* (1916), and *The Matrimaniac* (1916), he developed his screen persona as a dashing, reckless, and athletic hero. In this, his pre-costume era, he often played wealthy idlers who made good. After 1920, pirates and other outlaw figures became his primary mien in such films as *Robin Hood* (1922), *The Thief of Bagdad* (1924), and *The Black Pirate* (1926). His onscreen stunts, most of which he performed himself, were renowned for their daring (and included, among others, leaps from giant castle tapestries and ships' sails).

Even as a child, Fairbanks' athletic tendencies were apparent. According to an article that appeared in *Sunset Magazine* in 1928:

> He [Fairbanks] exhibited athletic tendencies first as a boy of eight or ten, there being no especial indication of any unusual muscular agility when he was younger.
>
> As a lad in Denver, Fairbanks is remembered vividly for his bodily nimbleness. He was seldom still and he performed all sorts of antics and feats which others of his age tried in vain to emulate....
>
> As he grew older he took an increasingly active part in neighborhood and school sports and displayed outstanding skill and dexterity. While still a youth he learned to fence.[119]

When Fairbanks arrived in Hollywood, he brought his aesthetic of constant motion with him, sometimes to the dismay of his new colleagues. According to Terry Ramsaye, D. W. Griffith, then a director at the Triangle Film Corporation, was irritated by Fairbanks' inability to keep still: "'Fairbanks seemed to have a notion that in a motion picture one had to keep eternally in motion, and he frequently jumped the fence or climbed a church at unexpected moments not prescribed by the script. Griffith advised him to go into Keystone comedies.'"[120]

Fairbanks did make one attempt at farce for Mack Sennett in 1916, but in the main he restricted himself to developing his burgeoning career as a symbol of all things enthusiastic, adventurous, and athletic. For instance, in 1917 he wrote an article entitled "Combining Playing With Work" in which he declared, "To my mind health and cheerfulness are the greatest assets one can have, whatever be one's walk in life.... With me, health [is] natural, and when one has health it ought to be just as natural to develop one's athletic side as it is for water to run down-hill.... I never look at a structure," Fairbanks continued, "without figuring how I could climb up the side of it."[121] This article includes active poses of Fairbanks exercising with a lasso and leaping a hedge. In 1921, his valet wrote a "tell all" piece in *Photoplay* that claimed to reveal Fairbanks' private habits. This valet, who never gives his name, complains that Mr. Fairbanks is a difficult man to serve because of his "nervous inability to hold still": "To use a vulgar but illuminating phrase of the day, he is as hard to keep one's finger on as a flea.... It is especially necessary that all his clothes be loose and comfortable, since one is never able to tell when he will take it into his head to perform those feats for which he is famous, and those exercises which he uses to keep himself fit and active."[122]

When Hollywood converted to sound film production in the period from 1928 to 1930, Fairbanks' popularity began to wane. His style of perpetual motion was ill suited to the more static medium of sound films, which, at least initially, had limited camera movement. Also, maintaining Fairbanks' legendary level of "pep and enthusiasm" was a tall order for any man, particularly one who had nearly reached the age of fifty by 1930. Even after Fairbanks' popularity began to wane, however, publicity articles trumpeted his continued athleticism. When he began work on a sound film with Bebe Daniels in early 1931, *Motion Picture Magazine* declared, "Douglas Fairbanks is coming back to this new medium as he originally came to Hollywood, lo, those many years ago. An actor, an athlete, and a blithe spirit."[123] And in January 1932, another article commented, "You can't get away from it—Doug, himself, is still most emphatically, Doug—with the same old dynamic pep and enthusiasm."[124] A few short years later, Fairbanks died of a heart attack, finally freed from his endless pursuit of athleticism.

Fairbanks may have been an unusual character, but when his restless energy was wed with Hollywood, it was a marriage destined to succeed. When Fairbanks arrived in Hollywood, the direction his screen persona would take was, to a large extent, predetermined by his background. He would be a screen athlete, a man in constant motion. Hollywood as a nascent center of physical culture and film as a dynamic visual medium were predisposed to exploit a man of exactly his talents. Hollywood was a land of physical culture, a place where outdoor activity and athleticism were appreciated and encouraged. In addition, Fairbanks' agility made him uniquely qualified to exploit the possibilities of cinema as a *moving* medium. When Fairbanks was onscreen, it was not just the camera and frames of film that moved; he added a third dimension of bold, vigorous *character* movement. Furthermore (as I argue in chapter 1), the 1920s was an era when men feared that the Industrial Age had feminized American culture; they turned to athletics as a way of proving their manhood. Fairbanks was a potent symbol of Anglo-Saxon masculinity, something that helps account for his wild popularity not only among women, but also among men. (Rudolph Valentino, another major romantic star of this period, never achieved the same level of acceptance among men, perhaps because of his Italian heritage and his "feminine" screen persona. See chapter 4.)

Fairbanks' status as an attractive male star in perpetual motion made athletes seem a natural for the screen, and a number of male athletes of the 1920s were given screen acting opportunities simply on the strength of their background in physical culture. Some athletes who achieved at least modest screen success include Fred Thompson, Maurice "Lefty" Flynn, George O'Brien, William Russell, Reginald Denny, Malcolm McGregor, Edmund Lowe, and George Walsh. "Great Athletes of the Screen," which appeared in *Motion Picture Classic* in 1926, provides biographical sketches for some of these actors, with an emphasis on details of body weight and muscle definition in lieu of a focus on specific films and/or film roles. For example, Maurice "Lefty" Flynn was an All-American fullback for Yale who went on to appear in action films. " 'Lefty' stands six feet two in his silk hosiery and weighs one hundred and ninety-five pounds, nearly every ounce of which is solid bone and muscle," gushes author Hal Wells.[125] George O'Brien was an all-around athlete, having been active in football, basketball, track and field, and swimming:

> O'Brien is believed to be the only motion picture actor in this country now holding a membership card in the American Athletic Union. . . .
>
> O'Brien trains as rigorously as any professional athlete. . . .
>
> For his weight, George has as magnificent a physique as any man in pictures. His muscles are flexible and rippling—never bunchy. He weighs a hundred and seventy-five pounds stripped. . . . His chest measurement is forty-four inches, and his waist thirty. He lives at the Hollywood Athletic Club, where he does most of his training.

William Russell, a boxer who was a "hopeless cripple" when he was sixteen, "succeeded so well in making his body whole again that ... he became amateur middleweight boxing champion of New York State.... Today Bill's weight is around the two-hundred mark, and there is not an ounce of superfluous flesh on his magnificent body."[126] (These fulsome compliments highlight the homoerotic component that was a frequent by-product of male physical display.)

For these men, athletic training was a valuable prerequisite to motion picture stardom. There was a limit to the benefits of athletic celebrity, however. Those athletes who reached the pinnacle of their chosen sport were usually unsuccessful on the screen, as an article in *Photoplay* noted in 1928. During the 1920s, several nationally famous athletes made attempts to parlay their fame into screen stardom. For instance, Duke Paoa Kahanamoku, an Olympic swimming champion from Hawaii whose name was a "household word both here and abroad," tried his hand at motion picture acting in several pictures but failed to build a fan base as a screen star:

> Duke Paoa Kahanamoku, most perfect specimen of his race, well over six feet in height, well over 200 pounds in weight, with a picturesque and splendid face and the carriage of an athlete, came to the screen already famous. He found that his name meant nothing. He had to start all over again. He had to build up with the extras. He was courageous in his efforts.... Now and then his name would be given screen credit. But in such fashion that few associated Duke Kahanamoku, the greatest swimmer, with Duke Kahanamoku, the petty chieftain of a native group, or Kahanamoku the pirate, or Kahanamoku the soldier, or Kahanamoku the body guard of the hero.[127]

Racial prejudice and/or racial typecasting no doubt affected Kahanamoku's chances of success as a screen star; Hawaiian men were (and still are) a rare sight in Hollywood films. But Kahanamoku was certainly not alone in his failure. Bill Tilden (tennis), Benny Leonard (boxing), Jack Dempsey (boxing), Red Grange (football), and Babe Ruth (baseball) were all nationally recognized athletes of this period who abandoned notions of a long-term screen career after testing the waters and finding that as screen stars, they were better paid and more famous as athletes.

Photoplay Magazine explained that it was presumptuous of athletes to assume that expertise in one field should so easily translate into success in another. Author Charley Paddock, himself an athlete who failed to find screen success, declared, "Again and again cropped up the old story of a celebrity thinking that he could achieve success in another field of endeavor without going through all the work and sacrifice that such success always demands."[128] In other words, screen stardom demanded acting skill that could only be developed through years of practice. This was not a principle that found widespread acceptance among athletes, who sometimes publicly discounted the difficulties involved in putting on a convincing screen performance. When George Walsh (brother of director Raoul Walsh), an athlete who had excelled at college baseball and football, was asked whether athletics might interfere with his ability to act, he replied, " 'Perhaps, but if they'll give me a *chance* to act, I think I can do it. In fact, I'm just conceited enough to think I know how to act. It's much easier to do than athletics.' "[129] Though Walsh was an example of an athlete who *did* achieve screen success, Hollywood insiders must have relished those instances when athletic celebrities failed to come across on the "silversheet." Those athletes who had achieved national fame were hampered both by their inability to act and by their association with a particular sport:

> One reason why many noted athletes have failed to ring the gong in pictures is that the public is not interested in them as actors but only as record-breakers. Unless the young man has an unusual personality an audience sits back, bored with his acting, and waiting for him to do the stunt that made him famous and usually when that feat is accomplished, *finis* is written to his screen career.[130]

Athletes who did find screen success were those of modest or moderate sporting fame who used their athletic prowess simply as a foot in the door—that is, as one asset among many in the competition for stardom. *Motion Picture Classic* concludes,

> The list of real athletes of the screen might be continued almost indefinitely. It is obvious that physical prowess, while far from being the sole prerequisite to success in pictures, is a highly important asset.
>
> For the American public, while it may occasionally raise a temporary furore [*sic*] over the sheik and other bizarre types, in the long run wants its heroes to be decidedly of the he-man variety, with the lithe muscles and the erect carriage of an athlete, and the training and ability to make those muscles really effective.

Such comments underline the connection between physical culture and motion picture stardom (as well as the presumed link between Anglo-Saxon athleticism and potent masculinity). An *athletic background alone* was sufficient to provide an entrée to the screen. Of course, such a background did not guarantee success. Other variables, such as acting ability and public appeal, were also of paramount importance. Yet Hollywood studios sought future stars among athletes because, in their view, the two professions demanded like qualifications. As a 1922 interview with screen star George Walsh noted, "He has the most glorious physique a he-men could ever have. Furthermore he has a fine, sympathetic nature and a headful of real ideas. What better combination for an actor?"[131]

"Bathing Girls" and Motion Picture Stardom

Just as the studios' interest in male athletes demonstrates an affinity between physical culture and motion picture stardom, so too does their predilection for female "bathing girls." Perhaps as yet another indication of women's association with more passive aspects of physical culture, athletic prowess was typically considered an impediment to a female's screen success. Women were consistently discouraged from pursuing forceful exercises that might mar their soft female beauty. For example, a 1931 fan magazine article declared, "No athletic type of girl has ever so much as reached first base in motion pictures."[132] This piece offers commentary from the ever-vocal Sylvia of Hollywood, who forcefully asserts, " 'No woman athlete is beautiful! Swimming, riding, golf and tennis are fine but shouldn't be overdone. Muscles are horrid things that must be pounded off. I allow the stars under my care no violent exercise in any form!' " In a culture concerned about feminization, muscular females were not admired; athleticism was the purvey of manly men. Consequently, while the "Athlete" became a screen type associated with males, the "Bathing Girl" emerged as a category of female stardom.

Traditionally, "bathing" (swimming) had simply provided an opportunity for physical exertion and/or a chance to indulge in the pleasures of water, sun, and sand, but in the early 1920s more revealing suits gained popularity and bathing became more of an *event*—an opportunity to be *seen* and *assessed*. Frederick Lewis Allen claims that the "bathing beauty" first emerged in 1921. In the summer of that year, when modest tunic bathing suits with long stockings were still the accepted fashion, there was a beauty show held at a beach near Washington, D.C. One of the contestants "daringly rolled her stockings below her knees."[133] Her gesture caught on, and that fall when Atlantic City held its first Beauty Pageant (which later became the Miss America Pageant), bare knees and skin-tight bathing suits were no longer banned. The cultural effects, says Allen, were immediate: "The one-piece suit became overnight the orthodox wear for bathing beauties ... promoters of seashore resorts began to plan new contests, and the rotogravure and tabloid editors faced a future bright with promise."[134]

The popularity of more daring bathing suits may have been *precipitated* by the actions of a few bold girls who bared their knees, but clearly the public was receptive to this new exposure of flesh. First, an increased awareness of sexuality after World War I helped add a dimension of sexual display to public bathing. (See chapter 1.) Furthermore, in this time of greater women's liberation, women may have found lighter, more revealing suits a convenient way to thwart the guidelines of conventional society. "In the 1920s, all hell broke loose," claims Malvina DeVries of *Retro*, an online magazine that focuses on 20th century popular culture. "Barer bathing costumes took on special significance as an expression of women's newfound freedom."[135] DeVries argues that skimpier suits were also a factor in the reducing craze:

"People became health-food, exercise and sun-worship fanatics in a major fitness fad, triggered by all that flesh out in public for the first time."[136] Though her article ignores other factors that contributed to the rise of reducing, clearly the advent of revealing bathing suits could have elicited interest in flesh-reducing techniques.

As men and women shed their cover-all bathing costumes in favor of formfitting, sleeveless wool tanks that ended at mid-thigh, bathing suits became a central symbol of sexuality, beauty, and physical culture. Motion picture stars were closely associated with this symbol through their participation in swimming, a popular pastime in southern California, and the subsequent popularity of the bathing suit as a mode for stars to display their bodies to the public. Also, from the beginning the terms "bathing beauty" and "bathing girl" referred not only to female beauty pageant contestants attired in swimwear, but also to their cinematic counterparts. As early as 1911, the bathing girl became an established screen type. Like beauty contestants, the primary duty of celluloid bathing girls was to *pose*—to be attractive in a bathing costume that exposed a significant amount of flesh. Bathing girls constituted an identifiable category of motion picture players whose chief requisites were youth and slenderness. They had their own subheading in *The Standard* (a casting directory mentioned earlier in the chapter). In the Bathing Girls section and no other, performers included information about their height, weight, and age. Being of modest weight was a key "professional qualification" for prospective bathing girls. For example, in July 1924, four bathing girls advertised their availability:

> Lackner, Myrtle, 5 ft. 3 in., 120 lbs., 18 yrs.
> Porteous, Jean, 5 ft. 3 in., 110 lbs., 22 yrs.
> Stuart, Isobel, 5 ft. 6 in., 135 lbs., 19 yrs.
> Willard, Ruth, 5 ft. 5 in., 125 lbs.[137]

It is worth noting that being a bathing girl was not only a potential *route* to stardom; for some girls, it constituted an entire screen career.

The most famous bathing girls of the screen were found in Mack Sennett's comedies. Mack Sennett produced scores of slapstick comedy films during the 1910s and 1920s, including those featuring the chaotic "Keystone Kops" as well as comic greats like Roscoe "Fatty" Arbuckle, Harry Langdon, and Charlie Chaplin. Sennett also gave female performers opportunities in his films, usually as one of his "Bathing Beauties." Sennett's original bathing beauty was comedienne Mabel Normand, who began appearing in a bathing costume in comedies like *The Diving Girl* (1911) and *The Water Nymph* (1912). Normand and other bathing beauties, including Phyllis Haver, Minta Durfee, Virginia Fox, Marie Prevost, and Gloria Swanson, quickly became a staple of Sennett's films, which typically featured a bevy of attractive girls clad in swimsuits as they flirted, posed, and cavorted through comic chaos.

Though their bathing costumes became more revealing as fashions evolved in the 1920s, from the beginning Sennett wanted his "beauties" to wear suits that defied traditional modesty:

> "Our wardrobe department supplied what it thought appealing in the way of bathing suits. They sent over high rubber shoes, black cotton stockings, dark blue bloomers and voluminous tunics with tatted neckpieces and ballooning sleeves. I howled in dismay and told them to junk all that stuff and design some bathing suits that showed what a girl looked like. The whole studio turned conservative on me in one of the most unexpected upheavals since the San Francisco earthquake. Even the comedians complained I was risque. But I went ahead and put the girls on film in the most abbreviated suits possible.... When the studio received hundreds of letters of protest from the women's clubs, I knew I had done the right thing."[138] (See figure 8.)

In what may be an indication of the limits of cinematic influence upon the public, however, the appearance of (relatively) scantily clad bathing girls in Sennett's film did not seem to spur major changes in bathing costume styles, which remained modest until the early 1920s. Apparently, additional factors, such as greater interest in sexuality and women's liberation, were necessary to precipitate the emergence of more revealing styles. Sennett's films helped establish the bathing girl as a screen type, however. *The Silents Majority*, a web site dedicated to the appreciation of silent films, claims that Normand's appearance in a bathing costume "set the nation on its ear and as a result made a woman in a bathing suit an icon in films ever after."[139]

Despite their popularity, bathing girls were clearly a minority of female motion picture performers, and most were not stars in the strict sense of the word. Though some bathing girls did become stars in their own right (for example, Mabel Normand and Gloria Swanson), typically they were no more than bit or featured players who provided an attractive backdrop for a film presenting other stars. Still, the fact that bathing girls became a category of screen performers provides further evidence that motion picture acting was a profession intimately associated with physical culture. Hollywood's bathing girls got onscreen work first and foremost because of their ability to look slim and attractive in bathing suits. Theirs was a category of stardom predicated upon an overt, direct relationship between low body weight and the opportunity for employment as a screen player.

CONCLUSIONS

During the 1920s, weight management became an integral part of being a motion picture star. The association between screen performance and physical culture, though it did not develop overnight, is nonetheless remarkable for the speed at which it took root, especially if we consider that there is no

Figure 8: Sennett bathing beauty in a typical costume (1916)

essential relationship between motion picture acting and weight control. Any associations that we have formed between the two are purely of our own construction. In the 1910s and 1920s, many factors, including concern about the camera's effect(s) upon the body and the establishment of a national film production center in a warm, sunny climate that afforded ample opportunity for physical display (see chapter 2), forged a link between cinema stars and physical culture. Little more than a decade passed between the emergence of the screen's first stars and wide acceptance of the notion that such stars needed to shun excess fat if they were to succeed in their profession. By the mid-1920s, keeping fit was a professional duty for motion picture stars. For prospective stars, excess weight might translate into a lack of screen opportunity; for established stars, it could mean a canceled or suspended contract. Stars became physical culture experts, regularly dispensing their dieting advice and tales of reducing woe to the public. The "How I Keep in Condition" story, which revealed intimate details of stars' physical caretaking rituals, became an important component of star discourse.

In essence, motion picture stars were the poster children of the 1920s reducing craze. Their fame and fortune, though ostensibly based on other factors such as acting skill or personality, were intimately associated with physical culture. There were other groups whose success depended upon keeping trim (such as athletes and physical culture experts), but individuals from those groups did not enjoy the public omnipresence characteristic of major motion picture stars. Such stars, aided by the mechanical reproduction of their images, expanded the scale of public fame. With their images multiplied tens of thousands of times across movie screens, fan magazines, newspapers, and advertisements, movie stars received unprecedented public attention. On or off the screen, their images and activities were incessantly reproduced, recorded, and reported. Details of their private lives, including their participation in physical culture, became fodder for public consumption. This extraordinary public presence enabled motion picture stars to influence public attitudes and behavior.

The nature of this influence is suggested by stars' relationship to public life. As discussed earlier in the chapter, subsequent to the emergence of the star system, stars functioned as the truth of films. Audiences sought information about stars' true identities, information that included their physical caretaking rituals. Stars also functioned as models of physical perfection, establishing new standards of attractiveness. And when they stepped off the screen, their fantasy lifestyles were models for the consumer society that developed in the postwar era. Body improvement products (including reducing and/or muscle-building products) were an important part of this rising tide of consumerism (see chapter 5). Finally, stars were examples of success for aspiring motion picture players, advising screen hopefuls that a trim body was an essential tool of the trade. In short, as screen stars of the 1920s drugged, dieted, pounded, and rolled themselves into shape, it is likely that they motivated at least some of their fans to do so as well.

The fans most susceptible to such influence would have been those who dreamt of stardom themselves. Across America, young men and women who hoped to grace the silver screen were told repeatedly that bodily discipline was essential to fame. Screen starlet Laura LaPlante warned prospective stars that directors would order any girl who was "the least bit fat" to reduce immediately, while male star Bert Lytell declared fat the "worst enemy" of screen players. For many stars, the preface to the "How I Keep in Condition" story could have been entitled "How I Became a Star." Losing weight became a part of the mystifying metamorphosis that fashioned motion picture dieties from everyday mortals. Fan magazine articles from the 1920s as well as later star biographies and autobiographies claimed that a program of reducing often provided screen hopefuls with a crucial career-igniting spark, while physical culture in general was a vital ingredient in the continued success of established personalities.

CHAPTER 4

Ascending the Celluloid Heavens
Reducing as Personal Transformation

The screen stars whose promotional discourse attributed at least a portion of their initial or enduring renown to physical culture are legion and include, among others: Norma Talmadge, Constance Talmadge, Gloria Swanson, Greta Garbo, Geraldine Farrar, Mae Murray, Clara Bow, Corinne Griffith, Lila Lee, Marion Davies, Joan Crawford, Mary Pickford, Mary Miles Minter, Nita Naldi, Elsie Ferguson, Agnes Ayres, Viola Dana, Betty Blythe, Evelyn Brent, Barbara La Marr, Pola Negri, Esther Ralston, Evelyn Brent, Owen Moore, Douglas Fairbanks, Ramon Novarro, Malcolm MacGregor, Rudolph Valentino, Richard Arlen, Jean Hersholt, Clive Brook, Gary Cooper, George Brent, and Harold Lloyd. To illustrate and illuminate the trope of "personal transformation" associated with stardom and physical culture, however, I present detailed case studies of two of the most popular stars from this list: Clara Bow and Rudolph Valentino, each of whom had a career that was both enriched and limited by the relationship between Hollywood and physical culture.

CLARA BOW: CURVE TROUBLES

> Nothing worries this ultra-flapper except adipose tissue and she treats it as ruthlessly as a vampire does the heart of man who should know better.
>
> —Glenn Chaffin, *Photoplay Magazine*, 1925

In 1957, when silent film actors, directors, and cameramen were asked to name the best screen artists of the 1910s and 1920s, "as expected, the actress most often cited was Greta Garbo. Unforeseen was her stiffest competition, which came not from Mary Pickford, Lillian Gish, or Gloria Swanson, but Clara [Bow], who ran a close second to Garbo and far ahead of everyone else."[1] Known as the legendary "It" Girl of the silver screen, Clara Bow may be the best example of a motion picture star whose physical culture regimen was influenced by the discourse surrounding post—World War I Hollywood. An avid movie fan who later became a star herself, Bow's life experience was shaped by the movies and motion picture magazines. Reliable information on her life and career was scarce until the publication of David Stenn's balanced, well-researched biography *Clara Bow: Runnin' Wild* in 1988. Stenn details Bow's beginnings in a miserable Brooklyn tenement, where she was born to Robert and Sarah Bow on July 29, 1905. Their first two offspring had died shortly after birth, so they assumed that their third baby would do so as well. Clara surprised them, however, and quickly developed into a robust, attractive child with auburn hair and dark eyes. "But health did not guarantee happiness, and Clara's life remained grim," notes Stenn.[2] Clara's father Robert was a self-centered, abusive, ne'er-do-well, while her mother battled mental illness and seizures (probably epilepsy).

As a withdrawn, self-conscious child, Clara Bow, like many children of her era, turned to the movies for solace. " 'In this lonesome time, when I wasn't much of nothin' and didn't have nobody, [there was] one place I could go and forget the misery of home and heartache of school,' she recalled years later. 'That was the motion pictures.' "[3] She read movie magazines (her favorite was *Motion Picture Magazine*) and fantasized about the day when she would become a star herself. "Just like the rest of her generation," says Stenn, "Clara was not only fascinated by the brand-new medium of the movies, but brainwashed to believe that stardom in them would provide fame, adulation, and, most elusive and important of all, love."[4]

Forced to leave school at age thirteen, Bow got jobs slicing hot dog buns and answering telephones. In January 1921, she read about a Fame and Fortune Contest in *Motion Picture Magazine*. Sponsored by Brooklyn-based Brewster Publications (which published *Motion Picture*, *Motion Picture Classic*, and *Shadowland*), the contest offered a part in a motion picture to the winner. "It was the only chance a nobody like Clara would get, and she was desperate to seize it."[5] With her father's help, she had a couple of cheap photographs of herself made at a Coney Island studio, then took the bus to Brewster Publications to drop them off. "It was a wise move: unbeknownst to Clara, the manager wrote 'Called in person—very pretty' across the bottom of her photos."[6] Soon, Bow was notified that she was a finalist. After extensive screen tests with the other finalists, Bow was declared the winner of the 1921 Fame and Fortune Contest.

It was at this point in her career that Bow's weight, which had not yet rated even a mention in Stenn's biography, apparently became a stumbling block in her career. Bow waited months for the movie role to which her contest victory supposedly entitled her, but none was forthcoming (the reasons for which are not made clear). Finally, she was offered a small role in the 1922 film *Beyond the Rainbow*, starring Ziegfeld Follies showgirl Billie Dove, a well-known beauty with whom Bow apparently compared unfavorably:

> Beside 'the Dove,' Clara was chubby nobody, and director Christy Cabanne wasted no time telling her so. 'Don't tell me *she* won a beauty contest,' hooted Cabanne to an assistant when Clara entered his office. Instead of

reminding him that the Fame and Fortune Contest had been based on ability, not beauty, a devastated Clara fled his office in tears. Afterward the Brewster organization persuaded Cabanne to hire her by promising free publicity for his film in its publications.[7]

Bow appeared in Cabanne's film, though her scenes were later cut. In 1922, she made the rounds, hopeful that another role would materialize. " 'I wore myself out goin' from studio t'studio, from agency t'agency, applyin' for every possible part,' " she said later. " 'I was too young, too little, or too fat. Usually I was too fat.' "[8]

As luck would have it, director Elmer Clifton was looking for someone to play the heroine's tomboy sister in a whaling film called *Down to the Sea in Ships*. Clifton felt Bow was perfect for the part; indeed, he liked her work so well that he padded the role for her, stretching two weeks of employment into thirteen. Shortly thereafter, Jack Bachman, a partner with B. P. Schulberg in Preferred Pictures, an independent production and distribution company based in Hollywood, offered Bow train fare to California and a three-month trial at fifty dollars a week.[9] Clara Bow arrived in Los Angeles in mid-1923, shortly before her eighteenth birthday. At first, Schulberg was critical of this "grubby Brooklyn girl," but when he found she could laugh or cry at the snap of a finger, he was won over. At the end of 1925, after Schulberg had spent more than two years "pimp[ing] Clara for profit"[10] (he loaned her out to other studios for $500 a week and paid her only $200), Preferred Pictures became part of Paramount, the studio where Bow remained until 1930. At Paramount, Bow cemented her image as a dynamic ultra-flapper. Adolph Zukor, the head of Paramount, said of Bow, " 'She danced even when her feet were not moving. Some part of her was always in motion, if only her great rolling eyes. It was an elemental magnetism, an animal vitality that made her the center of attraction in any company.' "[11] (See figure 9.)

Bow achieved her greatest fame in films like *Dancing Mothers* (1926), *Mantrap* (1926), *It* (1926), and *Red Hair* (1928), all of which showcased her appeal as a liberated, sexy heroine. *It*, the most famous of the four, was based on a novelette by Elinor Glyn that explored the concept of "It," better known as "sex appeal." Ben Schulberg ordered writers Louis Lighton and Hope Loring to junk Glyn's tale and come up with one tailored for Bow that would be based on "It." In the film, Bow's character is a shopgirl full of "It" who entices the owner of the department store where she works (played by Antonio Moreno). According to Stenn, *It* made Bow the "ranking Jazz Baby of the Jazz Age"; she was "the foremost symbol of sex in a decade preoccupied with the subject."[12]

What happened to Bow's weight between her appearance in her first film, *Beyond the Rainbow*, her subsequent role in *Down to the Sea in Ships*, and Schulberg's offer of a Hollywood contract is not entirely clear. Stenn calls Bow's character in *Down to the Sea in Ships* a "spunky, chunky girl," implying that Bow did *not* lose weight after *Beyond the Rainbow*. It is also

Clara
Bow

From a photograph
by W. F. Seely

You've heard
about that "come-
hither look," of
course, but you
probably never
had the good
luck to see it.
Well, here it is.
Little Miss Bow
illustrates it
rather well.
People say the
flapper is passing
out, her day is
done, and so
forth, but dont
you believe it.
As long as
Clara's irresist-
ible flappers
ornament the
screen, there's no
danger. Come
on, boys! Three
cheers for Clara!
Long may she
flap!

Figure 9: Bow demonstrates her sex appeal. *(Motion Picture Classic,* April 1925)

possible that Bow *did* lose weight after that initial film, making her more employable but still able to play a "chunky" girl onscreen. Finally, it may be that Bow lost weight after her role in *Down to the Sea in Ships*, which subsequently (along with her acting skills) stimulated the interest of Schulberg and Preferred Pictures. It would appear that the relationship of Bow's weight to her screen success (which is admittedly not the focus of Stenn's biography) is uncertain. Stenn raises the spectre of fat as a deterrent to screen fame, but does not clarify its effects on Bow's career.

Fan magazine articles that chronicled Bow's life and career were not so reticent, however. They attributed Bow's transformation from "ugly little thing" into motion picture actress to losing weight. In 1925, *Photoplay Magazine* chronicled Bow's "fat history": "A short time ago in her bungalow home ... she told me the story of the fat little girl who threw her ancient history at a school chum who told her that she was too fat to be a film actress."[13] After Bow's minor role in *Beyond the Rainbow* was cut, relates the article, she decided to "try anew":

> She'd show them, show them all. She'd be a star some day and—but first, she'd get thin.
>
> She locked herself in her bedroom, pushed her bed against the wall, lay down on the floor and rolled.
>
> "I'd roll around the room like a rubber ball until I was so dizzy that I couldn't move," she said. "Then I'd jump up and stagger to the looking glass to see if I'd lost any fat. Once I fell against the dresser and bumped my head awfully.
>
> "Say, I'll bet I rolled a hundred miles in that little room. I must be the champion roller of the world. And I starved myself, too. But it worked. Everybody noticed that I was getting thinner. I didn't tell a soul about the rolling. It was serious to me and I knew the kids would all laugh at me if I told them."[14]

After Bow rolled, she got a part in *Down to the Sea in Ships*. "Her work was praised but she was told that she was still too fat. She went home and rolled some more on the bedroom floor. Shortly afterwards ... B. P. Schulberg signed her for a five-year contract and she came to Hollywood."[15]

The veracity of this information is of course impossible to determine. At the very least, it is further proof of Hollywood's close association with physical culture; at most, the assertion that Bow became more slender after *Beyond the Rainbow* is not an unreasonable one. Articles in other fan magazines support this contention. In 1926, Bow told *Motion Picture Magazine* that after her role in her first film was cut, " 'I couldn't stand it. I made myself sick worrying about it and I suppose I lost weight—and besides, I grew a little.' "[16] Furthermore, rolling was a popular method for shedding fat. Bow says that she 'read somewhere' about rolling to grow thin. In 1922, *Motion*

Picture Magazine, Bow's favorite fan magazine, offered this advice: "The most effective exercise for rapid reducing is rolling.... Rolling should be done on the floor. The hard surface does not yield to the contour of the body as the bed does, but resists, and by its resistance crushes the cell of fat."[17] Did Bow read this article or others like it and take their advice to heart?

Even if a relatively ample figure did not prevent Bow from beginning her screen career, keeping that figure under control became a constant duty, especially at those times when she packed on additional pounds. In 1926, *Motion Picture Classic* noted that Bow exercised regularly to keep her figure in check: "She hikes over the hills.... She rides, too. Exercise keeps her slim—for her ambition."[18] In 1929, *Photoplay* did a piece called, "How They Manage Their Homes." Readers were told about Bow's "big, well-equipped gymnasium," which she used to "preserve the girlish figure that the public demands of its picture heroines."[19] Bow's cook prepared grapefruit juice and coffee for breakfast; an egg, a tomato, toast, and tea for lunch; and a lamb chop or steak, tomato, and coffee for dinner. " 'Yes, I'm dieting for dear life,' pouts Clara. 'I simply must not get fat—and, oh, I have such a good cook!' "[20]

1929 was a stressful year for Bow; in addition to being in an exploitative relationship with Broadway star Harry Richman (of "Puttin' on the Ritz" fame), who wanted to leverage her popularity to increase his own, she had to face the microphone as studios converted to sound film production. Fearful of sound technology after a disastrous sound test in mid-December 1928, Bow began shooting her first talkie, *The Wild Party*, in January 1929. Soon after, her hairdresser, Daisy DeVoe, took charge of her chaotic finances, ejecting freeloading relatives and corrupt employees from her home and establishing a trust fund into which Bow would deposit half her weekly salary. As part of her managerial duties, DeVoe put Bow on a diet to help her shed the weight she had begun to gain after *The Wild Party* finished shooting. Harry Richman was introduced to Bow that year, and he later said, " 'There stood one of the most luscious, sexiest women I ever saw in my life.... "Ripe" was the only word for that figure of hers.' "[21] In the summer of 1929, Richman and Bow visited Coney Island, where Bow had spent part of her youth. In a photograph taken during that visit, "[Bow's] face is puffy, her eyes are glazed, and her red hair runs amok in uncontrolled curls.... She looks fat, tired, and far too worn for a twenty-three-year old."[22]

By late 1929, Bow's weight had reached 132 pounds. (Her typical weight was around 110 pounds.[23] Her height is difficult to ascertain; based on her stature in films and photographs, she was probably in the range of 5'2" to 5'4" tall.) When her next talkie, *The Saturday Night Kid*, was released, "Most critics paid more attention to Clara's girth than her performance. Their verdict: The 'It' Girl had more 'It' than ever, especially around her midsection."[24] The year ended with Bow overcoming all of her obstacles, however. When her doctor advised the removal of one of her ovaries to resolve long-standing menstrual problems, Bow's convalescence after the operation melted thirty-two pounds from her figure. "Then an exhibitor's poll named her the top box office draw for the second year in a row, a citation which confirmed her success in talkies."[25]

Scandals quickly dampened her new confidence, however, and perhaps made her turn to food for comfort. In 1930 and 1931, Bow contacted the wife of a former lover, trying to recover "hush money" the studio had paid the woman to keep the affair quiet; went gambling and lost $13,900 when she thought she was only playing with fifty-cent chips; and was a witness at a sensational trial in which she accused her secretary Daisy DeVoe of trying to blackmail her. Shortly after the news of Bow's contact with the wife of a married ex-lover broke, a fan article asked, "What's to become of Clara Bow? Consider the scene. The eternal and wearying Richman publicity had died down to a murmur. Clara, whose billows had been causing wails and moans, had become slimmer and prettier than ever. A passable voice had suddenly popped out of that creamy throat. Then, from the cloudless Heavens, lightning snapped and crackled."[26] Especially damning was the trial, in which DeVoe made public many of the details of Bow's promiscuous love life and financial excesses. "Quit Pickin' on Me!" declared Bow in *Photoplay Magazine* in 1931 after being hounded by the press as each new scandal broke. "Surely Clara is entitled to some moderate dissipation," reasons the article in *Photoplay*. "Did you know that eating is one of the things Clara Bow is fondest of? When she's away from Hollywood, she doesn't miss boy friends, but her cook! Maybe this explains some of Clara's curve-trouble in the past!"[27]

Bow's "curve trouble" was not in the past, however. In June 1931, traumatized by further scandal (a tabloid paper called the *Coast Reporter* printed sensational—and false—details of incest, lesbianism, and drug addiction), Bow was unable to work. She left Paramount, the studio that had been her home since November 1925, and departed for the ranch of her newest beau, cowboy star Rex Bell. On the California-Nevada border, miles from the nearest neighbor, Bell's ranch afforded Bow the privacy she craved. While there, she ate heartily. " 'Gosh, how I could put away the grub!' she revealed later. 'I ate like a horse!' Within a month she had put on twenty-five pounds."[28] A fan magazine writer who visited Bow at her new digs remarked upon her weight gain:

> You're startled at Clara. First thing you notice is that she's far from slim. Clara never was svelte. She's further from it now than ever. "I've put on sixteen pounds," she says, because she notices you're noticing.
> "Sure," adds Earl Simpson, ranch superintendent, "and she eats plenty."
> There's a very definite double chin on Clara. Her face is moon round. Her arms and her what-Mencken-calls-sitzplatz are plenty.[29]

As long as Bow was off the screen, her additional adipose tissue was not a problem. Indeed, Stenn reports that Rex Bell was "delighted" by Bow's new figure and nicknamed her "Punkin." In December of 1931, the two were married in a quiet ceremony in Las Vegas.

Soon after, Bow began to think about a return to Hollywood. David O. Selznick, who had left Paramount for RKO, hired Bow's friend, writer Adela Rogers St. Johns, to write a film script for Bow's comeback. But when she visited Bow at the ranch, St. Johns informed Selznick that Bow was not ready to return to work. Clara was "fat, happy, and in no rush to change either condition."[30] Eventually, Bow signed with Fox, which offered her $250,000 for two pictures. Her contract, signed in the spring of 1932, included a weight clause requiring her to reduce to 118 pounds. If she didn't maintain that weight, Fox could cancel her contract with ten days' notice.[31] How quickly or easily she was able to reach 118 pounds (or less) is not clear. Stenn claims that Bow returned to Hollywood in June 1932 after "a crash diet had dropped the twenty-five pounds she gained at the Shack [the ranch]."[32] In November 1932 *Photoplay Magazine* implied that Bow's weight loss may have been a more arduous affair:

> Clara Bow, who has not set foot inside a studio—for working purposes— for almost two years, is ready to begin the first scene of *Call Her Savage*.
>
> There had been innumerable delays which Hollywood prophesied would put a jinx on the picture.
>
> First they had waited for Clara to lose the extra weight she had taken on since her illness.[33]

Bow, the article concludes, "is thinner but her figure is still well rounded. And she is more beautiful than ever."[34] Though Bow's precise weight and/or the reducing method(s) she used during this period will remain matters for conjecture, clearly her return to the screen necessitated yet another re-shaping of her body.

Call Her Savage, a film packed with "enough melodrama for three movies,"[35] was a huge box-office hit, proving that Bow was still a popular star. While Fox searched for a story for Bow's second film, she and husband Rex Bell went on a tour of Europe, a trip which was probably responsible for making her weight an issue once again. Interoffice correspondence from Fox's studio manager, J. J. Gain, to studio legal counsel Mr. Wasson indicates that, in the spring of 1933, Bow refused to be weighed: "In accordance with my letter of March 31, 1933, Miss Bow reported at this office this morning, accompanied by [husband] Rex Bell and [producer] Sam Rork, but refused to be weighed, her statement being that Mr. [W. I.] Gilbert [Bow's attorney] had explained the reasons for the refusal."[36] These "reasons" are made a bit clearer in a later letter from W. I. Gilbert dated April 3, 1933. At this point, it was apparently Fox's intention to cancel Bow's contract, but Gilbert argues against it. He reminds Fox that his client had hired a masseur "under your employ and upon your payroll. During a large portion of the time involved in the production of her first picture [*Call Her Savage*], Miss Bow was beyond that weight [118 pounds] and you did not exercise your option to cancel the contract on that basis." Gilbert further notes that Bow will be down to her contractually stipulated weight by the time her next film begins shooting; thus Fox has no right to terminate, and if they try, he will sue on his client's behalf.[37] Bow apparently did reach the weight specified in her contract; in the summer of 1933, she approved the script for *Hoopla*, a film in which she was to play an "amoral cooch dancer regenerated by love for a carnival barker's son,"[38] and shooting began shortly thereafter.

It would seem that the studio's stance regarding Bow's weight was inconsistent and contradictory. If, as Bow's attorney claims in his letter, Bow's weight was *over* 118 pounds during production of *Call Her Savage*, why then did Fox insist on Bow reaching that weight for her second film? Of course, we have incomplete information about the situation. Perhaps Bow's weight was not over 118 pounds while *Call Her Savage* was being shot. Certainly other sources, such as fan magazines and production stills taken during shooting (in which Bow appears slender), indicate that Bow had achieved one of the lowest weights of her career before she began production of her first comeback film. Bow's attorney may have lied to protect his client's interests. Or, if Bow's weight *was* over her contractually stipulated limit and production proceeded despite that fact, a number of conclusions are possible. First, Bow may have begun production well under her weight limit, but gained weight as shooting proceeded. In such a case, the studio may have avoided interrupting production simply to protect the considerable investment of time and money that had already been made. Second, an inconsistent application of the 118-pound weight limit may indicate its arbitrariness. The limit may not have been enforced for Bow's first film simply because no one bothered to do so. Perhaps the studio did not realize that Bow was over the limit. Perhaps she was only a pound or two beyond it, but gained additional weight during her trip to Europe and therefore made her weight more of an issue for her second film.

Though some of the details are lacking, one fact is plain: keeping relatively slim was one of Bow's professional responsibilities as a screen star. Her weight struggles were publicized repeatedly in fan magazines and became part of Hollywood's physical culture discourse, a discourse that intimately associated stardom with a slender figure. Of course, standards of slenderness in the 1920s were more forgiving than they became in later decades of the twentieth century. New concerns about shedding fat had reduced the female bodily ideal from the fleshy Junoesque type to one of rounded slenderness, but the "waif ideal" of the 1960s had yet to emerge. Even if, as I suggest in chapter 2, the motion picture camera prompted stars to keep their weight below what was considered "normal," Bow and other female screen stars were still neither required nor prodded to pursue extreme slenderness. Indeed, those star contracts that included weight clauses usually established what we would now consider rather generous weight limits. I have not been able to examine Bow's Paramount contracts, so I do not know if Paramount established a weight limit for her, although David Stenn, who has researched Bow's life extensively, claims that no weight clause appeared until Bow signed with the Fox Film Corporation in 1932. The evidence suggests that the limit of 118 pounds that Fox insisted upon was approximately ten pounds above Bow's typical weight, which is in keeping with the trend for weight clauses to establish limits that were above stars' usual weights.

In the end, ample weight did not prevent Bow from becoming a star. It seems that Bow's weight did fluctuate during her career, occasionally becoming as low as one hundred pounds. It is also apparent that Bow most often had what lover Harry Richman called a "ripe" figure. "Has the extreme boyish figure ever met with the entire approval of a beauty-loving public?" asked *Motion Picture Magazine* in March 1932. "Look at the favorites of the last few years! Clara Bow, no matter how she struggled and dieted, always had a tendency to curves." Slenderness, though an important ingredient in screen success, was never an absolute prerequisite. In the end, Bow's pert sexuality, dynamic personality, and magnetic screen presence "outweighed" any perceived imperfections in her body size. But even her tremendous talent was not enough to sweep weight considerations completely under the rug. Like other stars, she had to participate in Hollywood's physical culture discourse, detailing her battles with fat in fan magazine articles. Like other stars, she found her weight under constant scrutiny, both by her public and by her studio. Like other stars, she found that physical culture and motion picture stardom were inextricably intertwined.

After *Hoopla*, which was a critical and financial success, Bow retired from films. She wanted to be a housewife and mother. " 'I don't wanna be remembered as somebody who couldn't do nothin' but take her clothes off. I want somethin' real now,' "[39] she said. Once she was off the screen, Bow's weight seesawed mightily, typically on an upward swing. Whenever she returned to southern California or otherwise had contact with the public, she tried to lose weight, however. Her first pregnancy, which began soon after she left Fox, nearly doubled her weight: "Bored and nervous, she began binge-eating and ballooned to over two hundred pounds, nearly twice her normal weight."[40] When a second pregnancy ended in miscarriage, Bow was devastated. To improve her spirits, Rex encouraged her to return to work. "In September, 1937, the couple opened the 'It' Cafe on the corner of Hollywood Boulevard and Vine Street. Thin and glamorous once again, Clara informed reporters that she would be a constant presence at her restaurant."[41] She soon became pregnant again, however, and stayed in bed to avoid another miscarriage. After their second son was born, Clara and Rex returned to their ranch to raise their dream family.

Unfortunately, Bow chafed under the responsibilities of motherhood. Without the creative outlet of acting, she began to develop the symptoms of schizophrenia that had plagued her mother. She refused to socialize with her husband and yet did not want him to leave her home alone. In the late 1940s, she finally sought psychiatric help. At the Institute of Living in Hartford,

Connecticut, therapy uncovered suppressed childhood memories, including the fact that her father had raped her. Ultimately, "Clara's defense mechanisms proved impenetrable," and she left the institute in July 1950 without completing treatment.[42] She did not return to her family, but instead lived the rest of her days alone in a two-bedroom bungalow in Los Angeles, rarely going out. She died in 1965, the victim of a heart attack.

Stenn gives little detail about Bow's weight in these later years, though he does mention her sensitivity about it. "After hearing her joke about the weight she had gained since moving to Los Angeles, Tony [her younger son] sent his mother a postcard of an obese woman. The next time he visited, she would not allow him in the house."[43] Bow had not appeared in films for over two decades; clearly, hopes for continued employment would not have been a factor in any weight concerns she had. Like many retired stars, she probably felt at least some pressure to maintain an illusion of youthful slenderness—or least not to admit that her middle-aged body no longer matched her celluloid image. In 1980, popular screen star Joan Crawford tried to explain that once such an image is created, it can never be escaped:

> "[Director] Otto [Preminger] is totally right when he says that aging is hell for an actress.... [Once] the image is created ... it's up to you to keep fitting that image. If you try too hard—and I did it for several years—you look like a plastic caricature of yourself. Naturally, you do everything you can to shed years from your appearance. You try not to drink too much, and you diet like mad, and exercise, and get the right amount of sleep, and you exercise again, and you keep your sex life active, and it's one hell of a regimentation."[44]

Instead of engaging in the regimentation that Crawford describes, Bow simply withdrew from the world. She had virtually no face-to-face contact with anyone beyond a small circle of family and friends; if she needed to communicate with anyone outside that circle, she wrote letters. For most of the latter part of her life, perhaps in consideration of the fact that her body no longer matched her once-famous image, Bow kept her physical appearance a closely guarded secret.

RUDOLPH VALENTINO: PINK POWDER PUFF?

> Valentino has an almost perfect physique—a physique combining both beauty and strength: Apollo plus Dionysius. He is at once graceful and aggressively masculine.
>
> —*Photoplay Magazine*, February 1923

Perhaps the best way to elucidate screen idol Rudolph Valentino's significance to the 1920s is to begin by discussing his death, which occurred in August 1926 when he was only thirty-one years old. In that hot month, while he was in New York City to promote what became his last film, *The Son of the Sheik*, Valentino died very suddenly of complications from surgery done to repair a gastric ulcer and a ruptured appendix. Public response to his brief illness and subsequent death was unprecedented. While he lay in the Polyclinic Hospital, crowds of thousands gathered outside; telegrams and flowers wishing him a speedy recovery overwhelmed hospital staff. Later, when his body lay in state at Campbell's Funeral Parlor, over 100,000 people came to say good-bye to their screen idol. Thousands more lined the streets when Valentino's body was taken to St. Malachy's for his funeral, and when the train transporting his body to Hollywood for burial stopped over in Chicago, fifty thousand people crowded into the station. "Previously," says biographer Alexander Walker, "only the deaths of presidents or monarchs had aroused such a nation-wide response."[45]

Known as one of the screen's most passionate and exotic lovers, Rudolph Valentino rose to fame in 1921 as the South American character Julio in Rex Ingram's film *The Four Horsemen of the Apocalypse*. That film, which introduces Julio in a memorable tango scene, "assured Valentino's life-time patent on the [appellation of] 'Great Lover.' "[46] Shortly thereafter, *The Sheik*, the film that established Valentino as a desert lover with a cruel streak, was released to enthusiastic (mostly female) audiences, who quickly developed an ardent interest in the Middle East. "Libraries suddenly began to report record withdrawals of books about Arabia and Arabs; police sought hundreds of runaway girls whose destination was reported to be the Sahara; and women neglected their homes and flocked to the picture, even engaged in contests to determine who could see *The Sheik* most often."[47] From 1921 until his death in 1926, Valentino was a bona fide cultural phenomenon. Contemporary social commentators (mostly male) struggled to explain his popularity. In 1923, an "eminent psychologist" who wished to remain anonymous called Valentino the "greatest favorite on the screen" and speculated on the reasons for his appeal to women:

> Valentino would not be the national lover unless the country was in sore need of such a lover.... The American woman is starving for romantic love.... European men are far better versed in the game of love and the art of love-making than American men. They have, or take, more leisure. This is why a foreigner—especially a Latin—appeals so strongly to American women; and why so many American men lose out when competing with a European for a woman's favor.[48]

Unlike Douglas Fairbanks—whom Valentino admired and often tried to emulate in his films—Valentino's fame was not overtly based upon energetic Anglo-Saxon athleticism or adventurous derring-do. Rather, Valentino epitomized the "lure of romantic passion."[49] He was, as one fan magazine writer put it, "the first man in the movies to whom the term *sex appeal* was applied ... a real Latin lover ... [an] oily, jungle python of a lover who mastered [women] with silken cruelties."[50] Valentino's screen persona had no *direct* association with or dependence upon physical culture, and yet I will argue that it affected his career in two important ways. First, Valentino's participation in physical culture became part of his success story as a screen favorite, part of the process whereby he achieved and maintained his position as a star. Second, and perhaps even more importantly, physical culture functioned to recuperate Valentino's masculinity. As a man who began his show business career as a dancer, and as a recent Italian immigrant subject to racial prejudices, Valentino found his manhood frequently called into question, especially by male journalists. Physical culture activities, especially those that involved masculine sports like boxing, helped him to prove that he was a "real" man.

Valentino immigrated to the United States at the age of eighteen, arriving in New York City on December 23, 1923. The facts of his life prior to that journey remain controversial. Depending upon the source, Valentino's childhood is characterized either as one of genteel middle-class existence or as one of grinding poverty. An autobiography that was published in three installments in *Photoplay Magazine* in 1923 has presumably been the source for many of the later books and articles that elaborate upon Valentino's aristocratic background. In that series of articles, Valentino claimed that his full name was Rodolpho Alfonzo Raffaelo Pierre Filibert Guglielmi di Valentina d'Antonguolla. His mother supposedly explained the significance of all his names to him when he was a child; some of them had aristocratic connections. She told him, " 'The di Valentina is a papal title and the d'Antonguolla indicates an obscure right to certain royal property which is entirely forgotten now because one of your ancestors fought a duel.' "[51]

According to Valentino, his family lived in a "typical Italian farmhouse" with servants' quarters and stables, and his father practiced veterinary medicine. He died when Valentino was only eleven years old; Valentino subsequently attended Dante Alighieri College, which corresponds to grammar school in the United States. This was followed by the Collegio della Sapienze, a military school. Of his experiences there Valentino said, "The only thing I accomplished was [to join] the football team. While making that I failed all else and was compelled to go another year. By this time I was a gentleman of fifteen and felt I knew all there was to know."[52] His great ambition was to become an officer of the Italian cavalry, but his family didn't have enough money. "When my mother explained this we compromised on the Royal Academy. I did settle down to real study for once and got myself into excellent physical trim."[53] His chest expansion was one inch shy of the standard for admission, however. George Ullman, who was Valentino's business manager, claimed in a 1926 biography written shortly after Valentino's death (a biography whose first fifty pages recapitulated most of the details of the *Photoplay* series) that this episode was a seminal one in Valentino's young life. "This humiliation was like the flick of a whip on the back of a spirited horse. Rudy, of his own accord and with no one to force him, put himself into such marvelous physical shape that never, to the day of his death, did he lose any part of it."[54] Ullman's assertion, whether accurate or not, clearly associates Valentino's screen persona with physical culture; indeed, throughout his biography of Valentino, Ullman suggests that the star's success was a result of his "marvelous physical shape."

After Valentino failed to be admitted to the Royal Academy, he attended an agricultural academy. "I feel some satisfaction in the success I really did achieve at the agricultural school from which I was graduated with the highest honors of my class. It gave my mother happiness," he wrote in his autobiography.[55] After completing his studies there, he spent some time in Paris. When he depleted his funds, his family sent him to America. In a later affidavit for a court battle with Famous Players-Lasky, Valentino claimed that on his journey to America he was a first class passenger on the Steamship Cleveland of the Hamburg-American Line.[56] Biographer Irving Shulman offers a different version. "On December 9, 1913, Valentino set sail as a steerage passenger, with one American dollar sewn into the lining of his coat."[57] Valentino listed the amount as somewhat higher. "And so my mother got together about $4,000, all that she could spare, and gave it to me."[58]

Shulman also contests other items in Valentino's *Photoplay* autobiography, which he calls a "frothy catechism of pink icing."[59] Shulman was unable to verify Valentino's school information, since he found that records from the period(s) in question were no longer available. He is doubtful that Valentino ever attended school, however:

> There are snapshots showing Rodolpho in school uniform, but a number of expert photographers are convinced these are crude composites, the angle of the head not being quite right for the posture of the body. Also the paper on which they were printed was not of European manufacture.
>
> The truth is probably that Rodolpho's mother, distraught at her son's intractability, only wished she could have afforded to send the difficult boy to a boarding school, for he appears to have been a village scourge, constantly at odds with all adults.[60]

Shulman further contends that Valentino's autobiography was ghostwritten by Herbert Howe, a staff writer for *Photoplay*:

> What gratitude he [Valentino] showed when with a click of the typewriter keys Howe conferred nobility on him.... Valentino repeatedly called for Howe's reassurance that only his own name would really appear on the autobiography, and Howe promised. He kept that word, for only after Valentino's death, in several articles of reminiscence, did Howe admit that he had actually ghost-written the series.[61]

Even if the article was ghostwritten, however, more recent evidence indicates that at least some of its claims about Valentino's middle-class background may have been true. While doing research for his 1976 biography of Valentino, Alexander Walker managed to locate two snapshots of him aboard ship on his way to America in December 1913:

> These snapshots ... show a young Valentino, aged eighteen, which effectively kills the legend of the poor immigrant boy wearing sheets of newspaper under his shirt to keep out the cold. A smart young masher is the word for him, already self-composed and elegantly got-up, sporting a jaunty Jackie Coogan-like cap, with the 'V' of a white vest peeping from under a jacket which the wind on deck is whipping in close to the suggestion of a neat waist. The supple physique is already there.[62]

Walker also mentions Valentino's school records; apparently, unlike Shulman, he was able to examine them. "His school records speak of inattentiveness except at gymnastics and dancing-classes," observes Walker.[63]

Whatever the actual circumstances of Valentino's upbringing, what is clear is that his aristocratic background (or the pretense of it) was a key component in the construction of his masculinity. In her book on stardom and masculinity in the 1920s, Gaylyn Studlar has noted that the post—World War I era was an extremely xenophobic one characterized by fears of the "race suicide" that might result if Anglo-Saxon women mixed with the dark immigrant men streaming in from eastern and southern Europe.[64] One way for Hollywood to calm fears about the exoticism of its foreign stars was by giving them "the sheen of European aristocracy." But in Valentino's case, Studlar claims that this strategy was ineffective, and his low-class background, both as a youth in Italy and after his arrival in the United States, became common knowledge: "The revelation of Valentino's background linked him ... to those dark immigrants who wanted to hide what was believed to be their most dangerous characteristic: their racial/genetic inferiority. Through their false claims to aristocratic lineage, foreigners like Valentino, it was thought, tried to mask that inferiority while they attempted to appeal to the vanity and naïveté of American women."[65] Such revelations left Valentino open for criticism as a crude, superficial "Vaselino" who slicked his hair and used his dark appeal to lure and exploit women. An exotic model of masculinity was distinctly suspect to American men, many of whom considered Valentino effeminate and "woman-made," especially because he initially earned his living in America as a paid dance partner in New York cabarets.

Indeed, the charges of effeminacy that surfaced later in Valentino's career, though they were partly attributable to his status as a "dark foreigner," were almost certainly more closely related to his association with passionate ballroom dances. His status as a dancer made him the target of social commentators who had nursed a long-standing anxiety about the feminization of America. Michael S. Kimmel discusses this phenomenon—and its relationship to physical culture—in his excellent article, "Consuming

Manhood: The Feminization of American Culture and the Recreation of the Male Body, 1832–1920." According to Kimmel, as the Industrial Age took hold, many of the traditional bases for manhood began to erode. Instead of leading independent lives as skilled artisans or hardy farmers, men worked in offices or factories. In addition, the new separation of spheres (workplace vs. home) meant that the socialization of young boys was handled primarily by women. Men who wanted to reconstitute manhood had to somehow "rescue boys from the feminizing clutches of adult women. . . . While 'manhood' had historically been contrasted with 'childhood'. . . the new opposite of 'masculinity' was 'femininity,' traits and attitudes associated with women, not children."[66]

In such an atmosphere, men looked for alternative ways to prove their masculinity. They were "fanatical in their resolute avoidance of all emotions or behaviors seen as even remotely feminine. . . . [They] sought to sharpen the distinctions in manner, appearance, and style between the sexes as a way of muting the increasing similarities of everyday life."[67] Beards and moustaches became popular, and there was a new interest in physical culture as "men . . . attempted to develop manly physiques as a way of demonstrating that they possessed the virtues of manhood."[68] Muscle-building and sports such as boxing and baseball—or any others that at a minimum put men in the company of other men—were crucial aids in the fight against feminization. (Interestingly, when Valentino tried to grow a beard in 1924, he was roundly criticized. "Newspapers everywhere commented upon the fact [that Valentino had grown a beard]," says Shulman, "and general disapproval was expressed, showing that his public desired to see him as the clean-shaven youth which he had so endeared to his picture public."[69] Apparently the public was unwilling to accept so "masculine" an embellishment on Valentino's visage.)

Dancing was a physical activity, yet it was not considered manly enough to promote or reinforce masculinity. Indeed, though male dancers, especially those associated with ballet, developed admirable physiques, Gaylyn Studlar argues that their eroticized, often orientalized bodies

> ". . . threaten[ed] an athletic, physically based American masculinity. Dancing men were particularly dangerous because they seemed to suggest that the admirably fit male body in motion was not enough to guarantee a proper masculine character. . . . Prominent male dancers . . . undercut the foundation of the cult of the body since they were obviously muscular and athletic yet, at the same time, they were regarded as effeminate."[70]

Thus male dancers, especially those who not only participated in this feminine activity but also made their livings as the escorts of women, were an irritant to more right-thinking American males. Such dancing men were derided as lounge lizards or gigolos. The mere existence of such a breed of men was disheartening; the notion that one of them could become a romantic idol admired by millions of women was nearly unthinkable. When Valentino achieved such fame later in his career, his origins as a dancer made his masculinity the object of frequent criticism. Valentino's strategy for deflecting such barbs involved disavowing his career as a dancer and proving his expertise in more manly sports.

Valentino became a "lounge lizard" because he spent time in dance halls and cabarets where he learned popular ballroom dances. Eventually, he was hired at Maxim's, a trendy cabaret in New York City, as a partner for female customers. He was provided with meals and a room upstairs that he could use to give dancing lessons.[71] There, he may have held "tango teas," afternoon sessions in which "women rented male escorts to take them through the new steps [of popular ballroom dances such as the tango]."[72] Studlar claims that for many men of the period, "American women's challenge to traditional sexual roles and male domestic authority in the 1910s was exemplified by the popularity of nightclub dancing and tango teas."[73] At Maxim's, Valentino was a prime example of the feminization of American culture that men feared: he was a man who rented himself to women—a "woman-made" man. It was also at Maxim's that Valentino's first troubles with weight arose. He ate delicacies in the kitchen there, and soon began to gain weight. "The dancers at Maxim's had to be as slender as guardsmen. Rodolpho took to wearing a corset,"[74] says Shulman. Walker confirms this statement. "At this time, 1915–1916, the twenty-year-old dancer was wearing a corset under his evening clothes, which at least suggests he was eating well. He put on weight easily and had to watch his diet all through his career."[75]

Valentino practiced his dancing whenever possible and eventually was offered a substantive show-business opportunity. He became the partner of dancer Bonnie Glass, whose act with Clifton Webb was dissolving. After Bonnie retired to get married, he was hired to partner Joan Sawyer. In the summer of 1916, however, Sawyer dismissed him because of the "De Saulles affair." Apparently Valentino, in order to help his friend Bianca De Saulles sue her husband Jack for divorce, testified that he had seen his dance partner Joan Sawyer with Jack De Saulles. In revenge, Sawyer may have had Valentino arrested under false charges. The day after his testimony, he was arrested in the apartment of a Mrs. Georgia Thym on charges of blackmail. The disposition of the charge is not known, since, according to Shulman, the file is now empty. Perhaps, when Valentino later became famous, his studio had any embarrassing documents destroyed. In any case, "for the rest of his life this arrest plagued Valentino and he made numerous but unsuccessful attempts to have mention of it expunged from the *New York Times Index*."[76] Shortly thereafter, in 1917, he decided to try his luck on the West Coast. Initially, he landed in San Francisco, but he quickly made his way to Hollywood when actor Norman Kerry assured him that "the camera didn't emphasize the histrionic ability of an actor; what it did was record his personality. If the camera liked the actor's personality, success was assured, and the rewards could be fabulous. Rodolpho was sold."[77]

Initially, Valentino got work as an extra, though he supplemented his income dancing at Baron Long's Watts Tavern, a popular roadhouse. Eventually he began to get small featured roles as villainous foreign types in films like *The Married Virgin* (1918). In the fall of 1918, Valentino contracted the Spanish flu, which reportedly caused him to lose thirty pounds. "When I regained my strength after a careful diet of boiled fruits and broth, I started making the rounds of the studios," Valentino recalled later.[78] He had trouble finding screen work after his illness, however, and even considered going back to Italy, where his experience in Hollywood might have stood him in good stead. But Italian films required heroes with bodies like Hercules, claims Shulman, and Valentino, "lacked the physique suitable to a loincloth. The bald truth was that Rodolpho di Valentina was getting fat."[79]

Here, two points require clarification. First, Shulman's standard for applying the word "fat" is unclear. There are no extant photos of Valentino—including those of his life before he achieved stardom—that suggest he was anything other than trim and muscular. Other sources, such as Walker's biography, do indicate that Valentino had to watch his weight carefully, since he had a tendency to eat well and put on pounds. It seems unlikely, however, that Valentino's troubles with weight were ever a major issue in his career. Indeed, throughout most of his career his weight seems to have remained in the range of 160–165 pounds. In a 1923 fan magazine article, a photo of a document from the "Lasky Studio Engagement Department" lists Valentino's height as five feet ten and a half inches and his weight as one hundred sixty pounds.[80] Two years later, in November 1925, Valentino appeared at the Federal Building in New York City to apply for citizenship papers; there, he gave his height and weight as five feet eleven and a half inches and one hundred sixty-four pounds.[81] The second point is that Shulman's biography, though it is lengthy (500 pages) and well researched, includes many questionable pronouncements. This is not surprising, considering that his attitude toward Hollywood is openly critical and dismissive. He claims that Hollywood and its films are nothing more than "stupendous colossal stupidity." His motives for writing a Valentino biography seem to have been twofold: first, to patronize women for their worship of Valentino; and second, to debunk the Valentino myth, causing the keepers of that myth to froth at their "big fat mouths."

If Shulman is correct and Valentino had gained weight after recovering from the Spanish flu, a number of emotional and financial setbacks prompted him to lose it. In 1919, he received news of his mother's death and found little opportunity to earn an income, making it difficult to eat regularly. "Terribly hungry, out of sorts with everything, envious of everyone, he felt there was nothing left for him to do."[82] Then, through some of his Hollywood friends, he met Jean Acker, a friend of popular screen star Alla Nazimova (who was usually known simply as "Nazimova"). Valentino was enchanted. It was with Acker that he discussed changing his name from Rodolpho di Valentina to Rudolph Valentino; she agreed that it was a good idea. Two days after they met, Valentino proposed and they were married in a small ceremony at the house of Joseph Engel, the treasurer of Metro (where Acker was under contract at $200 a week). What followed remains a bizarre chapter in the history of matrimony. When they returned to Acker's residence at the Hollywood Hotel, she slammed the door on Valentino, telling him that their marriage had been a mistake. They never reconciled.

What happened? Alexander Walker has offered the best explanation. Nazimova was a lesbian and it was likely that Acker was one of her lovers:

> In the dedicated but highly competitive court circle where Nazimova, at the height of her power as a star and being paid $13,000 a week, would rotate her favourites, a minor talent like Jean Acker was bound to feel confused, insecure and frequently rejected. It was in such a mood that she apparently said yes to Valentino's proposal: it was a marriage of convenience, of companionship on her part, which immediately broke down once the consequence of having to share the marriage bed could no longer be postponed.[83]

In his autobiography, Valentino glosses over the abrupt end of his marriage to Acker, simply saying, "I left for New York after that. There I got work as a 'heavy' in a picture called *The Great Moment*.'"[84] Acker later sued for divorce based on Valentino's "failure to provide support." By that time, Valentino's first successful film as a "Great Lover," *The Four Horsemen of the Apocalypse*, had been released. As much as possible, he avoided discussion of their brief marriage, since his failure to consummate it was not the kind of publicity that would reinforce his image as an aggressive masculine lover.

The opportunity to play the leading role of Julio in *The Four Horsemen of the Apocalypse* came in New York in 1920. Screenwriter June Mathis (or so the story goes) had seen him in a small role in Clara Kimball Young's film *The Eyes of Youth* and thought him perfect for the male lead in the adaptation of Vicente Blasco-Ibáñez's novel. The plot involves a Frenchman who leaves his country in 1870 to escape military service and prospers in Argentina. His son Julio later returns to France and fights the Germans, dying a courageous death that atones for his father's earlier cowardice. It was this film that established Valentino as a bold, passionate screen lover.

Valentino's entrance into *The Four Horsemen* also made dancing an enduring part of the iconography of his romantic, domineering persona. According to Walker:

> Few film entrances are as stunningly designed as Valentino's in *The Four Horsemen of the Apocalypse*. One minute the screen is empty: the next, *he is there*, seen in close-up, teeth clenched determinedly on a cigarillo, smoke puffed boldly down his nostrils like a stud stallion on a frosty morning.

Deciding to cut in on a couple on the dance-floor, Valentino saunters over
in his gaucho costume, hand on hip, tapping the man meaningfully on the
shoulder, gazing with a very clear, unambiguous look at the girl, his right
eyelid ... quivering with ladykilling menace.[85]

This tango is a paradoxical one, for though it allows Valentino to demonstrate his physical prowess, the demonstration takes place in an arena
considered feminine by many American males. Thus Valentino's association
with the tango left him open to the sniping of males who were indignant
about his fame as the "Great Lover."

The sneering did not begin until Valentino reached the height of his popularity, however. After he completed work on *The Four Horsemen*, shot at
Metro, Nazimova requested him as her costar in *Camille*. Nazimova later
recalled that she told him to reduce before he would be granted the part. "'I
had already interviewed scores of young men,'" she said, "'but none seemed
to match my idea of a romantic star. Even Valentino didn't. He was too fat
and too swarthy.... Yet I saw that if he could reduce and pluck his eye-
brows, he would be the perfect Latin lover.'"[86] Nazimova does not mention
just how much weight she asked Valentino to lose. Certainly in *The Four
Horsemen*, he appears slender and muscular, especially in the film's later
battlefield scenes. It is possible that he gained weight after the production of
that film had concluded. What is noteworthy here, however, is not
Valentino's precise weight, but the fact that Nazimova considered slenderness
a qualification for a romantic screen star. Even if her comments were only an
attempt to be temperamental and/or controlling, it is still significant that she
considered weight a legitimate arena of criticism. Walker's biography also
suggests that Nazimova was not the only one who endorsed a reduction plan
for Valentino. He claims that Natacha Rambova, the production designer of
Camille, was also present when Nazimova interviewed Valentino. "As well
as recommending a diet and depilatory treatment, the two women at once
shampooed Valentino's shiny black skullcap of hair and fluffed it out with
hot tongs until it was more the style that a young French provincial ... might
have affected."[87]

Natacha Rambova was a clever, beautiful, egotistical, ambitious woman
whom many people considered the de facto director of *Camille*. Valentino
found her fascinating and quickly became infatuated. They had their first
date in December 1920; their ensuing romance put Valentino in an interesting position with Rambova as well as June Mathis and Nazimova: "Each
of them was tied to the others by strong bonds of temperamental affinity
and professional interest. Mathis had scripted three Nazimova films.
Rambova was her [Nazimova's] brilliant production designer. And all three
of them had advance knowledge of Valentino's capacity as an actor, a
romantic leading man, and his potential as a star."[88] Valentino's dependence
upon this triumvirate of women, as well as his connection to dancing, left
him open to charges that he was a woman-made man. Such charges became

more insistent when he eventually married Rambova (in March 1923) and it was rumored that she made all his career decisions as well as controlled production of his films.

The Four Horsemen was released in March 1921, and by the end of that month, Metro could claim to have the most successful film of the year. They balked at raising Valentino's salary from $400 to $450 a week, however, so shortly thereafter he signed with Famous Players-Lasky for $500 a week (an amount which was soon revised upward). In his first film for Jesse Lasky, *The Sheik*, Valentino played the character who became the icon of his career: Sheik Ahmed Ben Hassan, a desert marauder who kidnaps the militant feminist Lady Diana Mayo (Agnes Ayres) and makes her fall in love with him. To quiet fears of race mixing, Sheik Ahmed is later revealed to be the son of an Englishman and his Spanish wife, abandoned in the Sahara as a baby. In Sheik Ahmed, the ingredients of Valentino's appeal became clear: romantic menace combined with an underlying sensitivity. Studlar claims that this combination, which is metaphorically expressed in Valentino's tango in *The Four Horsemen*, is a typical feature of romantic narratives, especially during periods when women are unsure of their status. Such a situation "was surely applicable to many American women in the 1920s," says Studlar.[89] She cites Janice Radway, who explains that romantic narratives function to transform the darker elements of masculinity into a softer version that "reassure[s] the female ... that the patriarchal system is really benign."[90]

It was after the release of *The Sheik* in 1921 that Valentino began to reap the harvest of his dual association with passionate dancing and foreign exoticism. Most journalists did not openly attack Valentino's masculinity. Instead, they *defended* it. Because of Valentino's background, his masculinity was almost *automatically* called into question. A 1922 article asked readers to "dismiss the idea of the sleek and the insidious. There is nothing repellent, nothing unmasculine, about Valentino. Merely a heavy exoticism, compelling, fascinating, perhaps a little disturbing, as might be asphalt to the average cobbler."[91] Sympathetic journalists tried to recuperate Valentino's masculinity through a discussion of athletics. "I asked him how he preserved the splendid muscles that ripple over his back and biceps. Did he box, or swim or gymnasiumate?"[92] Valentino's answer acknowledges the role of dance in making his masculinity suspect. "'I do not make pretense to be an athaleet ... maybe because I have not the time. Because I dance once for a living, some...pipple say I was a lounge-lizard, but I do not theenk so, because I mus' dance or starve in America. I like better to dance.'"[93] Here, he uses the "I did it to survive, not because I actually liked it" defense. The article concludes by calling Valentino a "very Americanized foreigner" and listing his physical activities: walking four miles a day, climbing the Hollywood Hills, and galloping around on horses, "like Julio in the South American pampas."[94] Because Valentino was a dancer, because most of his fans were female, and because he seemed to allow the women in his life to make critical decisions for him, his masculinity required regular use of the "Physical Culture Defense." In 1925, well after wife Natacha Rambova's management of Valentino's career became the subject of speculation, *Motion Picture Magazine* declared, "Valentino Is Not a Henpecked Husband!" "The truth is," this article confided, "despite the matinée girls, Rudolph is a man's man. He has a handshake that brings the tears to your eyes and leaves you anxiously counting your bones. He is a wonderful boxer, and, as a former cavalry officer, rides well."[95]

Some journalists were not willing to be quite so supportive, however. Valentino's overwhelming popularity prompted a number of attacks in fan magazines as well as newspapers. Fan magazines, though they were more backhanded because of their function as promotional vehicles for Hollywood, echoed the assaults launched in other venues. In a 1922 article in *Photoplay*, Dick Dorgan declared:

> "I hate Valentino! All men hate Valentino. I hate his oriental optics; I hate his classical nose; I hate his Roman face; I hate his smile; I hate his glistening teeth; I hate his patent leather hair; I hate his Svengali glare; I hate him because he dances too well; I hate him because he's slicker; I hate him because he's the great lover of the screen; I hate him because he's an embezzler of hearts; I hate him because he's too apt in the art of osculation; I hate him because he's the leading man for Gloria Swanson; I hate him because he's too good looking."[96]

Of course, Dorgan's comments are tongue in cheek, but they are no less rancorous for it. Men who criticized Valentino often did it in an exaggerated, satirical tone, perhaps to suggest that Valentino's popularity was not worthy of serious analysis—a suggestion which is itself an indirect criticism. According to Shulman, Valentino was enraged by Dorgan's article. After he read it, he supposedly swore that he would " 'kill Dorgan on sight.' "[97]

In addition to Valentino's status as a dancer and a foreigner, Walker claims that the animus for much male hatred (or at the very least, discomfort) came from the final line in *The Sheik*, which became a catch phrase of the day. Lady Diana tells Sheik Ahmed, "I am not afraid with your arms around me, Ahmed, my desert love, MY SHEIK." According to Walker, this was "a line that the males in the audience had no response to: it asked the women to identify with Agnes Ayres and simply left the men feeling outclassed by Valentino. In it lies the making of much of the male antipathy he later suffered."[98]

The most infamous attack on Valentino's masculinity came in the summer of 1926, after he and Natacha Rambova had divorced (he protested that he would no longer stay with a woman who insisted upon having a career) and he was on his way to New York to promote his latest film, *The Son of the Sheik*. Ullman recounts that on the train he and Valentino read an editorial that had just been published in the *Chicago Tribune*. This editorial, which was entitled "Pink Powder Puffs," blamed Valentino for the feminization of the American male. The tone is admittedly ironic, but the rejection of the model of masculinity associated with Valentino is clear:

> "A new public ballroom was opened on the north side a few days ago, a truly handsome place and apparently well run. The pleasant impression lasts until one steps into the men's washroom and finds there on the wall a contraption of glass tubes and levers and a slot for the insertion of a coin. The glass tubes contain a fluffy pink solid, and beneath them one reads an amazing legend which runs something like this: 'Insert coin. Hold personal puff beneath the tube. Then pull the lever.'
>
> "A powder vending machine! In a men's washroom! Homo Americanus! Why didn't some one quietly drown Rudolph Guglielmi, alias Valentino, years ago?
>
> "And was the pink power machine pulled from the wall or ignored? It was not. It was used. We personally saw two 'men'—as young lady contributors to the Voice of the People are wont to describe the breed—step up, insert coin, hold kerchief beneath the spout, pull the lever, then take the pretty pink stuff and put it on their cheeks in front of the mirror....
>
> "It is time for a matriarchy if the male of the species allows such things to persist. Better a rule by masculine women than by effeminate men....
>
> "Do women like the type of 'man' who pats pink powder on his face in a public washroom and arranges his coiffure in a public elevator? Do women at heart belong to the Wilsonian era of 'I Didn't Raise My Boy to Be a Soldier'? What has become of the old 'caveman' line?
>
> "It is a strange social phenomenon and one that is running its course not only here in America but in Europe as well. Chicago may have its powder puffs; London has its dancing men and Paris its gigolos. Down with Decatur; up with Elinor Glyn. Hollywood is the national school of masculinity. Rudy, the beautiful gardener's boy [Valentino worked as a gardener for a brief period after his arrival in the United States], is the prototype of the American male.
>
> "Hell's bells. Oh, sugar."[99]

Ullman's rebuttal, published later that year in his biography of Valentino, staunchly defended the star but tacitly endorsed the feminine character of dance:

> What, I ask you, had the installation of a powdering machine in any public ballroom in Chicago to do with a dignified actor in New York and Hollywood? Had Valentino made dancing his profession, I grant you that there might have been some reason for this envious attack. But I have related how sincerely Valentino disliked the profession of dancing and what grave sacrifices he made . . . in repudiating the career of a dancer and suffering the privations necessary to become an actor in motion pictures.[100]

It was well known that Valentino did not truly repudiate dancing, however. His films often contained dance scenes. Furthermore, in the midst of a 1923 contract dispute with Famous Players-Lasky, when an injunction prevented him from working on the screen or the stage, Valentino and wife Natacha Rambova, through arrangements made by Ullman, staged a nationwide dancing tour to promote Mineralava Beauty Clay—a tour which not only made them $7,000 a week for seventeen weeks, but also demonstrated to studio executives the strength of Valentino's popularity *as a dancer.*

Valentino's response to the *Tribune*'s editorial, published within days of its appearance, was predictably grounded in physical culture: he publicly challenged the anonymous author of the piece to a boxing or wrestling match, whichever his opponent might prefer. " 'I will meet you immediately or give you a reasonable time to prepare, for I assume that your muscles must be flabby and weak, judging by your cowardly mentality, and that you will have to replace the vitriol in your veins for red blood—if there be a place in such a body as yours for red blood and manly muscle.' "[101] Valentino's tormentor never stepped forward. Ullman relates that soon after the challenge, however, Valentino did willingly get into the ring with boxer Buck O'Neil, who was suitably impressed by Valentino's pugilistic prowess. "I, as his friend," said Ullman, "make the statement that no cowboy on the Western plains nor athlete from the Marines could boast a more powerful physique than that of Valentino, nor more truly possess the right to the title of he-man."[102]

Physical culture was thus an essential component of Valentino's brief but intensely successful screen career. Walker claims that Valentino was obsessed with physical fitness and that such an obsession was probably grounded in the " 'less-than-virile' taunts that jealous males addressed to the 'Great Lover.' "[103] Valentino seemed to believe that if he simply proved conclusively that he had a muscular body, the taunts would cease. His films often exhibited his flesh. In *Monsieur Beaucaire* (1924), Valentino's well-muscled torso is displayed in a dressing scene in which he is naked to the waist. Walker includes a shot of this scene in his biography, remarking, "The cult of the body. Valentino valued his physical prowess and took every opportunity to display it. Dressing scenes were relished."[104] In *Son of the Sheik* (1926) Valentino's naked torso is again on exhibit during a whipping scene. (See figure 10.) Valentino displayed his well-muscled body in his publicity stills, as well, doing bare-chested sit ups and boxing with Jack Dempsey.[105] His Italian heritage undermined his efforts to publicize his athleticism, however. "The domineering behavior of the Sheik and an emphasis on Valentino's muscular physicality might have supported circulating views on manliness rooted in a cult of the body, but American men regarded Valentino as a foreign beauty rather than as an athlete," observes Studlar.[106] To them, Valentino was a feminized object of (homo)sexual display—as opposed to the active, athletic, heterosexual subjectivity Douglas Fairbanks was able to cultivate in his films and persona.

Figure 10: Rudolph Valentino in *Son of the Sheik* (1926)

Even after Valentino's death in 1926, the question of his masculinity was still not settled. Ullman's biography of Valentino is really no more or less than "he-man" propaganda that tries to prove Valentino was in perfect physical condition at all times—and therefore undeserving of attacks upon his manhood. Ever the faithful manager, Ullman protests that Valentino was "no weakling" and that he had a physique that was "the marvel of every one when he came into pictures." His protestations are tempered by a number of homoerotic passages that appear in his book, however. The most remarkable of these occurs when Ullman describes his first meeting with Valentino, an event which took place when Ullman approached him about doing a dancing tour for the Mineralava Beauty Clay Company:

> To say that I was enveloped by his personality with the first clasp of his sinewy hand and my first glance into his inscrutable eyes, is to state it mildly. I was literally engulfed, swept off my feet, which is unusual between two men. Had he been a beautiful woman and I a bachelor, it would not have been so surprising. I am not an emotional man. I have, in fact, often been referred to as cool-headed; but, in this instance, meeting a real he-man, I found myself moved by the most powerful personality I had ever encountered in man or woman.[107]

Here, Ullman waxes poetic about Valentino's status as an object of desire (both for women *and* men) while he simultaneously remarks upon Valentino's strength (and by extension, his "he-man" masculinity). Ullman's book is filled with such paradoxes; for example, he emphasizes Valentino's manly boxing and riding skills, yet uses a floral simile to describe the development of his artistic abilities: "Valentino bloomed like a gorgeous flower."[108]

By all reports, Ullman was a close friend and loyal manager of Valentino's. Indeed, after Valentino's death, he stayed on as executor of the Valentino estate, trying by every means possible to build value for Valentino's heirs (sister Maria and brother Alberto, as well as Natacha Rambova's aunt, Mrs. Teresa Werner, who had tried to help the couple work out their marital differences). It is then reasonable to assume that Ullman was sympathetic to Valentino's memory and that he would have attempted to forge a flattering account of Valentino's life. Yet he produced a document whose recuperation of Valentino's masculinity was at most incomplete. It is possible that a man of Valentino's era, even a sympathetic one, was simply unable to reconcile Valentino's masculinity with the standard Anglo-Saxon version. As a good-looking, mysterious, dancing foreigner whose career was "woman-made," Valentino's persona transgressed the American ideal of masculinity in too many ways for his manhood to be easily recovered with tales of physical prowess.

It is also possible that Ullman actually found Valentino physically attractive. Ullman's devotion to Valentino was unusually strong, persisting well after the latter's death. Did their relationship go beyond business? Both men were married during most of their association. Little is known of Ullman's marriage, but Valentino and Natacha Rambova apparently had little sexual interest in one another. "Neither Valentino nor his wife appears to have experienced any deep sexual need for each other. She would certainly have considered a family to be a serious block to a career. Her memoirs contain not one reference to any sexual intimacies, which is surprising considering that she was, after all, married to the screen's 'Great Lover.' "[109] Indeed, it is possible that they never consummated their marriage, as it is likely that Rambova, a close member of Nazimova's circle of lesbian protégés, was homosexual. It is also possible that Valentino himself was homosexual, though evidence is inconclusive in this area. He was often in the company of attractive young men. "The obvious pleasure he sought from the company of young men, often as handsome as himself," says Walker, "should not necessarily make us suppose he was homosexual.... Hanging around with the males in the gang, particularly if there was nothing else to do in a dead-end town, was part of the normal growing-up process for Italian youths and hadn't any ostensible sexual aspect."[110]

Whatever the truth may be about Valentino's sexual orientation, what is indisputable is that his brand of masculinity was one which was not compatible with the athletic Anglo-Saxon version accepted by many American men. For them, Valentino came to symbolize the race mixing taking place as dark immigrants flooded into United States from the far reaches of Europe as well as the feminization of American culture effected by women's increasing control over men's lives. More than most romantic stars, Valentino's background put the onus on him to prove that he was masculine. Thus he may have been under unusual pressure to build and display a body rippling with muscles.

Yet, such pressure was not absent for other male stars, particularly those in romantic roles. All screen lovers had to confront the public's expectation that romantic male figures would emulate the physical ideal of the day. During the reducing craze of the 1920s, that ideal was a well-muscled body without any superfluous fat. In addition, the effeminacy (and latent homosexuality) of the "Great Lover" figure in and of itself prompted even Anglo-Saxon romantic stars such as John Gilbert, Richard Barthelmess, and Ronald Coleman to participate in physical culture to prove their manhood. "There is always something inherently feminine in the 'Great Lover,' " says Walker, 'for it is his own narcissistic reflection he seeks in the depths of his beloved's eyes."[111] The price that male romantic stars paid for casting their reflections upon the silver screen as objects (rather than subjects) of desire was continual homage to the God of Physical Culture.

CHAPTER 5

Hollywood and Physical Culture
The 1920s and Beyond

Being beautiful isn't easy. Overcoming fat or building yourself up is a hard, hard job. But you *can* if you *will*.... You must give yourself the works, and not complain. I pledge you my word that if you will string along with me and do what I tell you to do, you will be as lovely as the stars of Hollywood—and lovelier!

—Sylvia of Hollywood, *No More Alibis*, 1933

The agrarian economy is out. Truth is still truth but human relations have changed.... The result of ... thrift today is merely nonbuying in an economic order which depends upon mass buying and ever greater and greater mass buying, for the welfare of all.

—Edward Filene, *The Consumer's Dollar*, 1934

HOLLYWOOD AND PHYSICAL CULTURE IN THE 1920s

What is perhaps most striking about the reducing craze of the 1920s is its apparent overdetermination. In addition to Hollywood, a virtual cascade of cultural forces nudged the American public in the direction of weight control in the early decades of the twentieth century, including but not necessarily limited to those detailed in chapter 1: World War I and its conclusion; the rise of consumerism; the decline of Victorian mores; Women's Suffrage; and the birth of the science of nutrition. All encouraged greater concern with physical appearance, particularly body size. Operating in the midst of such an imposing array of causes, the potential influence of Hollywood might seem a moot consideration.

Yet Hollywood became a prominent center of physical culture. Its serendipitous location in the temperate, sun-drenched climate of southern California in the symbolic freedom of the frontier, and its dependence upon a powerful yet unpredictable and fantastic industry where success often hinged on one's appearance, made it a place where bodily display was more acceptable than in eastern areas of the country. "[Hollywood's] amusements are noisy and intense," claimed *Photoplay Magazine* in 1921, "its habits artistically careless, its philosophy almost tropical—an island of motion pictures, that's all."[1] From its beginnings in the early 1910s, Hollywood

143

was seen as a place apart, a sunny, one-of-a-kind paradise inhabited by a cadre of young, strong, and beautiful motion picture players who lived glamorous lives both on- and offscreen. The features of its distinctive existence were exported to the world through films, advertisements, and newspaper and magazine articles, helping it to become not only the focal point of the reducing craze, but also, as a *Chicago Tribune* editorial writer lamented in the previous chapter, the "national school of masculinity," the place where male stars offered a muscle-based model of manhood predicated upon sexual display that replaced the inner-directed, achievement-oriented model of the nineteenth century. In addition, the optics of camera lenses played a key role in Hollywood's relationship to physical culture. The notion that the camera added from five to twenty pounds to the human body was accepted not only by the American public but by industry insiders as well. Weight control became one of the professional duties of motion picture stars, who subsequently became physical culture experts, regularly dispensing dieting advice to the public. Established stars who gained weight found their careers in jeopardy, while screen hopefuls who indulged in too many chocolate sundaes significantly diminished their chances of celluloid fame.

Furthermore, there is a fundamental mechanism that connects Hollywood with physical culture, a mechanism that arguably places Hollywood at the forefront of that overdetermined cascade of cultural factors that incited Americans to pursue physical culture in the 1920s. To identify this mechanism, I have been guided by the old adage that advises us to "follow the money." First and foremost, the reducing craze was an outgrowth of the dynamics between post—World War I consumerism and Hollywood. Both institutions emerged in the 1910s and 1920s, enriching one another in a convenient state of symbiosis. Physical culture as an *imperative*, as an activity in which consumers were *admonished* to engage, developed as a by-product of the intimate relationship shared by Hollywood and consumer culture.

The biggest and most profound changes that occurred in the post—World War I era were wrought by the exigencies of consumerism. Physically and psychologically, consumerism transformed people's daily lives. The remarkable increase in productivity that occurred after World War I, an increase attributable to the Industrial Age and to the new science of efficiency, allowed goods to be produced more rapidly and facilitated the advent of consumer culture. This culture of "excess" in which the public was urged to buy, buy, buy had a two-fold effect. First, youthfulness was at a premium, since "mechanized production depended heavily on the endurance and reflexes of youth. . . . Age, once a sign of accumulated productive know-how, came to be viewed as a detriment; compulsory retirement signified the transformation of labor from craftsmanship to unskilled machine-tending."[2] Second, the public was encouraged to adopt a "never satisfied" attitude that would promote perpetual consumption of goods and services. In 1926, an article in *The*

Saturday Evening Post remarked upon the ever-evolving array of body improvement products, ascribing the constant changes to the whims of a nebulous "Dame Fashion":

> Why is the personal reduction of American weight ... almost as eagerly sought as scaling down of American debts is sought abroad among the chancelleries of Europe?
>
> Partly because Dame Fashion is like that, never satisfied with anything about us "as is"; always trying to change something—our figures, our height, our complexions, our feet, our hair—just so as to give us a different look at least four times a year and make all our costumes *passé* long before they are half worn out. "Whatever is, is wrong" seems her motto.[3]

"Dame Fashion" was on the payroll of Madison Avenue, where advertising agencies quickly took root and produced a new breed of advertisements that fanned readers' dissatisfaction with their lives and pushed them to fulfill their roles as consumers. Advertisers enlisted the aid of social psychologists, who recommended that ads be constructed in a manner that would make consumers critical of themselves (and therefore more likely to buy): "The use of psychological methods ... attempted to turn the consumer's critical functions away from the product and toward himself. The determining factor for buying was self-critical and ideally ignored the intrinsic worth of the product."[4] A sampling of ads from the period provides ample evidence of these "psychological methods": "As she sits at the side of the man she adores, she is the picture of charm and beauty," begins a 1924 ad for Ab-scent anti-perspirant. "And yet, deep in her heart she suffers because he gives his attention to another. If she only knew that he would care for her were it not for the offense of perspiration."[5] A 1925 ad for a home hair treatment asks, "Could She Love Him Were He Bald?" and warns that men might lose their sweethearts if their hair begins to fall out.[6] Finally, a 1929 ad for the Delle Ross System of Reducing declares, "If you are fat, you cannot do your quota of work, nor have as many friends, nor as much self-respect, nor as good health as if you were normal weight."[7] If consumers could be convinced to be dissatisfied with themselves, they would have a general urge to buy. Such an urge is the engine of a consumer culture, and it is this engine that advertisers of the 1910s and 1920s attempted to build.

In this quest, they were aided and abetted by the motion picture industry. As detailed in chapter 2, the American motion picture industry flourished during the 1910s and 1920s. Production became centered in and around Hollywood, California; the vertically integrated studio system emerged; and by 1928, attendance at movie theaters had reached 65 million people per week.[8] Mike Featherstone argues that motion pictures, along with other mass media, allowed consumer culture to develop. Mass-circulated images promoted the new standards of behavior, appearance, and lifestyle to which the public was to aspire. Consumer culture was dependent upon the mass media to create desire and to encourage consumption. Indeed, in the early 1930s, a promotion booklet for advertisers in *Photoplay Magazine* declared:

> *Photoplay* ... is outstandingly tributary to the great sales-making, want building influence of the screen. . . . During that hour or two in the romantic world of make-believe, potent influences are at work. New desires are instilled, new wants implanted, new impulses to spend are aroused. These impulses may be at the moment only vague longings, but sooner or later they will crystallize into definite wants. . . . *The motion picture paves the way. Photoplay carries on, renewing the impulses caught on the screen.*[9]

This booklet includes a signed statement by the editor of *Photoplay*, James R. Quirk, who enthusiastically promotes Hollywood's relationship to consumer culture:

> "It became increasingly apparent to the publishers of *Photoplay* that the vast public who spent millions through motion picture box offices was interested in more than the stories flashed upon the screen; they were absorbing something beyond the vicarious emotions and adventures of the screen folk. The millions of young women who attended motion pictures began to realize that, closely observing the stars and leading women of the screen, they could take lessons to enhance their own attractiveness and personality. . . . When women go to the movies they see themselves not in the mirror, but in the ideal world of fancy."[10]

Here, manufacturers and advertisers are urged to base their products and ad campaigns upon the physical standards established by Hollywood films. (Quirk focuses his comments on women because the majority of *Photoplay*'s readers were young women.[11])

Obviously, consumer culture *did* depend upon the mass media to promote new lifestyle standards and to persuade consumers to buy. But the cinema occupied an unusual position in the media realm because unlike newspapers, magazines, or radio, it did not rely upon advertising revenue for its existence. Newspapers, magazines, and radio *had* to promote the ideology of consumerism. They were explicitly part and parcel of consumer culture. American motion pictures contained no explicit advertising messages. They were under no direct obligation to promote the values of consumer culture, and yet they did. Why? James Rorty offered one possible theory in 1934:

> Why does the motion picture with a high content of "romance," "beauty" and conspicuous expenditure represent the standard movie product of maximum salability? Because the dominant values of the society are material and acquisitive. And because the masses of the population, being economically debarred from the attainment of these values in real life, love

to enjoy them vicariously in the dream world of the silver screen. The frustrations of real life are both alleviated and sharpened by the pictures.[12]

Both Hollywood and consumer culture had the same goal: inspiring *want*, either to watch films or to purchase products. As Annette Kuhn has noted, films tend to offer an unattainable fantasy life to bring viewers back again and again.[13] This fantasy lifestyle provided rich fodder for advertisers, who urged consumers to pursue it. Motion pictures and consumer culture were the perfect complements for one another. Movies inspired wants that advertisers could exploit and advertisements stirred longings that movies could satisfy vicariously. Movies promoted consumer culture but were also *promoted by it*. Of course, this is not to say that the sole function of films was to inspire wants and/or to fulfill longing stirred by advertisements. However, the relationship between American cinema and consumer culture, as it emerged in the post—World War I period, was mutually supportive.

This interrelationship of consumer culture and Hollywood provided fertile ground for the growth of a physical culture trend. First, as Featherstone argues, consumer culture bases its appeal primarily upon the visual media, and such media tend to emphasize physical appearance. "Images make individuals more conscious of external appearance, bodily presentations and 'the look'.... A culture dominated by words tends to be intangible and abstract, and reduces the human body to a basic biological organism, whereas the new emphasis upon visual images [in the 1920s] drew attention to the appearance of the body, clothing, demeanour and gesture...."[14] As a moving visual medium, Hollywood cinema called attention to the body. It also allowed standards of appearance to be disseminated on a mass scale.

Second, the body provided an ideal arena of consumption. Each consumer had a body, each body was constantly changing (aging, losing or gaining weight), and each body had a nearly infinite number of features that could be "improved." If consumers could be convinced to be continually critical of their bodies, manufacturers and advertisers would benefit. Such companies took note of Hollywood's emphasis on the body, recognized the potential for profit, and began to produce and promote body improvement products. Consumers who absorbed the messages in body improvement ads began to idealize thin, muscular, wrinkle-free bodies; one way they could "have" such bodies was by watching them on the silver screen.

Again, consumers did not attend films simply to view attractive bodies. Yet, in terms of physical culture, Hollywood and consumer culture reinforced one another. As the major mass visual medium of the first half of the 20th century, Hollywood produced, distributed, and exhibited millions of images of the body. In the 1910s and 1920s, Hollywood films began to present more glamorous bodies. Lighting techniques improved and close-ups were used more frequently. Sets and costumes became more elaborate. Star personalities and feature films emerged. During this period, advertisements promoting physical perfection began to hammer away at consumers.

Hollywood films offered consumers the means of vicariously achieving the physical perfection which ads urged them to seek and made them more receptive to advertisements for physical culture products.

This cycle began with Hollywood's emphasis on physical appearance. Directly or indirectly, advertisements for physical culture products and methods that emerged in the 1910s and 1920s based their appeal on standards established by Hollywood. Such ads appeared much more frequently in motion picture fan magazines than in other popular magazines. Furthermore, many ads and physical culture guides specifically cited Hollywood stars or lifestyles as a means of establishing the value and desirability of losing weight or building muscles. This established a cycle, a cycle in which Hollywood's standards of attractiveness were reinforced by advertisements that urged consumers to reduce.

Thus, despite the wide range of factors eliciting concern with weight reduction in the early twentieth century, the reducing craze that developed during this period, characterized as it was by an aversion to fat and a subsequent urge to shed pounds, would not have been possible without the twin phenomena of Hollywood and consumer culture. Hollywood's slender benchmark of physical beauty was distributed on a mass scale and exhibited in a visual, moving medium. A burgeoning consumer culture, anxious to exploit potential avenues of consumption, latched onto this new model of bodily perfection and continually exhorted consumers to pursue it. Had either of these institutions been absent, any reducing trend that might have emerged would have been more moderate in scope, duration, and intensity.

Historians whose work deviates from this analysis include those cited extensively in chapter 1 of this study: Hillel Schwartz, Roberta Pollack Seid, and especially Peter Stearns. These scholars suggest that physical culture is a reaction to rather than an outgrowth of consumer culture; specifically, they argue that it is means of demonstrating restraint in an era of indulgence. According to Stearns:

> Even hucksters [in the 1920s and later] realized the moral force behind dieting as they continued to call for weight reduction as a sign of discipline and good character....
>
> Ultimately, the intensified concern about fat from the 1920s onward heightened the role of weight control, or worries about weight, as part of twentieth century morality. Here a basic ingredient of the initial culture of dieting persisted, even as it was overlaid by additional arguments about health or job efficiency. At its base, the need to fight fat remained a matter of demonstrating character and self-control in an age of excess.[15]

The Jazz Age, with its flappers, its speakeasies, and its emergent consumer culture, was arguably an era of excess. I do not discount the logic of asserting that excess in some areas may promote compensatory discipline in others, but as Stearns and others fail to note, the mantra of consumer culture was also the mantra of physical culture: "never satisfied." (Indeed, though Hillel Schwartz's work disagrees with my conclusions, his book is titled *Never Satisfied: A Cultural History of Diets, Fantasies and Fat*.) The strident moral tone that is present in ads for reducing products is present in ads for many other products as well. Advertisements in the 1920s urged consumers to keep their skin smooth (to avoid losing their mates), to educate themselves with home study courses (to avoid embarrassment at parties), and to avoid bad breath (lest they find themselves unemployed social outcasts). Ads for reducing products were strident not because of a new moral imperative to shed fat, but because the general tone of all advertising was shifting in order to compel people to become good consumers. The body was a frequent subject for such ads because it was a convenient site of consumption. And of course, Hollywood cinema, by calling attention to the body, made it a logical focus for consumer culture.

Caution must be exercised in applying these conclusions to other national cinemas, however. Hollywood's status as a symbol of physical culture and a focal point of conspicuous consumption make its relationship with consumer culture unique. Almost from its inception, Hollywood practiced a style of filmmaking that promoted the values of consumerism, a style that presented an "unattainable fantasy life." National cinemas that did not promote such values and/or lacked a production center similar to Hollywood (for example, those in non-capitalist nations) had a more tenuous, or even nonexistent, relationship with consumer culture (and therefore with physical culture).

Of course, Hollywood's influence was not limited to the United States; Hollywood films dominated the international market, especially in Europe, and what went on in Hollywood itself was news across the world. The extent of Hollywood's impact on physical culture in nations other than the United States is difficult to quantify, however, simply because the mechanisms that promoted Hollywood in the United States, as well as the synergy between Hollywood and American consumer culture, may have been present in lesser degrees or even absent completely in other nations. I have argued that films alone are not sufficient evidence of the relationship between cinema and physical culture. The fact that Hollywood cinema ruled the international film market does not necessarily imply that an appreciable impact upon physical culture followed. Such conclusions can only be drawn on a nation-by-nation basis after a detailed analysis of socio-cultural history, attitudes, and trends similar to the one offered in this study has been performed.

Nonetheless, there is at least indirect evidence that America's reducing craze had a ripple effect on other nations. In the early 1930s, reports of embryonic reducing fads in other countries began to appear sporadically in the *New York Times*. In July 1930, the *Times* noted that in Turkey "certain Constantinople matrons . . . have gone in for reducing alone western lines."[16] The article explained that the trend dated from the winter of 1929–30, when Mubedjel Namik Hanoum, who followed a strict physical culture regime (the exact nature of which is not made clear) and lost thirty-three pounds, became Miss Turkey. In 1932, the *New York Times* reported that women in Italy had begun "starv[ing] themselves to achieve slim, youthful figures."[17] In 1933, the paper observed that schoolgirls in Budapest, Hungary were trying to lose weight and speculated that a recent birth trend in London may have been the result of reducing diets. Apparently, more boy babies than girl babies had been born in recent years. Dr. J. W. Munro, a London entomologist, explained that experiments with beetles had shown that partial starvation influenced the sex ratio of offspring, so it was possible that female reducing diets "had set up a male-determining physiological condition in many prospective mothers."[18] (Let us hope that the use of insect data to draw conclusions regarding English females is not a reflection of women's status in the United Kingdom at this time!)

Articles about reducing in European countries appeared well *after* the American reducing craze had peaked and even begun to wane, suggesting that it simply took time for Hollywood's influence, in the form of films, fan magazines, and other promotional materials, to travel abroad. The delayed and muted character of reducing trends that emerged in European countries suggests that cultural factors worked to mitigate the effects of Hollywood. In Turkey, for example, doctors warned that women should eat for strength, not beauty, and the *New York Times* concluded, "Considering the heavy consumption of sugars, fats and starches in this country, it will be a long time before Turkey changes its preconceived opinions regarding the feminine form."[19] In Italy, Benito Mussolini instructed newspapers to "avoid any references likely to implant in the minds of women the idea [that] there is anything fashionable in being thin; or that there is anything to be ashamed of in being plump." Italian newspapers responded by "ridicul[ing] women who live on salads or do their daily dozen to rid themselves of superfluous flesh."[20] Finally, in Hungary, where it was discovered that girls at a Budapest High School had "vied with one another to see who could lose the most weight within a given time," parents, teachers, and doctors met and decided to "depict in lectures the fatal consequences of the habit of getting thin, and [to] praise in public the girls who were prudent enough to free themselves from it."[21] Though Hollywood's influence was being felt, social authorities in Turkey, Italy, and Hungary, where ideals of female beauty emphasized strength and health rather than slenderness, quickly attempted to dampen budding physical culture fads. Their actions reinforce the need for caution in asserting Hollywood's power to influence physical culture in Europe and elsewhere.

BEYOND THE 1920s

Ultimately, the reducing craze was curtailed by two factors: reducing "sanity" and the Great Depression. When in 1926 *Photoplay Magazine* promised, in the name of public safety, not to "admit to its advertising columns any internal reducing preparations or questionable methods," physical culture advertising in that publication became less frequent. In 1925, *Photoplay* published over 135 physical culture ads; in 1926, that number declined to 74, and in 1927, to only 39 ads. But then it began to climb again; in 1928, 74 physical culture ads appeared, and in 1929, 88. *Photoplay* quickly broke its promise not to advertise any "internal reducing preparations" or "questionable methods," but more articles and advertisements did mention the need for "sane reducing." The surge in physical culture advertising in 1928 and 1929 seems to indicate that the cautionary *Photoplay* articles (as well as similar articles that appeared in other publications) diminished but did not dissipate the desire for reducing products.

This desire was further dampened by the Depression. From a peak of over 100 ads per year in motion picture fan magazines such as *Photoplay*, *Motion Picture Magazine*, and *Motion Picture Classic*, the number of physical culture ads stabilized at 40–80 ads per year (per magazine) in the early 1930s. Reducing was no longer a craze, a fad, or a mania, but it did not go away. Advertisements for physical culture products continued to appear. Interestingly, perhaps as a result of the Depression, ads for methods to gain weight began to outnumber ads for reduction methods. After World War II, weight loss products enjoyed a renewed (and even more instense) popularity. But although standards of attractiveness shifted, consumers were consistently exhorted to spend money on molding their bodies. The relationship between consumer culture and Hollywood had been established and continued to exert its influence during the Depression and beyond.

Today, in the first decade of the new millennium, the pattern established during the 1920s' physical culture movement is still readily apparent. Bodily ideals have fluctuated and Hollywood has expanded its production capacity to include electronic media, but the essential relationship between Hollywood and consumer culture remains. Both institutions reinforce and depend upon one other. Physical culture, as a subset of consumer culture, is a ramification of that affinity. Other factors do exert waxing or waning effects upon physical culture as historical circumstances dictate, but interest in shaping the body will not disappear as long as the interactively parallel institutions of Hollywood and consumer culture survive.

Finally, one of the principal goals of this study is to recast the study of the relationship between physical culture and mass visual media into one in which circumstances of production, distribution, and exhibition are given at least an equal footing with content analyses. Media institutions include not only the movies or television programs or web pages that they produce, but also the mechanisms that support such production, including personnel; advertisements and promotional materials; and associated lifestyle(s). It is my hope that future considerations of the dynamics between mass visual media and physical culture will take all aspects of these unwieldy, multi-faceted institutions into account.

Notes

CHAPTER ONE: CINEMA AND PHYSICAL CULTURE

1. See Kristen Harrison and Joann Cantor, "The Relationship Between Media Consumption and Eating Disorders," *Journal of Communication* 47.1 (1997): 44.

2. The "Wholesale Murder and Suicide" series was published in *Photoplay Magazine* in July, August, and September of 1926. For this quote, see Catherine Brody, "Wholesale Murder and Suicide," *Photoplay Magazine* July 1926: 31.

3. W. Charisse Goodman, *The Invisible Woman: Confronting Weight Prejudice in America* (Carlsbad, CA: Gürze Books, 1995): 47.

4. See Harrison and Cantor 62. For other correlational studies, see Eaaron and Donna Henderson-King, "Media Effects on Women's Body Esteem: Social and Individual Difference Factors," *Journal of Applied Social Psychology* 27 (1997): 399–417; Larry A. Tucker and Glenn M. Friedman, "Television Viewing and Obesity in Adult Males," *American Journal of Public Health* 79 (1989): 516–518; and Larry A. Tucker and Marilyn Bagwell, "Television Viewing and Obesity in Adult Females," *American Journal of Public Health* 81 (1991): 908–911.

5. See Laura Mulvey, "Visual Pleasure and Narrative Cinema," 1975, *Issues in Feminist Film Criticism*, ed. Patricia Erens (Bloomington/Indianapolis: Indiana University Press, 1990); Linda Williams, "Film Body: An Implantation of Perversions," *Explorations in Film Theory: Selected Essays from Ciné-Tracts, 1976–1983*, ed. Ron Burnett (Bloomington: Indiana University Press, 1991); and Mary Ann Doane, "Woman's Stake: Filming the Female Body," *October* 17 (Summer 1981): 23–36. For a good survey of continental theories of the body, see the *The Body: Classic and Contemporary Readings*, ed. Donn Welton (Malden, MS: Blackwell Publishers, 1999).

6. See Steven Cohan and Ina Rae Hark, eds., *Screening the Male: Exploring Masculinities in Hollywood Cinema* (London/New York: Routledge, 1990); Brian Caldwell, "Muscling in on the Movies: Excess and the Representation of the Male Body in Films of the 1980s and 1990s," *American Bodies: Cultural Histories of the Physique*, ed. Tim Armstrong (New York: New York University Press, 1996): 133–140; and Peter Lehman, *Running Scared: Masculinity and the Representation of the Male Body* (Philadelphia: Temple University Press, 1993).

7. See Susan Jeffords, *Hard Bodies: Hollywood Masculinity in the Reagan Era* (New Brunswick, NJ: Rutgers University Press, 1994); Gaylyn Studlar, "Barrymore, the Body, and Bliss: Issues of Male Representation and Female Spectatorship in the 1920s," *Fields of Vision: Essays in Film Studies, Visual*

Anthropology, and Photography (Berkeley: University of California Press, 1995): 160–180; and Gaylyn Studlar, *This Mad Masquerade: Stardom and Masculinity in the Jazz Age* (New York: Columbia University Press, 1996).

8. See Hillel Schwartz, *Never Satisfied: A Cultural History of Diets, Fantasies and Fat* (New York: Macmillan, 1986); Roberta Pollack Seid, *Never Too Thin: Why Women Are at War with Their Bodies* (New York: Prentice Hall, 1989); and Peter N. Stearns, *Fat History: Bodies and Beauty in the Modern West* (New York: New York University Press, 1997).

9. Seid 23.

10. See Susie Orbach, *Fat Is a Feminist Issue* (New York: Berkeley Publishing Group, 1978); Marcia Millman, *Such a Pretty Face: Being Fat in America* (New York: W.W. Norton & Company, 1980); Kim Chernin, *The Obsession: Reflections on the Tyranny of Slenderness* (New York: HarperCollins Publishers, 1981); Naomi Wolf, *The Beauty Myth: How Images of Beauty Are Used Against Women* (New York: Doubleday, 1991); and Susan Bordo, *Unbearable Weight: Feminism, Western Culture and the Body* (Berkeley: University of California Press, 1993).

11. Bordo 206.

12. See Lary May, *Screening Out the Past: The Birth of Mass Culture and the Motion Picture Industry* (New York: Oxford University Press, 1980), especially pages 114 and 167.

13. See Mike Featherstone, "The Body in Consumer Culture," *The Body: Social Process and Cultural Theory*, ed. Mike Featherstone, Mike Hepworth, and Bryan S. Turner (London: Sage, 1991): 170–196.

14. René Girard, "Hunger Artists: Eating Disorders and Mimetic Desire," *The Body Aesthetic: From Fine Art to Body Modification*, ed. Tobin Siebers (Ann Arbor: The University of Michigan Press, 2000): 179–198, especially page 194.

15. May 167.

16. Schwartz 42, 45–47.

17. Seid 76.

18. Seid 65, 69, and 72.

19. Stearns 4.

20. Seid 82–83.

21. Stearns 58, 60.

22. Schwartz 147.

23. Seid 94.

24. Stearns 18.

25. Samuel G. Blythe, "Get Rid of that Fat," *Saturday Evening Post* 23 April 1927: 10–11.

26. "The Cult of Slimness," *Living Age* 28 Feb. 1914: 572–573.

27. Dr. Dudley A. Sargent, "Are You Too Fat, or Too Thin?" *The American Magazine* Nov. 1921: 13.

28. H. I. Phillips, "It Is Never Too Late To Shrink," *The American Magazine* Nov. 1925: 38.

29. "Cult of Slimness," 573.

30. Wendell C. Phillips, M. D., Introduction, *Your Weight and How to Control It*, 1926, ed. Morris Fishbein, M. D. (Garden City: Doubleday, Doran and Company, 1929): x.

31. Harlow Brooks, M. D., "The Price of a Boyish Form," *Your Weight and How to Control It*, 1926, ed. Morris Fishbein, M. D. (Garden City: Doubleday, Doran and Company, 1929): 30.

32. Brooks 30.

33. "Penalties of Obesity," *Journal of the American Medical Association* 89 (1927): 694–695.

34. "Find No Sure Guide to Women's Weight," *New York Times* 23 Feb. 1926: 17.

35. An ad campaign by the "Corrective Eating Society" provides an excellent illustration of this trend. A 1915 ad in *The American Magazine* offered "Eugene Christian's Course in Scientific Eating," promising that purchasers could "Eat to Live 100 Years." This ad was simply informative, making no attempt to humiliate readers or persuade them to lose weight; it only recommended a particular course of eating in order to maintain health. Soon, however, the tone of the Corrective Eating Society's ads began to change. In July 1916, a tag line read, "The Crimes We Commit Against Our Stomachs." Later in the ad, readers were told, "A man's success in life depends more on the co-operation of his stomach than on any other factor." In an April 1919 ad, the Society revealed "Why Some Foods Explode in the Stomach." Meanwhile, in *Photoplay*, where no ads for the Corrective Eating Society had previously appeared, a full-page ad on page seven of the August 1921 issue announced, "New Discovery Takes Off Flesh Almost 'While You Wait'!" The Society was still offering a course by Eugene Christian, but it was now entitled "Weight Control—The Basis of Health." The ad noted that by taking off "useless fat," women could wear attractive clothing styles and men could enjoy a miraculous return of youthful energy. In April 1922, a full-page ad for the Corrective Eating Society appeared in *The American Magazine*. As in *Photoplay*, the ad was now about weight control instead of merely eating for health: "Doctor's Wife Takes off 40 Pounds Through New Discovery." In 1922, some of the Society's ads in *Photoplay* began to adopt a forceful tone: "It's a Crime to Be Fat—When It's So Easy to Be Slender."

36. Allen 348.

37. Seid 101.

38. Frederick Lewis Allen, *Only Yesterday: An Informal History of the Nineteen-Twenties* (New York: Harper, 1931): 20, 247–248.

39. Schwartz 141–142.

40. Dr. Lulu Hunt Peters, *Diet and Health—With Key to the Calories* (Chicago: Reilly and Britton, 1918): 12–13.

41. Schwartz 143–144.

42. See *Photoplay Magazine* Oct. 1918: 104.

43. Allen 25, 77.

44. Seid 82.

45. Schwartz 88.

46. See Michael S. Kimmel, "Consuming Manhood: The Feminization of American Culture and the Recreation of the Male Body, 1832–1920," *Michigan Quarterly Review* 33.1 (1994): 7–36 and Gaylyn Studlar, *This Mad Masquerade: Stardom and Masculinity in the Jazz Age* (New York: Columbia University Press, 1996).

47. Kimmel 17.

48. See Stuart Ewen, *Captains of Consciousness: Advertising and the Roots of the Consumer Culture* (New York: McGraw-Hill, 1976) and Mike Featherstone, "The Body in Consumer Culture," *The Body: Social Process and Cultural Theory*, ed. Mike Featherstone, Mike Hepworth, and Bryan S. Turner (London: Sage, 1991): 170–196.

49. Robert Bocock, *Consumption* (New York: Routledge, 1993): 50.

50. William Leach, *Land of Desire: Merchants, Power, and the Rise of a New American Culture* (New York: Vintage Books, 1993): 3.

51. James Rorty, *Our Master's Voice: Advertising* (New York: The John Day Company, 1934): 29.

52. Rorty 24.

53. Ewen 32.

54. Ewen 24–26.

55. Ewen 31–32.

56. Allen 169.

57. Robert and Helen Lynd, *Middletown: A Study in American Culture* (New York: Harcourt, Brace and Company, 1929): 3. (Data collection concluded in 1925.)

58. Robert and Helen Lynd 82.

59. Allen 196.

60. Stearns 58.

61. Stearns 59.

62. See Featherstone, "The Body in Consumer Culture."

63. Stearns 18, 67.

64. Stearns 67.

65. Anthony S. Kern, *Anatomy and Desire: A Cultural History of the Human Body* (New York: Bobs-Merrill, 1975): 5–6.

66. Featherstone 177.

67. Allen 119.

68. Allen 99.

69. Allen 99.

70. Robert and Helen Lynd 123–125.

71. Allen 94.

72. "The Cult of Slimness" 572.

73. Woods Hutchinson, M.D., "Fat and Fashion," *The Saturday Evening Post* 21 Aug. 1926: 64.

74. Seid 81.

75. Seid 82, 91.

76. Woods Hutchinson, M.D., "A Defense of Fat Men," *The Saturday Evening Post* 7 June 1924: 8.

77. Morris Fishbein, M. D., "The Craze for Reducing," *Your Weight and How to Control It*, ed. Morris Fishbein, M. D. (Garden City, NY: Butterick Publishing, 1926): 25.

78. Allen 97.

79. Adela Rogers St. Johns, "New American Beauty," *Photoplay Magazine* June 1922: 26–27.

80. Bordo 206.

81. Allen 108.

82. Fishbein 24.

83. Seid 84.

84. Allen 108–109.

85. Wolf 184.

86. Hutchinson, "A Defense of Fat Men": 8.

87. H. I. Phillips 38.

88. Allen 98, 199, 197.

89. Benjamin Harrow, Ph.D., *What to Eat in Disease and Health* (New York: E.P. Dutton and Company, 1923): Photograph opposite page 1.
90. Qtd. in Schwartz 133.
91. Stearns 30.
92. Marise de Fleur, "Reducing the Fat of the Land" *Sunset Magazine* August 1925: 72.
93. Peters 24, 37.
94. Henry T. Finck, *Girth Control for Womanly Beauty, Manly Strength, Health and a Long Life for Everybody* (New York/London: Harper and Brothers, 1923): 104.
95. Finck 115–116.
96. Seid 89.
97. Schwartz 135, 139.
98. Lewellys F. Barker, "How Glands Affect Weight," *Your Weight and How to Control It*, 1926, ed. Morris Fishbein, M.D. (New York: Doubleday, Doran and Company, 1929): 67.
99. Barker 73.
100. *Photoplay Magazine* Oct. 1923: 21.
101. "The Sangrina and Silph Chewing Gums Frauds," *Journal of the American Medical Association* 87 (1926): 689.
102. Catherine Brody, "Wholesale Murder and Suicide," *Photoplay Magazine* July 1926: 92.
103. *Photoplay Magazine* Aug. 1923: 13.
104. *Photoplay Magazine* May 1924: 149.
105. Blythe 11.
106. Barker 72.
107. Schwartz 156.
108. Finck 14.
109. Eugene Lyman Fisk, M. D., "How Much Fat Will You Give?" *Good Housekeeping* Jan. 1918: 76.
110. Dr. Dudley A. Sargent, "Are You Too Fat, or Too Thin?" *The American Magazine* Nov. 1921: 13.
111. These are the weights cited in tables compiled from insurance data. See sample tables in Sargent, page 13.
112. *Photoplay Magazine* June 1918: 110.
113. Harriette Underhill, "The Movies Give the World a Boyish Form: Motion Pictures Have Transformed the Public Taste in Feminine Pulchritude," *Motion Picture Classic* Nov. 1925: 30.
114. Katherine Albert, "Diet—The Menace of Hollywood," *Photoplay Magazine* Jan. 1929: 30.
115. See May, particularly pages 189–190.

CHAPTER 2: THE DRAMA-CANNING INDUSTRY HEADS WEST

1. Bruce T. Torrence, *Hollywood: The First Hundred Years* (New York: Zoetrope, 1979): 9.
2. Torrence 9.
3. Torrence 68.

4. Kevin Brownlow, *Hollywood: The Pioneers* (New York: Alfred P. Knopf, 1979): 90.

5. Brownlow 91.

6. Kenneth L. Roberts, "Flaming Hollywood," *The Saturday Evening Post* 12 July 1924: 4.

7. Lary May, *Screening Out the Past: The Birth of Mass Culture and the Motion Picture Industry* (New York: Oxford University Press, 1980): 189.

8. Roberts 4.

9. Roberts 3.

10. Richard Koszarksi, *An Evening's Entertainment: The Age of the Silent Feature Picture, 1915–1928. History of the American Cinema*, vol. 3. (Berkeley: University of California Press, 1990): 102, 104.

11. Brownlow 91.

12. Torrence 68.

13. Robert Sklar, *Movie-Made America: A Cultural History of American Movies* (New York: Vintage Books, 1976): 68.

14. Brownlow 91.

15. Sklar 67.

16. George Fitzmaurice, "What Future Has Hollywood as a Moving Picture Producing Center?" *The Truth About the Movies—By the Stars*, ed. Laurence A. Hughes (Hollywood, CA: Hollywood Publishers, Inc., 1924): 19.

17. Koszarski 26.

18. See William Allen Johnston, "In Motion Picture Land," *Everybody's Magazine* Oct. 1915, p. 448: "To-day Los Angeles is the hub of the photo-play world, the producing center of an industry now rated a fifth in size the country." The exact ranking of the motion picture industry is uncertain; a 1932 article claims that it is *not* the fourth or fifth American industry in terms of size, but that it does "rank first as our most conspicuous industry." See Jerome Beatty, "Hullabaloo Town," *The American Magazine* May 1932: 26.

19. May 177.

20. "Movie Myths and Facts as Seen by an Insider," *The Literary Digest* 7 May 1921: 38, 42.

21. "Health—Hollywood's Greatest Asset," *Photoplay Magazine* Nov. 1926: 33.

22. Dorothy Donnell, "Are the Movies to Blame for Hollywood's Suicides?" *Motion Picture Classic* Oct. 1927: 70.

23. Katharine Fullerton Gerould, "Hollywood: An American State of Mind," *Harper's Magazine* May 1923: 693.

24. Gerould 692.

25. Preston K. Harris, "Who Are the Beautiful Girls of Hollywood?" *Motion Picture Classic* Sept. 1925: 28.

26. Charles Donald Fox, *Mirrors of Hollywood* (New York: Charles Renard Corporation, 1925): 11–12.

27. "The Right Weigh," *Motion Picture Magazine* Jun 1925: 106.

28. "The Swimming Pools of Hollywood," *Photoplay Magazine* Oct. 1922: 22–23.

29. "Health—Hollywood's Greatest Asset" 33.

30. Mary Winship, " 'Oh, Hollywood!'—A Ramble in Bohemia," *Photoplay Magazine* May 1921: 21.

31. "Talmadge Sisters, Film Stars, Arrive," *New York Times* 25 Feb. 1922: 9.

32. Dorothy Calhoun, "Taking the Die Out of Diet," *Motion Picture Magazine* July 1930: 28, 112.

33. Harriet Parsons, "The Weigh of all Flesh," *Photoplay Magazine* Oct. 1929: 64.

34. Dorothy Calhoun, "The 18-Day Diet," *Motion Picture Magazine* Oct. 1929: 45.

35. Parsons 43.

36. Roberta Pollack Seid, *Never Too Thin: Why Women Are at War with Their Bodies* (New York: Prentice Hall, 1989): 96.

37. E. W. Bowers, M.D., "The Stars Tell How They Keep Those Girlish Lines," *Photoplay Magazine* Sept. 1924: 28.

38. Qtd. in Bowers 30.

39. "Signore Valentino Herewith Presents His New Leading Lady, Fräulein Banky," *Motion Picture Magazine* Nov. 1925: 24.

40. Harriette Underhill, "The Movies Give the World a Boyish Form," *Motion Picture Classic* Nov. 1925: 31.

41. "Do You Want to Reduce?" *Photoplay Magazine* Oct. 1920: 64.

42. Corliss Palmer, "The Slender Silhouette," *Motion Picture Magazine* Nov. 1921: 60.

43. Carolyn Van Wyck, "Friendly Advice on Girls' Problems," *Photoplay Magazine* July 1926: 94.

44. Milton H. Berry (as reported by Wagner White), "You Can Keep a Youthful Figure if You Treat Your Muscles Right," *The American Magazine* Aug. 1927: 43.

45. Lois Shirley, "The Enemy of Beauty—Over-Exercise," *Photoplay Magazine* Aug. 1931: 30.

46. Carolyn Van Wyck, introduction, *No More Alibis*, Sylvia of Hollywood (New York: MacFadden Book Company, 1934): 9.

47. Schwartz 164.

48. Schwartz 155.

49. Schwartz 166.

50. Per an e-mail from *The Ladies' Home Journal*, circulation figures are as follows: December 1916: 1,604,903; June 1927: 2,498,310; and December 1934: 2,545,857. *The American Magazine* announced a circulation of over 2,000,000 on the cover of several issues throughout the 1920s. On page 193 of *An Evening's Entertainment: The Age of the Silent Feature Picture* (Berkeley: Univ. of California Press, 1990), Richard Koszarski notes that *Photoplay*'s circulation in 1918 was 204,434. On page 252 of *Our Master's Voice: Advertising* (New York: The John Day Company, 1934), James Rorty cites a 1930s promotion pamphlet for *Photoplay* that lists a circulation of over 600,000.

51. These figures represent my tally of the number of physical culture ads for the periods cited. I have counted only those ads that promote physical culture activities, per my definition of such activities. My figures include *all* physical culture ads, irrespective of their size, which ranges from a small fraction of a page to a full page. Since it is often difficult to draw the line between cosmetic devices and physical culture products, others may arrive at slightly different statistics.

52. Here are some representative figures for *Motion Picture Magazine*: 1917: 16 physical culture ads published; 1921: approximately 59 physical culture ads; 1925: 116 physical culture ads; and 1930: 76 physical culture ads. *Motion Picture Classic* began publication in 1915 as *Motion Picture Supplement*, a supplement to *Motion Picture Magazine*. In 1916, it became *Motion Picture Classic*. Based on the issues I have been able to examine, I offer the following

statistics for physical culture ads in *Motion Picture Classic*: Nov. 1915—Aug. 1916: 13 ads; Mar. 1921—Feb. 1922: 60 ads; 1925: 64 ads; 1930: 59 ads. *Motion Picture Classic* published fewer physical culture ads than *Photoplay Magazine* or *Motion Picture Magazine*, but this may have been because the advertising sections in *Motion Picture Classic* were 25 to 50 pages shorter than those in *Photoplay* or *Motion Picture Magazine*.

53. For example, from 1921 through 1924 the Corrective Eating Society advertised a weight control course in both *Photoplay* and *The American Magazine*. During this period, sixteen ads appeared in *Photoplay*; thirteen of those were full-page ads in the front advertising section. Comparably, in *The American Magazine* only two ads for the Corrective Eating Society's weight control course appeared, both in the rear advertising section. Although the message of the ads was similar in both publications, the ads appeared more frequently and more prominently in *Photoplay*.

54. *Photoplay Magazine* June 1915: 170.

55. *Photoplay Magazine* Aug. 1925: 135.

56. *Motion Picture Magazine* Nov. 1925: 116.

57. *Motion Picture Classic* Feb. 1928: 81.

58. *Photoplay Magazine* Mar. 1929: 113.

59. *Photoplay Magazine* May 1929: 147.

60. *Photoplay Magazine* Jan. 1930: 14.

61. *Motion Picture Magazine* Mar. 1930: 10.

62. Koszarski 100.

63. May 183.

64. Rosten 16.

65. Budd Schulberg, *The Disenchanted* (New York: Random House, 1950): 99.

66. Frederick Van Vranken, "Women's Work in Motion Pictures," *Motion Picture Magazine* Aug. 1923: 29.

67. Winship 112.

68. "Movies Arraigned by Senator Myers," *New York Times* 30 June 1922: 9.

69. Rosten 194.

70. George Ade, "Answering Wild-Eyed Questions about the Movie Stars at Hollywood," *The American Magazine* May 1922: 52.

71. Ade 52.

72. "Depicts Hollywood as Homelike City," *New York Times* 18 Sept. 1926: 25.

73. George Walsh, "Athletics and the Screen," *Breaking into the Movies*, ed. Charles Reed Jones (New York: The Unicorn Press, 1927): 77–78.

74. Billie Dove, "Physical Culture and Poise," *Breaking into the Movies*, ed. Charles Reed Jones (New York: The Unicorn Press, 1927): 88.

75. Ade 52.

76. "Talmadge Sisters, Films Stars, Arrive" 9.

77. "Depicts Hollywood as Homelike City" 25.

78. Gerould 692.

79. Rosten 13.

80. Betty Compson, "Not a Life of Ease," *The Truth About the Movies—By the Stars*, Laurence A. Hughes, ed. (Hollywood, CA: Hollywood Publishers, Inc., 1924): 133.

81. Rob Wagner, "Sudden Stars," *Opportunities in the Motion Picture Industry— And How to Qualify for Positions in its Many Branches*, vol. 1. (Los Angeles: Photoplay Research Society, Bureau of Vocational Guidance, 1922): 79.

82. Katherine Albert, "They Must Suffer to Be Beautiful," *Photoplay Magazine* Oct. 1929: 31.

83. "The Right Weigh," *Motion Picture Magazine* June 1925: 57.

84. F. A. Datig, "Are You a Screen Personality?" *Opportunities in the Motion Picture Industry—And How to Qualify for Positions in its Many Branches*, vol. 1. (Los Angeles: Photoplay Research Society, Bureau of Vocational Guidance, 1922): 48.

85. Rosten 122.

86. Rosten 45, 122.

87. Herbert Howe, "Returning to Hollywood," *Photoplay Magazine* May 1925: 109.

88. Howe 110.

89. Rosten 39.

90. Ruth Biery, "Hollywood's Age of Fear," *Photoplay Magazine* July 1931: 58.

91. Biery 127.

92. Jan and Cora Gordon, *Star-Dust in Hollywood* (London: George G. Harrap & Co. Ltd., 1930): 154.

93. "Elinor Glyn Thinks Hollywood Abused," *New York Times* 14 Apr. 1922: 17.

94. Howe 30.

95. Bert Lytell, "Can I Appear on the Screen?" *Opportunities in the Motion Picture Industry —And How to Qualify for Positions in its Many Branches*, vol. 1. (Los Angeles: Photoplay Research Society, Bureau of Vocational Guidance, 1922): 40, 42.

96. May 126.

97. See Mike Featherstone, "The Body in Consumer Culture," *The Body: Social Process and Cultural Theory*, ed. Mike Featherstone, Mike Hepworth, and Bryan S. Turner (London: Sage, 1991): 170–196 and Stuart Ewen, *Captains of Consciousness: Advertising and the Social Roots of the Consumer Culture* (New York: McGraw-Hill, 1976).

98. May 190.

99. This information is courtesy of the Warner Brothers/First National Archives, University of Southern California, Los Angeles.

100. Rosten 39, 53.

101. May 232–233.

102. Gaylyn Studlar, *This Mad Masquerade: Stardom and Masculinity in the Jazz Age* (New York: Columbia University Press, 1996): 164.

103. Walker 59.

104. Rudolph Valentino, "Keeping in Condition," *The Truth About the Movies—By the Stars*, ed. Laurence A. Hughes (Hollywood, CA: Hollywood Publishers, Inc., 1924): 275.

105. Adele Whitely Fletcher, "Who Has the Best Figure in Hollywood—And Why," *Photoplay Magazine* Mar. 1931: 34.

106. Norma Talmadge, "What Percentage of Girls Who Come to Hollywood Actually Achieve Success," *The Truth About the Movies—By the Stars*, ed. Laurence A. Hughes (Hollywood, CA: Hollywood Publishers, Inc., 1924): 62.

107. Qtd. in Charles Higham, *Hollywood Cameramen: Sources of Light* (Bloomington, IN: Indiana University Press, 1970): 78.

108. Katherine Albert, "They Must Suffer to Be Beautiful," *Photoplay Magazine* Oct. 1929: 30+.

109. Editor's Note, "How I Keep in Condition," by Corinne Griffith, *Photoplay Magazine* Nov. 1921: 33.

110. David Wark Griffith, "Youth, the Spirit of the Movies," *Illustrated World* Oct. 1921: 194.

111. Louis W. Physioc, "Does the Camera Lie?" *American Cinematographer* Jan. 1927: 21.

112. Qtd. in Fletcher 86.

113. Fletcher 34–35.

114. "The Stars Tell How They Keep Those Girlish Lines," *Photoplay Magazine* Sept. 1924: 28.

115. Harriette Underhill, "The Movies Give the World a Boyish Form," *Motion Picture Classic* Nov. 1925: 30, 73.

116. Underhill 31.

117. Qtd. in Underhill 31.

118. Lois Shirley, "The Enemy of Beauty—Over-Exercise," *Photoplay Magazine* Aug. 1931: 30, 112.

119. Catherine Brody, "Wholesale Murder and Suicide," *Photoplay Magazine* Aug. 1926: 105.

120. Bert Lytell, "Can I Appear on the Screen?" *Opportunities in the Motion Picture Industry—And How to Qualify for Positions in its Many Branches*, vol. 1 (Los Angeles: Photoplay Research Society, Bureau of Vocational Guidance, 1922): 39–40, 42.

121. See Jameson Sewell, "What Is Camera Beauty?" *Photoplay Magazine* Aug. 1925: 38.

122. Albert 31–32.

123. Physioc 21+.

124. Carl Girod, "Re: Camera's Distortion of Body Weight," e-mails to the author, 1 Apr. 1999 and 5 Apr. 1999.

125. Steven Poster, "Re: Camera's Distortion of Body Weight," e-mail to the author, 2 Apr. 1999.

126. Iain Neil, Executive Vice President at Panavision International, telephone interview, 5 Apr. 1999.

127. Poster e-mail.

128. David Stenn, personal interview, Feb. 1999.

129. Louis W. Physioc, "Movie Make-Up: A Technical and Artistic Analysis of Motion Picture Make-Up with an Historical Sketch," *American Cinematographer* Feb. 1928: 25.

130. Max Factor, "Movie Make-Up: A Master of the Arts Sets Forth That Make-up Is the Cinematographer's Best Ally," *American Cinematographer* Apr. 1928: 8.

131. Sewell 39.

132. Physioc 21.

133. Rob Wagner, "Shining up the Stars," *Collier's* 6 Mar. 1926: 7–8.

134. Physioc 24.

135. Joseph Dubray, "Movie Make-Up," *American Cinematographer* Mar. 1928: 8.

136. Editor's Note, "Taking the Die Out of Diet," by Dorothy Calhoun, *Motion Picture Magazine* July 1930: 28.
137. Dr. H. B. K. Willis, "Eat and Be Merry." *Photoplay Magazine* Aug. 1929: 107.
138. Glenn Chaffin, "She Rolls Her Own Fat Away," *Photoplay Magazine* June 1925: 78, 112.
139. Dorothy Calhoun, "Diet Quickies: Three Stars Tell How to Lose Weight Fast Without Fasting," *Motion Picture Magazine* Sept. 1930: 33.
140. Bob Thomas, *Joan Crawford* (New York: Simon and Schuster: 1978): 58–59.
141. Laura LaPlante, "Breaking in as an Extra," *Breaking into the Movies*, ed. Charles Reed Jones (New York: The Unicorn Press, 1927): 18–19.
142. Dorothy Calhoun, "Don't Diet! Curves Are Coming Back!" *Motion Picture Magazine* Mar. 1932: 30, 89.
143. Katherine Albert, "Why the Hollywood Stars Quit Those Freak Diets," *Photoplay Magazine* July 1930: 58.

CHAPTER 3: CAPITALIZING THEIR CHARMS

1. Jack Grant, "What Do You Mean—'STAR'?" *Motion Picture Classic* Dec. 1930: 73.
2. Richard deCordova, *Picture Personalities: The Emergence of the Star System in America* (Urbana/Chicago: University of Illinois Press, 1990): 7.
3. deCordova 8.
4. deCordova 5–6.
5. deCordova 26.
6. deCordova 34.
7. deCordova 36.
8. deCordova 46.
9. deCordova 46.
10. Alexander Walker, *Stardom: The Hollywood Phenomenon* (New York: Stein and Day, 1970): 21.
11. deCordova 82, 84.
12. deCordova 84.
13. deCordova 88, 92.
14. deCordova 120.
15. deCordova 140.
16. deCordova 112.
17. deCordova 145.
18. deCordova 46.
19. Walker 55–56.
20. Walker 47.
21. Walker 35.
22. Campbell MacCulloch, "What Makes Them Stars?" *Photoplay Magazine* Oct. 1928: 44.
23. Dyer 21–22.
24. Walker 235.
25. David Robinson, *Hollywood in the Twenties* (New York/South Brunswick: A.S. Barnes and Company, 1968): 143–144.
26. Richard Dyer, *Stars* (1979; London: British Film Institute, 1998): 20.

27. Walker 121.
28. Lary May, *Screening Out the Past: The Birth of Mass Culture and the Motion Picture Industry* (New York: Oxford University Press, 1980): 190.
29. Walker 126.
30. Walker 127.
31. Walker 127.
32. Katharine Gerould Fullerton, "Hollywood: An American State of Mind" *Harper's Magazine* May 1923: 691.
33. William Allen Johnston, "In Motion Picture Land" *Everybody's Magazine* Oct. 1915: 445.
34. See "Hollywood Warns Film-Struck Girls," *New York Times* 4 Dec. 1923: 23.
35. Gladys Hall, "Heartbreaking into Pictures," manuscript for *Modern Screen*, March 1934, Gladys Hall Collection, Margaret Herrick Library, Bevery Hills: 1.
36. Hall 2.
37. Dorothy Manners, "The Flesh and Blood Racket," *Motion Picture Magazine* April 1929: 119.
38. Reverend Neal Dodd, "The Truth About Hollywood," *Opportunities in the Motion Picture Industry—And How to Qualify for Positions in its Many Branches*. Vol 1. Photoplay Research Society (Los Angeles: Photoplay Research Society, Bureau of Vocational Guidance, 1922): 117.
39. Helen Broderick, "Pretty Soft to Be a Star, Eh?" *Photoplay Magazine* Sept. 1921: 43.
40. Editor's Note, "How I Keep in Condition," by Corinne Griffith, *Photoplay Magazine* Nov. 1921: 33.
41. Ruby De Remer, "How I Keep in Condition," *Photoplay Magazine* Sept. 1921: 45.
42. "The Penalties of Being a Star," *Photoplay Magazine* Dec. 1922: 32.
43. "The Stars Tell How They Keep Those Girlish Lines," *Photoplay Magazine* Sept. 1924: 29.
44. Harriet Works Corley, "The Deuce with Reducing," *Photoplay Magazine* July 1925: 46.
45. Qtd. in Dorothy Spensley, "The Torture Chambers of Hollywood," *Motion Picture Magazine* June 1929: 53.
46. Dorothy Calhoun, "The 18-Day Diet," *Motion Picture Magazine* Oct. 1929: 107.
47. Katherine Albert, "They Must Suffer to be Beautiful," *Photoplay Magazine* Oct. 1929: 30.
48. Qtd. in Albert 33.
49. Dorothy Calhoun, "Taking the Die Out of Diet," *Motion Picture Magazine* July 1930: 28.
50. Stewart Robertson, "Weight and Hope," *Photoplay Magazine* July 1930: 126.
51. Lois Shirley, "The Enemy of Beauty—Over-Exercise," *Photoplay Magazine* Aug. 1931: 30.
52. "How Jackie Coogan Keeps Fit," *Photoplay Magazine* Oct. 1924: 70.
53. "How They Keep in Trim," *Photoplay Magazine* Dec. 1922: 50.
54. "Keeping Fit," *Motion Picture Classic* Sept. 1925: 52.
55. Calhoun, "Die Out" 112.
56. Francis X. Bushman, *So You Want to Act, Do You?* (Hollywood, CA: Francis X. Bushman, Inc., 1937): 28.

57. Roberston 44.
58. Robertson 45.
59. Robertson 128.
60. Contract dated Feb. 28, 1925 between Warner Bros. and Clive Brook, clause 15. "Clive Brook Contract File," Warner Brothers/First National Archives, University of Southern California, Los Angeles.
61. Lila Lee, "How I Keep in Condition," *Photoplay Magazine* Dec. 1921: 31.
62. Qtd. in Lee 102.
63. Lee 102.
64. See the "Biographies of Film Folk" section of *Mirrors of Hollywood,* by Charles Donald Fox (New York: Charles Renard Corporation, 1925). This section provides about three lines of biographical info for dozens of period stars, including height and weight, though the source(s) of this information are not cited. Lila Lee's height is 5'6", while her weight is listed as 125 lbs.
65. Qtd. in "The Right Weigh," *Motion Picture Magazine* June 1925: 106–107.
66. Katherine Albert, "Diet—The Menace of Hollywood," *Photoplay Magazine* Jan. 1929: 32.
67. Dorothy Manners, "138 Lbs. Ringside!" *Motion Picture Magazine* Mar. 1931: 98.
68. Manners, "Ringside" 98.
69. Manners, "Ringside" 98.
70. Harriette Underhill, "The Movies Give the World a Boyish Form," *Motion Picture Classic* Nov. 1925: 31.
71. Gordon R. Silver, "My Contract Won't Let Me," *Motion Picture Classic* Sept. 1927: 63.
72. Editor's Note, "Taking the Die Out of Diet," by Dorothy Calhoun, *Motion Picture Magazine* July 1930: 28.
73. Harriet Parsons, "The Weigh of All Flesh," *Photoplay Magazine* Oct. 1929: 143.
74. Silver 63.
75. Silver 63, 91.
76. Dorothy Donnell, "Contracts Is Contracts," *Motion Picture Magazine* Dec. 1927: 37.
77. John Held, Jr., "Cella Lloyd Becomes Pleasingly Plump," *Motion Picture Classic* Sept. 1926: 28.
78. Albert, "Diet" 33, 113.
79. See full-page adverstisement on page 26 of the July 1933 issue of *Photoplay Magazine.*
80. David Stenn, personal interviews, February 1999.
81. "Irene Rich Contract File," Warner Brothers/First National Archive, University of Southern California, Los Angeles.
82. "Richard Barthelmess Contract File," Warner Brothers/First National Archive, University of Southern California, Los Angeles.
83. Lois Shirley, "Starving Back to Stardom," *Photoplay Magazine* Aug. 1928: 120.
84. Shirley 120.
85. "Molly O'Day Contract File," Warner Brothers/First National Archive, University of Southern California, Los Angeles.
86. This memo is from a Mr. Rowland to a Mr. Perkinds. See "Molly O'Day Contract File," Warner Brothers/First National Archive.

87. "Reduces Weight by Knife," *New York Times* 4 Sept. 1928: 14.

88. Albert, "Diet" 33.

89. Qtd. in Manners, "Flesh" 118.

90. Manners 35.

91. Carroll Graham, "Clause and Effect: Option Day in Hollywood and How it Is Observed," *Motion Picture Magazine* Dec. 1929: 55.

92. *Hollywood Undressed: Observations of Sylvia as Noted by Her Secretary* (New York: Brentano's, 1931): See jacket cover.

93. *Hollywood Undressed* 10–12.

94. *Hollywood Undressed* 176.

95. Dorothy Calhoun, "Don't Diet! Curves Are Coming Back!" *Motion Picture Magazine* Mar. 1932: 31–32.

96. Catherine Brody, "Wholesale Murder and Suicide," *Photoplay Magazine* July 1926: 30.

97. Myrtle West, "The Price They Paid for Stardom," *Photoplay Magazine* Nov. 1926: 29.

98. Dr. H. B. K. Willis, "Diet for Health and Beauty," *Photoplay Magazine* Feb. 1929: 90.

99. Manners, "Flesh" 118.

100. Manners, "Flesh" 34.

101. Qtd. in Manners, "Flesh" 118.

102. Dorothy Spensley, "The Torture Chambers of Hollywood," *Motion Picture Magazine* June 1929: 53, 96.

103. Albert, "Suffer" 31, 33.

104. Rubye De Remer, "How I Keep in Condition," *Photoplay Magazine* Sept. 1921: 45.

105. Corinne Griffith, "How I Keep in Condition," *Photoplay Magazine* Nov. 1921: 33.

106. Qtd. in "The Stars Tell How They Keep Those Girlish Lines," *Photoplay Magazine* Sept. 1924: 117.

107. Qtd. in "The Right Weigh" 56.

108. See Part One of *Hollywood Undressed: Observations of Sylvia as Noted by Her Secretary* (New York: Brentano's, 1931).

109. Qtd. in "Right Weigh" 107.

110. Qtd. in Harriet Works Corley, "The Deuce With Reducing," *Photoplay Magazine* July 1925: 47.

111. I examined several issues of *The Standard—Casting Directors Directory* from 1923 and 1924, available at the Margaret Herrick Library, Academy of Motion Picture Arts and Sciences, Beverly Hills,.

112. See Scrapbook #8 in the Jean Hersholt Collection, Margaret Herrick Library, Academy of Motion Picture Arts and Scienes, Beverly Hills. The cartoon from the *Los Angeles Record* is dated Sept. 22, 1928. The source and date of the photograph are unidentified.

113. Dorothy Calhoun, "Diet Quickies," *Motion Picture Magazine* Sept. 1930: 35.

114. Charles Carter, "How Tony Keeps in Trim," *Picture-Play Magazine* March 1920: 78.

115. "The Way to Keep Fit," *Motion Picture Magazine* Aug. 1924: 66.

116. "Where the Screen Stars Train," *Photoplay Magazine* 1924: 86.

117. Douglas Fairbanks, "Health Plus Enthusiasm," *The Truth About the Movies—By the Stars*, ed. Laurence A. Hughes (Hollywood: Hollywood Publishers, 1924): 51.

118. John C. Tibbetts and James M. Welsh, *His Majesty the American: The Cinema of Douglas Fairbanks, Sr.* (South Brunswick and New York: A. S. Barnes and Company, 1977): 11.

119. C. H. Vivian, "What Kind of a Boy Was Doug?" *Sunset Magazine* Oct. 1928: 60.

120. Qtd. in Tibbetts and Welsh 23.

121. Douglas Fairbanks, "Combining Play With Work," *The American Magazine* July 1917: 33–34.

122. "Autobiographical Memoirs of M._____," *Photoplay Magazine* Nov. 1921: 31, 110.

123. Dorothy Manners, "What Is Doug Doing?" *Motion Picture Magazine* Feb. 1931: 55.

124. Mary Webster, "Doug Carves a New Career for Himself," *Motion Picture Magazine* Jan. 1932: 75.

125. Wells 70.

126. Wells 84.

127. Charley Paddock, "Why Athletes Fail in Pictures," *Photoplay Magazine* Sept. 1928: 124.

128. Paddock 126.

129. Qtd. in Truman B. Handy, "If You Dont [*sic*] Weaken," *Motion Picture Classic* May 1922: 83.

130. May Allison Quirk, "Muscling In," *Photoplay Magazine* Jan. 1933: 102.

131. Handy 36.

132. Lois Shirley, "The Enemy of Beauty—Over-Exercise," *Photoplay Magazine* Aug. 1931: 30.

133. Frederick Lewis Allen, *Only Yesterday: An Informal History of the Nineteen-Twenties* (New York: Harper & Harper, 1931): 80.

134. Allen 80–81.

135. Malvina DeVries, "In the Swim: The Evolution of the 20th Century Bathing Suit," *Retro Magazine* Mar. 1998 <http://www.retroactive.com/mar98/swimsuit.html>.

136. DeVries, "In the Swim"

137. See *The Standard—Casting Directors Directory* July 1924: 106. I examined it at the Margart Herrick Library, Beverly Hills, CA.

138. Qtd. in "Mack Sennett Bathing Beauties," *The Silents Majority* July 1998 <http://www. silentsmajority.com/FeaturedPerformer/0798.htm>. Sennett's quote is "as told to" Cameron Shipp in the 1954 book *King of Comedy.*

139. "Mack Sennett Bathing Beauties"

CHAPTER 4: ASCENDING THE CELLULOID HEAVENS

1. David Stenn, *Clara Bow: Runnin' Wild* (New York: Doubleday, 1988): 278.

2. Stenn 10.

3. Qtd. in Stenn 12.

4. Stenn 14.

5. Stenn 16.

6. Stenn 16.
7. Stenn 21.
8. Qtd. in Stenn 23.
9. Stenn 29.
10. Stenn 44.
11. Qtd. in Stenn 70.
12. Stenn 87.
13. Glenn Chaffin, "She Rolls Her Own Fat Away," *Photoplay Magazine* June 1925: 78.
14. Chaffin 112.
15. Chaffin 112.
16. Qtd. in Alice L. Tildesley, "She Wants to Succeed," *Motion Picture Classic* June 1926: 90.
17. Corliss Palmer, "Exercise for the Stout Figure," *Motion Picture Magazine* Feb. 1922: 108.
18. Tildesley 90.
19. Alice Whitaker, "How They Manage Their Homes," *Photoplay Magazine* Sept. 1929: 78.
20. Qtd. in Whitaker 78.
21. Qtd. in Stenn 173.
22. Stenn 175.
23. A table of stars' weights that appears in *Motion Picture Magazine* lists Bow's weight as 108 pounds. This was after Bow lost the extra weight she gained in 1929. See Dorothy Calhoun, "Taking the Die Out of Diet," *Motion Picture Magazine* July 1930: 30.
24. Stenn 180.
25. Stenn 186.
26. Leonard Hall, "What About Clara Bow?" *Photoplay Magazine* Oct. 1930: 60.
27. Paul Jarvis, "Quit Pickin' on Me!" *Photoplay Magazine* Jan. 1931: 33.
28. Stenn 236.
29. Harry Lang, "Roughing It With Clara," *Photoplay Magazine* Sept. 1931: 102.
30. Stenn 240.
31. David Stenn, "Re: Clara Bow's Contracts," e-mail to the author, 2 March 1999. Stenn gathered this information from the Fox Legal Files at UCLA Research Library, Arts Special Collections, Box 835 (Clara Bow/*Call Her Savage* Files).
32. Stenn 241.
33. Henry Crosby, "The Return of Clara Bow," *Photoplay Magazine* Nov. 1932: 27.
34. Crosby 27.
35. Stenn 241.
36. See the Fox Legal Files at UCLA Research Library, Arts Special Collections, Box 835.
37. See letter dated April 3, 1933 from W. I. Gilbert to William Fox in the Fox Legal Files at UCLA Research Liberary, Arts Special Collections, Box 835.
38. Stenn 245.
39. Stenn 245.
40. Stenn 249.
41. Stenn 250.
42. Stenn 266.

43. Stenn 270.
44. Qtd. in Roy Newquist, *Conversations with Joan Crawford* (Seacaucus, NJ: The Citadel Press, 1980): 161.
45. Alexander Walker, *Rudolph Valentino* (London: Elm Tree Books/Hamish Hamilton Ltd., 1976): 44.
46. Walker 46.
47. Irving Shulman, *Valentino* (New York: Trident Press, 1967): 166–167.
48. "The Vogue of Valentino," *Motion Picture Magazine* Feb. 1923: 100.
49. "Vogue" 27.
50. Don Ryan, "Has the Great Lover Become Just a Celebrity?" *Motion Picture Classic* May 1926: 78.
51. Qtd. in Rudolph Valentino, "My Life Story—Part I," *Photoplay Magazine* Feb. 1923: 31.
52. Valentino 35.
53. Valentino 35.
54. S. George Ullman, *Valentino As I Knew Him* (New York: A. L. Burt Company, 1926): 22.
55. Valentino 104.
56. This affadavit of Sept. 18, 1922, which was later destroyed, was printed by *Movie Weekly* October 21, 1922 through January 6, 1923. See *The Silents Majority* <http://www.silentsmajority.com/FeaturedStar/ star50d.htm>.
57. Shulman 95.
58. Valentino 105.
59. Shulman 94.
60. Shulman 93.
61. Shulman 216.
62. Walker 11.
63. Walker 11.
64. Gaylyn Studlar, *This Mad Masquerade: Stardom and Masculinity in the Jazz Age* (New York: Columbia University Press, 1996): 164.
65. Studlar 181.
66. Michael S. Kimmel, "Consuming Manhood: The Feminization of American Culture and the Recreation of the Male Body, 1832–1920," *Michigan Quarterly Review* 33.1 (Winter 1994): 15–16.
67. Kimmel 20.
68. Kimmel 17.
69. Shulman 101.
70. Studlar 185–186.
71. Rudolph Valentino, "My Life Story: Chapter Two," *Photoplay Magazine* Mar. 1923: 112.
72. Studlar 161.
73. Studlar 159.
74. Shulman 104.
75. Walker 14.
76. Shulman 115.
77. Shulman 118.
78. Rudolph Valentino, "My Life Story—Chapter III," *Photoplay Magazine* Apr. 1923: 52.

79. Shulman 125–126.
80. "Vogue" 29.
81. Shulman 289.
82. Shulman 129.
83. Walker 34.
84. Valentino, "Chapter III" 96.
85. Walker 22.
86. Shulman 145.
87. Walker 36.
88. Walker 34–35.
89. Studlar 175.
90. Studlar 172–173.
91. Willis Goldbeck, "The Perfect Lover," *Motion Picture Magazine* May 1922: 40.
92. Gordon Gassaway, "The Erstwhile Landscape Gardener," *Motion Picture Magazine* July 1921: 92.
93. Gassaway 92.
94. Gassaway 92.
95. Harry Carr, "Valentino Is Not a Henpecked Husband!" *Motion Picture Magazine* Aug. 1925: 33.
96. Qtd. in Shulman 201.
97. Qtd. in Shulman 202.
98. Walker 50.
99. Qtd. in Ullman 182–184.
100. Ullman 185.
101. Qtd. in Ullman 188.
102. Ullman 190.
103. Walker 73.
104. Walker 69.
105. See photos in Walker 71–72.
106. Studlar 186.
107. Ullman 59.
108. Ullman 135.
109. Walker 99.
110. Walker 119.
111. Walker 119.

CHAPTER 5: HOLLYWOOD AND PHYSICAL CULTURE

1. Mary Winship, "Oh, Hollywood!—A Ramble in Bohemia," *Photoplay Magazine* May 1921: 21.
2. Stuart Ewen, *Captains of Consciousness: Advertising and the Roots of the Consumer Culture* (New York: McGraw-Hill, 1976): 142.
3. Woods Hutchinson, M.D., "Fat and Fashion," *The Saturday Evening Post*, 21 Aug. 1926: 56.
4. Ewen 37–39.
5. *Motion Picture Magazine* Sept. 1924: 123.
6. *Motion Picture Magazine* Jan. 1925: 7.
7. *The American Magazine* Oct. 1929: 165.

8. Attendance data from *An Evening's Entertainment: The Age of the Silent Feature Picture* by Richard Koszarski (Berkeley: Univ. of California Press, 1990): 26.

9. Quoted in James Rorty, *Our Master's Voice: Advertising* (New York: The John Day Company, 1934): 252, 254.

10. Qtd. in Rorty 253–254.

11. See Rorty pg. 252.

12. Rorty 256.

13. Annette Kuhn, *The Power of the Image: Essays on Representation and Sexuality* (London/New York: Routledge, 1985): 13.

14. Featherstone 179.

15. Peter N. Stearns, *Fat History: Bodies and Beauty in the Modern West* (New York/London: New York University Press, 1997): 67, 116–117.

16. "Physicians Defend Plump Turkish Lines As 'Miss Turkey' Starts Fad of Reducing," *New York Times* 27 July 1930, sec. 3: 4.

17. "Italian Press Is Instructed to Taboo Slim Style," *New York Times* 20 Feb. 1932: 8.

18. See "Dieting School Girls in Budapest Defy Parents and Doctors in Order to Be Slim," *New York Times* 19 Feb. 1933, sec. 4: 1 and "Reducing Diets Believed Factor in Birth of Boys," *New York Times* 15 Oct. 1933, sec. 1: 16.

19. "Physicians Defend Plump Turkish Lines," sec. 3: 4.

20. "Italian Press Is Instructed to Taboo Slim Style" 8.

21. "Dieting School Girls in Budapest Defy Parents and Doctors," sec. 4: 1.

Bibliography

Ade, George. "Answering Wild-Eyed Questions About the Movie Stars at Hollywood." *The American Magazine* May 1922: 52+.

Albert, Katherine. "Diet—The Menace of Hollywood." *Photoplay Magazine* Jan. 1929: 30+.

———. "They Must Suffer to Be Beautiful." *Photoplay Magazine* Oct. 1929: 30+.

———. "Why the Hollywod Stars Quit Those Freak Diets." *Photoplay Magazine* July 1930: 58+.

Allen, Frederick Lewis. *Only Yesterday: An Informal History of the Nineteen-Twenties*. New York: Harper & Brothers, 1931.

Allen, Robert C. and Douglas Gomery. *Film History: Theory and Practice*. New York: McGraw-Hill, 1985.

Alton, John. *Painting with Light*. New York: Macmillan, 1949.

"Autobiographical Memoirs of M._____." *Photoplay Magazine* Nov. 1921: 30+.

Baldwin, Mabel E., Ph.D. *Diet and Like It: A Guide to Pleasant and Healthful Dieting for Those Who Would Reduce and Those Who Would Not Gain*. New York/London: D. Appleton-Century Company, 1935.

Bandura, A. *Social Learning Theory*. Englewood Cliffs, NJ: Prentice-Hall, 1977.

Beatty, Jerome. "Hullabaloo Town." *The American Magazine* May 1932: 22+.

Berry, Milton H. (as reported by Magner White). "You Can Keep a Youthful Figure if You Treat Your Muscles Right." *The American Magazine* Aug. 1927: 43+.

Biery, Ruth. "Hollywood's Age of Fear." *Photoplay Magazine* July 1931: 58+.

Blythe, Samuel G. "Get Rid of that Fat." *The Saturday Evening Post* 23 April 1927: 10+.

Bocock, Robert. *Consumption*. New York: Routledge, 1993.

Bordo, Susan. *Unbearable Weight: Feminism, Western Culture, and the Body*. Berkeley: University of California Press, 1993.

Bordwell, David and Noël Carroll, eds. *Post-Theory: Reconstructing Film Studies*. Madison, WI: University of Wisconsin Press, 1996.

Bowers, E.W., M.D. "The Stars Tell How They Keep Those Girlish Lines." *Photoplay Magazine* Sept. 1924: 28+.

Broderick, Helen. "Pretty Soft to Be a Star, Eh?" *Photoplay Magazine* Sept. 1921: 43+.

Brody, Catherine. "Wholesale Murder and Suicide." *Photoplay Magazine* July 1926: 30+.

———. "The Second Article on Wholesale Murder and Suicide." *Photoplay Magazine* Aug. 1926: 36+.

———. "The Happy Ending of Wholesale Murder and Suicide." *Photoplay Magazine* Sept. 1926: 30+.

Brownlow, Kevin. *Hollywood: The Pioneers.* New York: Alfred P. Knopf, 1979.

Bushman, Francis X., with Elmore J. Andre. *So You Want to Act, Do You?* Hollywood: Francis X. Bushman, Inc., 1937.

Caldwell, Brian. "Muscling in on the Movies: Excess and the Representation of the Male Body in Films of the 1980s and 1990s." *American Bodies: Cultural Histories of the Physique.* Ed. Tim Armstrong. New York: New York University Press, 1996: 133–140.

Calhoun, Dorothy. "Diet Quickies: Three Stars Tell How to Lose Weight Fast Without Fasting." *Motion Picture Magazine* Sept. 1930: 33–35.

———. "Don't Diet! Curves Are Coming Back!" Mar. 1932: 30+.

———. "The 18-Day Diet." *Motion Picture Magazine* Oct. 1929: 44+.

———. "Taking the Die Out of Diet." *Motion Picture Magazine* July 1930: 28+.

Carr, Harry. "That Town—Hollywood." *Motion Picture Classic* Mar. 1926: 24+.

———. "Valentino Is Not a Henpecked Husband!" *Motion Picture Magazine* Aug. 1925: 32+.

Carter, Charles. "How Tony Keeps in Trim." *Picture-Play Magazine* Mar. 1920: 78.

Chaffin, Glenn. "She Rolls Her Own Fat Away." *Photoplay Magazine* June 1925: 78+.

Chernin, Kim. *The Obsession: Reflections on the Tyranny of Slenderness.* 1981. New York: Harper, 1994.

Cohan, Steven and Ina Rae Hark, eds. *Screening the Male: Exploring Masculinities in Hollywood Cinema.* London/New York: Routledge, 1993.

Corley, Harriet Works. "The Deuce With Reducing." *Photoplay Magazine* July 1925: 46+.

Crosby, Henry. "The Return of Clara Bow." *Photoplay Magazine* Nov. 1932: 27.

"Cult of Slimness." *Living Age* 28 Feb. 1914: 572–574.

Davies, Nathaniel Edward. *Foods for the Fat: A Treatise on Corpulency and a Dietary for Its Cure.* Philadelphia: J. B. Lippincott, 1889.

deCordova, Richard. *Picture Personalities: The Emergence of the Star System in America.* Urbana/Chicago: University of Illinois Press, 1990.

de Fleur, Marise. "Reducing the Fat of the Land." *Sunset Magazine* Aug. 1925: 72–74.

"Depicts Hollywood as Homelike City." *New York Times* 18 Sept. 1926: 25.

De Remer, Ruby. "How I Keep in Condition." *Photoplay Magazine* Sept. 1921: 45+.

DeVries, Malvina. "In the Swim: The Evolution of the 20th Century Bathing Suit." *Retro Magazine* Mar. 1998. <http://www.retroactive.com/mar98/swimsuit.htm>.

"Dieting School Girls in Budapest Defy Parents and Doctors in Order to Be Slim." *New York Times* 15 Oct. 1933, sec. 4: 1.

Doane, Mary Anne. "Woman's Stake: Filming the Female Body" *October* 17 (Summer 1981): 23–36.

Donnell, Dorothy. "Are the Movies to Blame for Hollywood's Suicides?" *Motion Picture Classic* Oct. 1927: 18+.

————. "Contracts Is Contracts." *Motion Picture Magazine* Dec. 1927: 36+.

Dove, Billie. "Physical Culture and Poise." *Breaking into the Movies.* Ed. Charles Reed Jones. New York: The Unicorn Press, 1927: 83–89.

"Do You Want to Reduce?" *Photoplay Magazine* Oct. 1920: 64+.

Dubray, Joseph. "Movie Make-Up." *American Cinematographer* Mar. 1928: 8+.

Dyer, Richard. *Stars.* 1979. London: British Film Institute, 1998.

"Elinor Glyn Thinks Hollywood Abused." *New York Times* 14 Apr. 1922: 17.

Ewen, Stuart. *Captains of Consciousness: Advertising and the Social Roots of the Consumer Culture.* New York: McGraw-Hill, 1976.

Factor, Max. "Movie Make-Up: A Master of the Arts Sets Forth that Make-up Is the Cinematographer's Best Ally." *American Cinematographer* Apr. 1928: 8+.

Fairbanks, Douglas. "Combining Play With Work." *The American Magazine* July 1917: 33+.

Featherstone, Mike. "The Body in Consumer Culture." *The Body: Social Process and Cultural Theory.* Ed. Mike Featherstone, Mike Hepworth, and Bryan S. Turner. London: Sage, 1991: 170–196.

Filene, Edward A. *The Consumer's Dollar. The John Day Pamphlets.* No. 41. New York: The John Day Company, 1934.

Finck, Henry T. *Girth Control for Womanly Beauty, Manly Strength, Health and a Long Life for Everybody.* New York/London: Harper and Brothers, 1923.

"Find No Sure Guide to Women's Weight." *New York Times* 23 Feb. 1926: 26.

Fishbein, Morris, M.D., ed. *Your Weight and How to Control It.* Garden City, NY: Butterick Publishing, 1926.

Fisk, Eugene Lyman, M.D. "How Much Fat Will You Give?" *Good Housekeeping* Jan. 1918:76+.

Fletcher, Adele Whitely. "Who Has the Best Figure in Hollywood—and Why." *Photoplay Magazine* Mar. 1931: 34+.

Fox, Charles Donald. *Mirrors of Hollywood.* New York: Charles Renard Corporation, 1925.

Garner, David M. and Ann Kearney-Cooke. "Body Image 1996." *Psychology Today* March/April 1996: 55–61.

Gassaway, Gordon. "The Erstwhile Landscape Gardener." *Motion Picture Magazine* July 1921: 40+.

Gerould, Katharine Fullerton, "Hollywood: An American State of Mind." *Harper's Magazine* May 1923: 689–696.

Girard, René. "Hunger Artists: Eating Disorders and Mimetic Desire." *The Body Aesthetic: From Fine Art to Body Modification.* Ed. Tobin Siebers. Ann Arbor: The University of Michigan Press, 2000: 179–198.

Girod, Carl. "Re: Camera's Distortion of Body Weight." E-mails to the author. 1 Apr. 1999 and 5 Apr. 1999.

Goldbeck, Willis. "The Perfect Lover." *Motion Picture Magazine* May 1922: 40+.

Goodman, W. Charisse. *The Invisible Woman: Confronting Weight Prejudice in America.* Carlsbad, CA: Gürze Books, 1995.

Gordon, Jan and Cora. *Star-Dust in Hollywood.* London: George G. Harrap & Co. Ltd., 1930.

Graham, Carroll. "Clause and Effect: Option Day in Hollywood and How it Is Observed." *Motion Picture Magazine* Dec. 1929: 55+.

Grant, Jack. "What Do You Mean—'STAR'?" *Motion Picture Classic* Dec. 1930: 73+.

Gregory, Deborah. "Heavy Judgement: A Sister Talks About the Pain of 'Living Large.'" *Essence* Aug. 1994: 57+.

Griffith, Corinne. "How I Keep in Condition." *Photoplay Magazine* Nov. 1921: 33+.

Griffith, David Wark. "Youth, the Spirit of the Movies." *Illustrated World* Oct. 1921: 194–196.

Hall, Gladys. "Heartbreaking into Pictures." Manuscript for *Modern Screen*, March 1934. Gladys Hall Collection, Margaret Herrick Library, Beverly Hill, CA.

Hall, Leonard. "What About Clara Bow?" *Photoplay Magazine* Oct. 1930: 60+.

Halprin, Sara. *"'Look at my Ugly Face!': Myths and Musings on Beauty and Other Perilous Obsessions with Women's Appearance.* New York: Penguin, 1995.

Haly, B. *The Healthy Body and Victorian Culture.* Cambridge, MA: Harvard University Press, 1979.

Handy, Truman B. "If You Dont [*sic*] Weaken." *Motion Picture Classic* May 1922: 36+.

Harris, Preston K. "Who Are the Beautiful Girls of Hollywood?" *Motion Picture Classic* Sept. 1925: 28+.

Harrison, Kristen and Joanne Cantor. "The Relationship Between Media Consumption and Eating Disorders." *Journal of Communication* 47.1 (1997): 40–67.

Harrow, Benjamin, Ph.D. *What to Eat in Disease and Health*, New York: E.P. Dutton & Company, 1923.

"Health Appeal." *Journal of the American Medical Association* 91 (1927): 1806–1807.

"Health—Hollywood's Greatest Asset." *Photoplay Magazine* Nov. 1926: 32–33.

Held, Jr., John. "Cella Lloyd Becomes Pleasingly Plump." *Motion Picture Classic* Sept. 1926: 28–29.

Henderson-King, Eaaron and Donna Henderson-King. "Media Effects on Women's Body Esteem: Social and Individual Difference Factors." *Journal of Applied Social Psychology* 27 (1997): 399–417.

Higham, Charles. *Hollywood Cameramen: Sources of Light.* Bloomington, IN: Indiana University Press, 1970.

Hollywood Undressed: Observations of Sylvia as Noted by Her Secretary. New York: Brentano's, 1931.

"Hollywood Warns Film-Struck Girls." *New York Times* 4 Dec. 1923: 23.

"How Jackie Coogan Keeps Fit." *Photoplay Magazine* Oct. 1924: 70.

"How They Keep in Trim." *Photoplay Magazine* Dec. 1922: 50–51.

Howe, Herbert. "Returning to Hollywood." *Photoplay Magazine* May 1925: 30+.

Hughes, Laurence A., ed. *The Truth About the Movies—By the Stars.* Hollywood, CA: Hollywood Publishers: 1924.

Hutchinson, Woods, M.D. "A Defense of Fat Men." *The Saturday Evening Post* 7 June 1924: 8+.

———. "Fat and Fashion." *The Saturday Evening Post* 21 Aug. 1926: 58+.

"Italian Press is Instructed to Taboo Slim Style." *New York Times* 20. Feb. 1932: 8.

Jarvis, Paul. "Quit Pickin' on Me!" *Photoplay Magazine* Jan. 1931: 32–33.

Jeffords, Susan. *Hard Bodies: Hollywood Masculinity in the Reagan Era.* New Brunswick, NJ: Rutgers University Press, 1994.

Jones, Charles Reed. *Breaking into the Movies.* New York: The Unicorn Press, 1927.

Johnston, William Allen. "In Motion Picture Land." *Everybody's Magazine* Oct. 1915: 437–448.

Kern, S. *Anatomy and Destiny: A Cultural History of the Human Body.* New York: Bobbs-Merrill, 1975.

"Keeping Fit." *Motion Picture Classic* Sept. 1925: 52.

Kimmel, Michael S. "Consuming Manhood: The Feminization of American Culture and the Recreation of the Male Body, 1832–1920." *Michigan Quarterly Review* 33.1 (1994): 7–36.

Koszarski, Richard. *An Evening's Entertainment: The Age of the Silent Feature Picture, 1915–1928.*

History of the American Cinema. Vol. 3. Berkeley: University of California Press, 1990.

Krupp, Charla. "Fat Crimes: Let's Stop Persecuting Women Stars for Weight Gain." *Glamour* Oct. 1993: 160.

Kuhn, Annette. *The Power of the Image: Essays on Representation and Sexuality.* London/New York: Routledge, 1985.

Lang, Harry. "Roughing It With Clara." *Photoplay Magazine* Sept. 1931: 30+.

Leach, William. *Land of Desire: Merchants, Power, and the Rise of a New American Culture.* New York: Random House, 1993.

Lee, Lila. "How I Keep in Condition." *Photoplay Magazine* Dec. 1921: 31+.

Lehman, Peter. *Running Scared: Masculinity and the Representation of the Male Body.* Philadelphia: Temple University Press, 1993.

Lieb, Clarence W. *Eat, Drink and Be SLENDER: What Every Overweight Person Should Know and Do.* New York: The John Day Company, 1929.

Lynd, Robert and Helen. *Middletown: A Study in American Culture.* New York: Harcourt, Brace and Company, 1929.

MacCulloch, Campbell. "What Made Them Stars?" *Photoplay Magazine* Oct. 1928: 44+.

"Mack Sennett's Bathing Beauties." *The Silents Majority* Jul 1998 <http://www.silentsmajority.com/FeaturedPerformer/0798.htm>.

Manners, Dorothy. "The Flesh and Blood Racket." *Motion Picture Magazine* April 1929: 34+.

———. "138 Lbs. Ringside!" *Motion Picture Magazine* Mar. 1931: 58+.

———. "What Is Doug Doing?" *Motion Picture Magazine* Feb. 1931: 55+.

May, Lary. *Screening Out the Past: The Birth of Mass Culture and the Motion Picture Industry.* New York: Oxford University Press, 1980.

Millman, Marcia. *Such a Pretty Face: Being Fat in America.* New York: W. W. Norton, 1980.

"Movie Myths and Facts as Seen by an Insider." *The Literary Digest* 7 May 1921: 38–45.

"Movies Arraigned by Senator Myers." *New York Times* 30 June 1922: 9.

Mulvey, Laura, "Visual Pleasure and Narrative Cinema." 1975. *Issues in Feminist Film Criticism*. Ed. Patricia Erens. Bloomington/Indianapolis: Indiana University Press, 1990.

Nash, Roderick. *The Nervous Generation: American Thought, 1917–1930*. Chicago: Rand McNally, 1970.

Neil, Iain. Telephone interview. 5 Apr. 1999.

Newquist, Roy. *Conversations with Joan Crawford*. Seacaucus, NJ: The Citadel Press, 1980.

Opportunities in the Motion Picture Industry—And How to Qualify for Positions in its Many Branches. Vol. 1. Los Angeles: Photoplay Research Society, Bureau of Vocational Guidance, 1922.

Orbach, Susie. *Fat Is a Feminist Issue*. 1978. New York: Berkley Publishing Group, 1990.

Paddock, Charley. "Why Athletes Fail in Pictures." *Photoplay Magazine* Sept. 1928: 52+.

Palmer, Corliss. "Exercise for the Stout Figure." *Motion Picture Magazine* Feb. 1922: 62+.

———. "The Slender Silhouette." *Motion Picture Magazine* Nov. 1921: 60+.

Parsons, Harriet. "The Weigh of all Flesh." *Photoplay Magazine* Oct. 1929: 64+.

"Penalties of Being a Star, The." *Photoplay Magazine* Dec. 1922: 32.

"Penalties of Obesity." *Journal of the American Medical Association* 89 (1927): 694–695.

Peters, Dr. Lulu Hunt. *Diet and Health—With Key to the Calories*. Chicago: Reilly and Britton, 1918.

Peterson, Theodore. *Magazines in the Twentieth Century*. Urbana, IL: University of Illinois Press, 1956.

Phillips, H. I. "It Is Never Too Late To Shrink." *The American Magazine* Nov. 1925: 38+.

"Physicians Defend Plump Turkish Lines as 'Miss Turkey' Starts Fad of Reducing." *New York Times* 27 July 1930, sec. 3: 4.

Physioc, Louis W. "Does the Camera Lie?" *American Cinemaotographer* Jan. 1927: 21+.

———. "Movie Make-Up: A Technical and Artistic Analysis of Motion Picture Make-Up with an Historical Sketch." *American Cinematographer* Feb. 1928: 6+.

Poster, Steven, A.S.C. "Re: Camera's Distortion of Body Weight." E-mail to the author. 2 Apr. 1999.

Quirk, May Allison. "Muscling In." *Photoplay Magazine* January 1933: 72+.

"Reduces Weight by Knife." *New York Times* 4 Sept. 1928: 14.

"Reducing Diets Believed Factor in Birth of Boys." *New York Times* 15 Oct. 1933, sec. 1: 16.

Richardson, F. H. "Effect of Distance of Projection and Projection Angle Upon the Screen Image." *Transactions of the Society of Motion Picture Engineers* Oct. 1922: 67–74.

"Right Weigh, The." *Motion Picture Magazine* June 1925: 56+.

Roberts, Kenneth L. "Flaming Hollywood." *The Saturday Evening Post* 12 July 1924: 3+.

Robertson, Stewart. "Weight and Hope." *Photoplay Magazine* July 1930: 44+.

Robinson, David. *Hollywood in the Twenties*. New York/South Brunswick: A.S. Barnes and Company, 1968.

Rorty, James. *Our Master's Voice: Advertising*. New York: The John Day Company, 1934.

Ryan, Don. "Has the Great Lover Become Just a Celebrity?" *Motion Picture Classic* May 1926: 20+.

St. Johns, Adela Rogers. "New American Beauty." *Photoplay Magazine* June 1922: 26+.

"Sangrina and and Silph Chewing Gum Frauds, The." *Journal of the American Medical Association* 87 (1926): 688–691.

Sargent, Dr. Dudley A. "Are You Too Fat, or Too Thin?" *The American Magazine* Nov. 1921: 13+.

Schneider, Karen S., et al. "Too Fat? Too Thin? How Media Images of Celebrities Teach Kids to Hate Their Bodies." *People Weekly* 3 June 1996: 64+.

Schulberg, Budd. *The Disenchanted*. New York: Random House, 1950.

Schwartz, Hillel. *Never Satisfied: A Cultural History of Diets, Fantasies and Fat*. New York: MacMillan, 1986.

Seid, Roberta Pollack. *Never Too Thin: Why Women Are at War with Their Bodies*. New York: Prentice Hall, 1989.

Sewell, Jameson. "What Is Camera Beauty?" *Photoplay Magazine* Aug. 1925: 38+.

Shirley, Lois. "The Enemy of Beauty—Over-Exercise." *Photoplay Magazine* Aug. 1931: 30+.

———. "Starving Back to Stardom." *Photoplay Magazine* Aug. 1928: 80+.

Shulman, Irving. *Valentino*. New York: Trident Press, 1967.

"Signore Valentino Herewith Presents His New Leading Lady, Fräulein Banky." *Motion Picture Magazine* Nov. 1925: 24+.

Silver, Gordon R. "My Contract Won't Let Me." *Motion Picture Classic* Sept. 1927: 63+.

Sinclair, Upton. *The Fasting Cure*. New York: Mitchell Kennerley, 1911.

Sklar, Robert. *Movie-Made America: A Cultural History of American Movies*. New York: Vintage Books, 1976.

Spensley, Dorothy. "The Torture Chambers of Hollywood." *Motion Picture Magazine* June 1929: 52+.

Spitzack, Carole. *Confessing Excess: Women and the Politics of Body Reduction*. Albany: State University of New York Press, 1990.

"Stars Tell How They Keep Those Girlish Lines." *Photoplay Magazine* Sept. 1924: 28+.

Stearns, Peter N. *Fat History: Bodies and Beauty in the Modern West*. New York: New York University Press, 1997.

Stenn, David. *Clara Bow: Runnin' Wild*. New York: Doubleday, 1988.

———. Personal interview. Feb. 1999.

Studlar, Gaylyn. "Barrymore, the Body, and Bliss: Issues of Male Representation and Female Spectatorship in the 1920s." *Fields of Vision: Essays in Film Studies,*

Visual Anthropology, and Photography. Ed. Leslie Deveraux and Roger Hillman. Berkeley: University of California Press, 1995: 160–180.

———. *This Mad Masquerade: Stardom and Masculinity in the Jazz Age*. New York: Columbia University Press, 1996.

"Swimming Pools of Hollywood, The." *Photoplay Magazine* Oct. 1922: 22–23.

Sylvia of Hollywood. *No More Alibis*. New York: MacFadden Book Company, 1934.

Székely, Éva. *Never Too Thin*. Toronto: The Women's Press, 1988.

"Talmadge Sisters, Film Stars, Arrive." *New York Times* 25 Feb. 1922: 9.

Thomas, Bob. *Joan Crawford*. New York: Simon and Schuster: 1978.

Thompson, Vance. *Eat and Grow Thin*. New York: E. P. Dutton and Company, 1914.

Thornley, Betty. "Merrily We Roll Along." *Collier's* 7 Dec. 1929: 19+.

Tibbetts, John C. and James M. Welsh. *His Majesty the American: The Cinema of Douglas Fairbanks, Sr.* South Brunswick: A. S. Barnes and Company, 1977.

Tildesley, Alice L. "She Wants to Succeed." *Motion Picture Classic* June 1926: 36+.

Torrence, Bruce T. *Hollywood: The First Hundred Years*. New York: Zoetrope, 1979.

Tucker, Larry A. and Marilyn Bagwell. "Television Viewing and Obesity in Adult Females." *American Journal of Public Health* 81 (1991): 908–911.

Tucker, Larry A. and Glenn M. Friedman. "Television Viewing and Obesity in Adult Males." *American Journal of Public Health* 79 (1989): 516–518.

Ulbeck, Sylvia. *No More Alibis*. New York: MacFadden Book Company, 1934.

Ullman, S. George. *Valentino As I Knew Him*. New York: A. L. Burt Company, 1926.

Underhill, Harriette. "The Movies Give the World a Boyish Form: Motion Pictures Have Transformed the Public Taste in Feminine Pulchritude." *Motion Picture Classic* Nov. 1925: 30+.

Valentino, Rudolph. "My Life Story—Part I." *Photoplay Magazine* Feb. 1923: 30+.

———. "My Life Story: Chapter Two." *Photoplay Magazine* Mar. 1923: 54+.

———. "My Life Story—Chapter III." *Photoplay Magazine* Apr. 1923: 49+.

Van Vranken, Frederick. "Women's Work in Motion Pictures." *Motion Picture Magazine* Aug. 1923: 28+.

Van Wyck, Carolyn. "Friendly Advice on Girls' Problems." *Photoplay Magazine* July 1926: 94+.

———. "Introduction." *No More Alibis*. Sylvia of Hollywood. New York: MacFadden Book Company, 1934: 7–10.

Vivian, C. H. "What Kind of a Boy Was Doug?" *Sunset Magazine* Oct. 1928: 38+.

"Vogue of Valentino, The." *Motion Picture Magazine* Feb. 1923: 27+.

Wagner, Rob. "Shining up the Stars." *Collier's* 6 Mar. 1926: 7+.

Walker, Alexander. *Rudolph Valentino*. London: Elm Tree Books, 1976.

———. *Stardom: The Hollywood Phenomenon*. New York: Stein and Day, 1970.

"Way to Keep Fit, The." *Motion Picture Magazine* Aug. 1924: 66.

Webster, Mary. "Doug Carves a New Career for Himself." *Motion Picture Magazine* Jan. 1932: 75+.

Wells, Hal K. "Great Athletes of the Screen." *Motion Picture Classic* Sept. 1926: 40+.

Welton, Don, ed. *The Body: Classic and Contemporary Readings*. Malden, MS: Blackwell Publishers, 1999.

West, Myrtle. "The Price They Paid for Stardom." *Photoplay Magazine* Nov. 1926: 28+.

"Where the Screen Stars Train." *Photoplay Magazine* Aug. 1924: 86.

Whitaker, Alice. "How They Manage Their Homes." *Photoplay Magazine* Sept. 1929:64+.

Williams, Linda. "Film Body: An Implantation of Perversions." *Explorations in Film Theory: Selected Essays from Ciné-Tracts, 1976–1983.* Bloomington: Indiana University Press, 1991.

Willis, Dr. H. B. K. "Diet for Health and Beauty." *Photoplay Magazine* Feb. 1929: 69+.

———. "Eat and Be Merry." *Photoplay Magazine* Aug. 1929: 72.

Winship, Mary. " 'Oh, Hollywood!'—A Ramble in Bohemia." *Photoplay Magazine* May 1921: 21+.

Wolf, Naomi. *The Beauty Myth: How Images of Beauty Are Used Against Women.* New York: Doubleday, 1991.

Index

Acker, Jean, 132–133
advertising. *See also* physical culture
    critical attitudes toward body, 3
    emergence of modern, 13–14, 145,
        149
    psychological methods, 145
Albert, Katherine, 80, 85, 97
Allen, Frederick Lewis, 10, 14, 18, 21,
        22, 108
American Cinematographer, 58, 61
American Magazine, The, 41, 42, 43,
        155n35, 159n50
American Medical Association, 7, 26
Arbuckle, Fatty, 48, 99
assimilation, 55
Astor, Mary, 88
athletics, 102–7
Atwater, Wilbur, 24
avoirdupois, 23. *See also* fat or corpu-
        lence
Ayres, Agnes, 135, 136

Balsinger, W. E., 92–93, 96
Banky, Vilma, 40, 86
Barker, Lewellys, 7–8, 25
barrel distortion, 62–63
Barrymore, Ethel, 39
Barthelmess, Richard, 88, 90, 141
bathing girls, 85–86, 108–10
bathing suit evolution, 108–10
Battle of the Sexes (1928), 101
beauty pageants, 108
Bell, Rex, 121, 122, 124
Berry, Milton H., 40–41
Beyond the Rainbow (1922), 116,
        117, 119
birth control, 16, 18

Blondell, Joan, 88
Blythe, Betty, 99
body. *See also* physical ideal
    and Hollywood's social freedom, 48
    as instrument of pleasure in
        consumer culture, 16
    as object of display, 16, 18
Bordo, Susan, 3, 21, 22
Bow, Clara, 65, 115–25
    childhood, 116
    images of, 30
    "It" Girl, 115
    and reducing as duty, 120, 123–24
    retirement, 124–25
    and rolling, 65, 119–20
    scandals, 121
    as sex symbol, 117
    and sound, 120
    weight as obstacle to screen career,
        116–20, 121–22, 168n23
    weight clause in contract, 122–24
Bow, Robert and Sarah, 116
Brody, Catherine, 1, 69, 95
Brook, Clive, 83, 88
Brownlow, Kevin, 35
bulimia. *See* snapping cookies
Bushman, Francis X., 82

Calhoun, Dorothy, 66, 69, 80, 82, 94
California, southern. *See* Hollywood
calorie, 24–25
camera. *See* motion picture camera
casting directory, 100–1
Chernin, Kim, 2
Chittenden, Russell, 24
Clifton, Elmer, 117
close-ups, 63

183